KT-547-890

Documentary Storytelling
for Film and Videomakers

THE LIBRARY
GUILDFORD COLLEGE
of Further and Higher Education

Documentary Storytelling for Film and Videomakers

WITHDRAWN

Sheila Curran Bernard

AMSTERDAM • BOSTON • HEIDELBERG • LONDON
NEW YORK • OXFORD • PARIS • SAN DIEGO
SAN FRANCISCO • SINGAPORE • SYDNEY • TOKYO

Focal Press is an imprint of Elsevier

ELSEVIER

Focal
Press

136854

136854
791. 436 BER

Focal Press is an imprint of Elsevier
200 Wheeler Road, Burlington, MA 01803, USA
Linacre House, Jordan Hill, Oxford, OX2 8DP, UK

Copyright © 2004, Sheila Curran Bernard. All Rights Reserved.

No part of this publication may be reproduced, stored in a retrieval system,
or transmitted in any form or by any means, electronic, mechanical, photocopying, recording, or otherwise, without the prior written permission of the
publisher.

Permissions may be sought directly from Elsevier's Science & Technology Rights
Department in Oxford, UK: phone: (+44) 1865 843830, fax: (+44) 1865 853333,
e-mail: permissions@elsevier.com.uk. You may also complete your request
on-line via the Elsevier Science homepage (http://elsevier.com), by selecting
"Customer Support" and then "Obtaining Permissions."

∞ Recognizing the importance of preserving what has been written, Elsevier prints
its books on acid-free paper whenever possible.

Library of Congress Cataloging-in-Publication Data
Application submitted.

British Library Cataloguing-in-Publication Data
A catalogue record for this book is available from the British Library.

ISBN: 0-240-80539-9

For information on all Focal Press publications
visit our website at www.focalpress.com

03 04 05 06 07 08 10 9 8 7 6 5 4 3 2 1

Printed in the United States of America

In memory of Henry Hampton.

Table of Contents

Acknowledgments

My thanks go to colleagues and friends who've made documentary filmmaking, and storytelling in general, an ongoing joy and a lifelong opportunity for learning. For help with this book, special thanks go to Jon Else, Boyd Estus, Kenn Rabin, and Holly Stadtler, as well as to Michael Ambrosino, Steven Ascher, Paula Apsell, Liane Brandon, Ric Burns, Barbara Decharo, Gail Dolgin, Martha Fowlkes, Susan Froemke, Jim Gilmore, Jeanne Jordan, Robert Lavelle, Xan Parker, Sam Pollard, Kate Roth, Susanne Simpson, Bennett Singer, Eric Stange, and Melanie Wallace. For their review of the draft manuscript, thanks go to Debbie Brodsky, Jennifer Lawson, and some academic reviewers whose notes were very much appreciated. Thanks also to Elinor Actipis and Theron Shreve at Focal Press, to Christine Brandt at Kolam, and to my agent, Deborah Schneider. For everything else, I need to thank my parents, David and Kathleen Bernard; my sisters, brother, and their families; and Joel, who has helped more than he knows.

1

Introduction

Whether you're a producer, director, writer, editor, cinematographer, researcher, commissioning editor, or executive producer, issues of documentary storytelling—structure, point of view, balance, style, and more—will confront you throughout your career. Storytelling lies at the heart of most good documentaries—strong characters, compelling tension, and a credible resolution. It's a must for many, if not most, programmers and financiers and a necessity for audiences.

Yet even as filmmakers are increasingly expected to tell strong and competitive stories, information on how to do so is scarce. Bookstore shelves are crowded with guides to dramatic screenwriting, many of which are excellent. But documentary filmmakers work with fact, not fiction; we're not free to invent plot points or character arcs and instead must find them in the raw material of real life. Our stories depend not on creative invention but on creative arrangement, and our storytelling must be done without sacrificing journalistic integrity. It's a tall order.

To that end, this book offers some basics of documentary storytelling—what it is, how it's done, and what mistakes to look out for. It also offers a range of examples to demonstrate that, rather than promote formula and predictability, mastery of the skills of storytelling, and application of those skills sooner rather than later in a production, will help filmmakers find their own creative voices as they focus on diverse subjects and turn them into films that are original, challenging, humorous, educational, and entertaining.

DEFINING DOCUMENTARY

Documentaries bring viewers into new worlds and experiences through the presentation of factual information about real people, places, and events, generally portrayed through the use of actual images and artifacts. A young American woman goes to Vietnam to meet her birth mother *(Daughter From Danang)*; a prisoner consoles her lawyer even though she's the one about to be put to death *(The Execution of Wanda Jean)*; pioneering families are trapped by snow en route to California *(The Donner Party)*. But factuality alone does not define documentary films; it's what the filmmaker does with those factual elements, weaving them into an overall narrative that strives to be as compelling as it is truthful and, at its best, results in a film that is greater than the sum of its parts. "The documentarist has a passion for what he *finds* in images and sounds—which always seem to him more meaningful than anything he can *invent*," wrote Erik Barnouw in his 1974 book, *Documentary*. "Unlike the fiction artist, he is dedicated to *not* inventing. It is in selecting and arranging his findings that he expresses himself."

Story is the device that enables this arrangement. A story begins as a hypothesis or a series of questions and is refined and shaped every step of the way from idea to screen, until it has a compelling beginning, an unexpected middle, a satisfying end, and the kind of twists and turns that will get people talking. The clearer the story is from the beginning of the production process, the fewer the wrong turns and missed opportunities, and— perhaps ironically—the greater the freedom to follow the unexpected. No filmmaker can plan for those surprise moments that make a good film great, but a smart filmmaker, armed with a story, is best prepared to recognize and take full advantage of those moments when they occur.

SUBJECTIVITY

Like any form of communication, documentary filmmaking involves choice-making on the part of the communicator, and is therefore unavoidably subjective, no matter how balanced or neutral the presentation. Which stories are being told and why? What information or material is included or excluded? What choices are made concerning style, tone, point of view, and format? "To be sure, some documentarists claim to be 'objective,' " notes Barnouw, "a term that seems to renounce an interpretive role. The claim may be strategic but is surely meaningless."

Within that subjectivity, however, there are some basic ethical guidelines for documentary film making. Audiences trust documentaries; that trust is key to the films' power and relevance. Betraying it by implying that important events happened in a way that they did not, selecting only those facts that support your essay, or bending the facts in service of a more "dramatic" story undermines the form and your film. This doesn't mean that you can't have and present a very strong and overt point of view, or, for that matter, that you can't create work that is determinedly neutral. It does means that your argument, or your neutrality, needs to be grounded in accuracy.

WHO WANTS DOCUMENTARY STORIES?

In today's documentary marketplace, nearly everyone is looking for strong stories. A small sampling:

- From the web site for the Sundance Documentary Fund: "In supporting independent vision and creative, compelling stories, the Sundance Documentary Fund hopes to give voice to the diverse exchange of ideas crucial to developing an open society." (www.Sundance.org)

- From the Discovery Channel web site for producers, a list of "Required Materials" includes: "One- to two-page treatment that describes the proposed program, story line, visual approach, acts, and production team." (http://discovery.com/utilities/about/submissions/faq.html)
- From the PBS web site for producers: "Program topics should be interesting to a wide audience and be of a high caliber throughout all elements of the production, with a well-crafted story line, strong visuals, and a clear purpose." (www.pbs.org/producers)
- From the web site for the PBS showcase, INDEPENDENT LENS: "Programs accepted for the series must be compelling stories, well told, with elements suited to attracting a national audience. INDEPENDENT LENS seeks work that is

innovative, provocative, character driven, and well-crafted."
(www.pbs.org/producers/news/2003_ind_lens. html)
- From the web site for the National Endowment for the
Humanities, which funds public media: "NEH . . . seeks
to fund those films that will best bring the issues, approaches, and materials of the humanities to broad public
audiences. Producers should have a well-thought-out story
outline, define the target audience, and have a strong commitment to the project." (www.NEH.gov)

WHO TELLS DOCUMENTARY STORIES?

The range and breadth of documentary filmmaking in the United
States and worldwide is actually quite astonishing. Some documentary filmmakers work within production houses or stations.
Many work independently, with varying degrees of financial and
technical support. Some filmmakers strive for national theatrical or
broadcast release; others work to reach regional or local audiences,
including community groups. But a common element at all levels
of production is story. In 1992, for example, musician Peter Gabriel
co-founded a group called Witness, which provides video equipment and training to people worldwide who want to document
injustice as part of a struggle for human rights. The first chapter of
the group's *Practical Guide for Activists*, available on the web
(www.witness.org), is called "How to Tell a Story." And the other
end of the production spectrum, some of the longest-running and
most influential documentary series on public television today,
including FRONTLINE and NOVA, are founded on the notion that
complex ideas can best be conveyed through powerful storytelling.

DOCUMENTARIES TODAY

The dawn of the 21st century is proving to be both a challenging
and promising time for documentary filmmakers. The emergence
of lower-cost production technology has created new opportunities
for more diverse stories and storytellers. The rise in cable programming has increased broadcast outlets, and the potential for theatrical release has been bolstered by the recent success of films,
including *Bowling for Columbine*. At the same time, a combination

of economic and political forces has eroded financial support for independent and public television production, pushing growing numbers of producers into a competitive commercial marketplace that affects, and often limits, what stories can be told, by whom, and how well.

It seems, too, that general awareness of the documentary form has been confused by a crowded schedule of "reality" programming that is often anything but and by programming that is rightly called "documentary" but is often mediocre, if not stale—stories of predators and prey, autopsies, deadly weather, and celebrities. Like junk food, it may be temporarily satisfying but offers little in the way of actual nourishment. Documentaries should do more than help viewers pass the time; they should demand their active engagement, challenging them to think about what they know, how they know it, and what more they might want to find out. Documentaries expand our horizons and inform civic dialogue; they are a critical part of our democracy.

A good documentary confounds our expectations, pushes boundaries, and takes us into worlds—both literal worlds and worlds of ideas—that we did not anticipate entering. To do this, they generally must grab us first by playing on our very basic desire for a good story well told. When the audience is caught up in a life-and-death struggle for a union (*Harlan County, U.S.A.*), in Mick Jagger's futile efforts to calm the crowd at a free Rolling Stones concert (*Gimme Shelter*), or in the story of a family's rift over the issue of whether or not a deaf child should be given a chance to hear (*Sound and Fury*), there is nothing as powerful as a documentary. Jeanne Jordan and Steven Ascher learned that their film, *Troublesome Creek: A Midwestern*, about the efforts of Jordan's parents to save their Iowa farm from foreclosure, had influenced farming policy in Australia; Jon Else's CADILLAC DESERT, the story of water and the transformation of nature in the American West, was screened to inform policy-makers on Capitol Hill. Whether they entertain, inform, or both, documentaries matter.

STORYTELLING, NOT WRITING

Documentary storytelling does not refer specifically or exclusively to writing. Instead, it describes the conceptual process that begins at the moment an idea is raised and continues through production and post-production. A film's author is the person (or people) with primary responsibility for the film's story and structure, which often means it's the producer and/or director, working as or in tandem with a writer and editor. Whether the film is formally written out in a progression from treatment to final script or whether it's merely outlined for the convenience of the production team, the filmmakers routinely address story issues that are familiar to other types of authors, from playwrights to novelists. "Who are your characters? What do they want? What are the stakes if they don't get it? Where is the tension? Where is the story going? Why does it matter?" And so on.

When a writer is credited on a documentary film, the job performed may vary. At times, it refers to someone integrally involved in the film's development and production; at other times, it's a credit for scripted narration. But note that there is no documentary counterpart to the lone screenwriter working "on spec" (unpaid) on the Great American Screenplay, which he or she hopes to sell to Hollywood. Documentary filmmakers may toil (unpaid) for months or years on a project, but they're pushing the entire project along, not just a script, and often the script is the last element to take shape. What people generally pitch and sell are documentary concepts, usually presented at some stage of pre-production or production as an outline, treatment, rough cut, or finished film.

ABOUT THE BOOK

The idea for this book emerged from my own experience as a documentary filmmaker and, over the past ten years, my work as a writer, story editor, and consulting producer on a range of projects, large and small. Working with established, as well as emerging filmmakers, it became clear to me that there are underlying issues of story and structure that can generally be applied to documentaries regardless of style or length, and many filmmakers lack a common vocabulary for addressing these problems.

It was also clear to me that new technologies and the growing popularity of nonfiction programming were fueling a misperception about documentary filmmaking, that it's better and more "real" to shoot first and find the story later. There are exceptions, but in general, and especially for newer filmmakers, to do this risks missing a story entirely or realizing in the editing room that you didn't shoot the elements you need to tell the story you want to tell. The result is likely to be a cobbled-together film in which many of the elements simply don't work, or they don't do as powerful a job as they might have with a little preparation and forethought. Last-minute narration, no matter how well-written, can't compensate for a flawed structure, and gimmicks and hype—whether pumped-up music, flashy editing, or hints of danger around every corner—will only distract from a story that's weak or missing altogether.

INTENDED READERSHIP

This book is for anyone working in documentary filmmaking who has an interest in understanding how story and structure work. It's written with both the experienced and novice filmmaker in mind, as well as those people who watch documentaries or use them in their work. It's my hope that by understanding the storytelling choices filmmakers make, viewers will become better and more critical consumers of documentary programming. They'll have a clearer understanding of why something does or does not feel "true," why some films seem to carry greater emotional or intellectual weight, why some programs leave them feeling manipulated or bored, and how shifts in point of view or tone can change the nature of the presentation. In today's television-saturated world, media literacy is more important than ever.

FORMAT AND METHODOLOGY

The sections of this book are intended only as a guide; there may be information throughout the book that will prove useful to someone editing a film, for instance, not just in the section on editing. Generally speaking, Part I introduces concepts of story and structure and applies them to the initial stages of a film's conception. Part II explores story issues that emerge during a film's development and pre-production. Part III looks at storytelling in the field and in the editing room. Part IV includes conversations about documentary storytelling with professionals whose work is diverse in both content and style, from direct cinema to archival film making. Additional material from these interviews, and from conversations with several other filmmakers, is interspersed throughout the book.

The stages of film making generally described here are the following: research, development, outline, treatment, shooting treatment, assembly, and assembly script, further revised as rough cut, fine cut, picture lock, and script lock. Not all films follow this path, however, and throughout the book I've tried to acknowledge the many variants that exist, whether for reasons of budget, schedule, or production style. Docudramas and essay programs are sometimes scripted prior to production, for example; some treatments are long documents, while others consist of a few pages submitted for the approval of an executive producer. There are also times when an event demands an immediate response from filmmakers, in which case shooting sooner rather than later is the only way to go. I trust that filmmakers can pick and choose from this information as needed to suit their circumstances.

Examples in this book that are drawn from actual films are identified as such. Otherwise, the examples were created by me for illustration purposes, and any resemblance to actual films, whether produced or proposed, is purely coincidental. At the back of the book, I've included a list of many of the films cited; these may be available for rent either at video stores or libraries, and some continue to be rebroadcast. In addition, a web search by title will tell which films are available for purchase and may direct readers to additional resources such as the filmmakers' own web sites.

OBSERVATIONS

In preparing this book, I screened a wide variety of films and spoke with a range of filmmakers, many of whom raised the same basic points:

- The availability of lower-cost digital video technology in many ways increases the need for filmmakers to shoot smarter. It's very possible to shoot everything and end up in the editing room with nothing.
- Time is an increasingly rare commodity for filmmakers, especially during pre-production and editing. Yet time is what enables a film to have depth, in terms of research, themes, and layers of storytelling; it can enhance creativity.

As a group, we need to resist the push to turn out documentary *products*, rather than documentary *films*. While some excellent documentary programming has been produced quickly and/or inexpensively, not all stories lend themselves to rapid or low-cost turnaround.

- Story does not have to mean three-act drama, and it definitely does not mean artificial tension that is imposed from without. Story comes from within the material and the ways in which you, the filmmaker, structure it. The bottom line is if it works, it works.

There are many ways to tell a quality documentary story, many stories to be told, an increasing number of filmmakers to tell them, and high-quality, lower-cost technology to tell them with. So tell an honest story and a good one. Contribute to our understanding of who we are, where we've been, and what we might become. Be open-minded. Be rigorous. Have fun. Just please don't call them "docs." They're usually so hard to make, and so carefully wrought, that they deserve all five syllables—and then some.

Part I

INITIAL CONCEPT

2

Story Basics

A story is the narrative, or telling, of an event or series of events, crafted in a way to interest the audience, whether they are readers, listeners, or viewers. At its most basic, a story has a beginning, middle, and end. It has compelling characters, rising tension, and conflict that reaches some sort of resolution. It engages the audience on an emotional and intellectual level, motivating viewers to want to know what happens next.

Strategies for good storytelling are not new. The Greek philosopher Aristotle first set out guidelines for what he called a "well-constructed plot" in 350 BCE, and those basics have been applied to storytelling—on stage, on the page, and on screen—ever since. Expectations about how storytelling works seem hardwired in audiences, and meeting, confounding, and challenging those expectations is no less important to the documentarian than it is to the dramatist.

Don't be confused by the fact that festivals and film schools commonly use the term "narrative" only to describe works of dramatic fiction. Most documentaries are also narrative, which simply means they tell stories (whether or not those stories are also *narrated* is an entirely different issue). How they tell those stories and what stories they tell separates the films into subcategories such as genre or style, from cinéma vérité to film noir.

A few storytelling terms:

EXPOSITION

Exposition is the information that grounds you in a story: who, what, where, when, and why. It gives the audience members the

13

tools they need to follow the story that's unfolding, and more importantly, it allows them *inside* the story. It doesn't mean giving away everything, just giving away what the audience needs, when the audience needs it. Exposition is occasionally discussed as "Something To Be Avoided," but it is necessary to an audience's understanding of the film, and its presentation—usually in the first act—doesn't have to be heavy-handed.

Exposition in theater used to be handled by the maid who bustled onstage at the start of a play and said, to no one in particular, or perhaps to a nearby butler, "Oh, me, I'm so very worried about the mistress, now that the master has gone off hunting with that ne'er-do-well brother of his, and without even telling her that his father, the Lord of Pembrokeshire, has arranged to sell this very house and all of its belongings before a fortnight is up!" In documentary films, the corollary might be those programs that are entirely front-loaded with narration that tells you information you were unprepared for or didn't really need to know—and when you *did* need the information, you generally couldn't remember it. Front loading also frequently occurs when filmmakers decide to put the entire backstory—all of the history leading up to the point of their story's attack—at the beginning of the film.

Exposition can be woven into a film in many ways. Sometimes expository information comes out when people argue, "Yeah? Well, we wouldn't even be in this mess if you hadn't decided to take your paycheck to Atlantic City!" Sometimes it's revealed through headlines or other printed material, as much of the exposition is conveyed in *The Thin Blue Line*. Good narration can deftly weave exposition into a story, offering viewers just enough information to know where they are. (Voice-over material drawn from interviews can sometimes do the same thing.) Exposition can also be handled through visuals: an establishing shot of a place or sign; footage of a sheriff nailing an eviction notice on a door (*Roger & Me*); the opening moments of an auction (*Troublesome Creek*). Toys littered on a suburban lawn say, "Children live here." Black bunting and a homemade shrine of flowers and cars outside a fire station say, "Tragedy has occurred." A long shot of an elegantly dressed woman in a large, spare office high up in a modern building says, "This woman is powerful." A man on a subway car reading *The Boston Globe* tells us where we are, as would a caption on screen that reads, "Boston, 1983." Time-lapse photography, title cards, and animation can all be used to accomplish exposition, as the creators of *South Park* demonstrated in their cartoon history of the United States in *Bowling for Columbine*.

Again, it all goes back to story. You want the storytelling to motivate the presentation of exposition; in other words, you want the audience to *want* to know the information you're giving them. When exposition involves backstory—how we got to where we are now—it's often a good idea to get the present-day story moving forward before looking back. In *Troublesome Creek: A Midwestern*, the filmmakers alert their audience to the danger ahead—the Jordans may be losing their family farm—and introduce them to the protagonists *before* they explore the colorful past of the Jordan family, which has owned the farm since 1867.

Offer too many details too soon, and the film will feel didactic or preachy. But tell too few, and viewers will eventually give up trying to figure things out and disengage. It's no fun being on the outside looking in, even if the footage *seems* like it should be compelling. You can watch a scene in which group of people go into a board room and come out looking ashen, and one or two might even be sobbing, but if you don't know what the meeting was about or what was at stake, you won't care. If you'd gone into that meeting *with* those people, rooting for their company and knowing that the principals had gambled everything on a land deal that required an emergency loan, and that the stern-faced guy shaking his head was the banker, then you'd be feeling what they're feeling, and your hopes would be crushed, too.

THEME

In literary terms, theme is the general underlying subject of a specific story, a recurring idea that often illuminates an aspect of the human condition. EYES ON THE PRIZE, in fourteen hours, tells an overarching story of America's civil rights movement. The underlying themes include race, poverty, and the power of ordinary people to accomplish extraordinary change. Themes in *The Day After Trinity*, the story of J. Robert Oppenheimer's development of the atomic bomb, include scientific ambition, the quest for power, and efforts to ensure peace and disarmament when both may be too late.

The best documentary stories, like memorable literary novels or thought-provoking dramatic features, not only engage the audience with an immediate story—one grounded in plot and action—but with themes that resonate beyond the particulars of the event being told. *Sound and Fury*, for example, is not only about a little girl and her family trying to decide if she should have an operation that might enable her to hear, it's also about universal issues of identity, belonging, and family.

"Theme is the most basic lifeblood of a film," says filmmaker Ric Burns. "Theme tells you the tenor of your story. *This* is what this thing is about." Burns chose to tell the story of the ill-fated Donner Party and their attempt to take a shortcut to California in 1846, not because the cannibalism they resorted to would appeal to prurient viewers but because their story illuminated themes and vulnerabilities in the American character. These themes are foreshadowed in the film's opening quote from Alexis de Tocqueville, a French author who toured the United States in 1831. He writes of the "feverish ardor" with which Americans pursue prosperity, the "shadowy suspicion that they may not have chosen the shortest route to get it," and the way in which they "cleave to the things of this world," even though death steps in, in the end. These words presage the fate of the Donner Party, whose ambitious pursuit of a new life in California will have tragic consequences.

ARC

The arc refers to the way or ways in which the events of the story transform your characters. An overworked executive learns that his family should come first; a mousy secretary stands up for himself and takes over the company; a rag-tag group of kids that nobody ever notices wins the national chess tournament. In pursuing a goal, the protagonists learn valuable lessons about themselves and their place in the world, and those lessons change them—and may, in fact, change their desire for the goal.

In documentary films, story arcs can be hard to find. Never, simply in the interest of a good story, presume to know what a character is thinking or feeling. Only present evidence of an arc if it can be substantiated by factual evidence. For example:

- In *The Day After Trinity*, Physicist J. Robert Oppenheimer, a left-leaning intellectual, successfully develops the world's

Build up for Characters' goals [handwritten marginal note]

first nuclear weapons and is then horrified by the destructive powers he's helped to unleash. He spends the rest of his life trying to stop the spread of nuclear weapons and in the process falls victim to the Cold War he helped to launch; once hailed as an American hero, he is accused of being a Soviet spy.

- In *The Thin Blue Line*, we hear and see multiple versions of a story that begins when Randall Adams's car breaks down on a Saturday night and a teenager named David Harris offers him a ride. Later that night, a police officer is shot and killed by someone driving Harris's car, and Adams is charged with the murder. The deeper we become immersed in the case, the more clearly we see that Adams's imprisonment and subsequent conviction are about politics, not justice. He is transformed from a free man to a convicted felon, and that transformation challenges the viewer's assumptions about justice and the basic notion that individuals are innocent until proven guilty.

PLOT AND CHARACTER

Films are often described as either plot- or character-driven. Character-driven means that the action of the film emerges from the wants and needs of the characters. Plot-driven means that characters are secondary to the events that make up the plot. (Many thrillers and action movies are plot-driven.) In documentary, both types of films exist, and there is much gray area between them. Errol Morris's *The Thin Blue Line* imitates a plot-driven *noir* thriller in its exploration of the casual encounter that leaves Randall Adams facing the death penalty. Circumstances act *upon* Adams; he doesn't set the plot in motion except inadvertently, when his car breaks down and he accepts a ride from David Harris. In fact, part of the film's power comes from Adams' inability to alter events, even as it becomes apparent that Harris, not Adams, is likely to be the killer.

In contrast, *Daughter From Danang* is driven by the wants of its main character, Heidi Bub, who was born in Vietnam and given up for adoption in 1975. Raised in Tennessee and taught to deny her Asian heritage, Bub is now estranged from her adoptive mother; she sets the events of the film in motion when she decides to locate and reunite with her birth mother.

As in these two examples, the difference between plot- and character-driven films can be subtle, and one often has strong elements of the other. The characters in *The Thin Blue Line* are distinct and memorable; the plot in *Daughter From Danang* is strong and takes unexpected turns. It's also true that plenty of memorable documentaries are not "driven" at all in the Hollywood sense. *Where Did You Get That Woman?*, for example, offers a portrait of a Chicago washroom attendant, and in the light-hearted *Gefilte Fish*, three generations of women explain how they prepare a traditional holiday dish (the third generation, the filmmaker, unscrews a jar). Frederick Wiseman's documentaries are elegantly structured but not "plotted" in the sense that each sequence makes the next one inevitable. Still other films are driven not by characters or plot but by questions—an essay. This was Michael Moore's strategy in *Bowling for Columbine*, an exploration of the forces behind the tragic 1999 shooting at Columbine High School in Littleton, Colorado. In all of the films cited, however, a narrative through line binds the overall elements.

DRAMATIC STORYTELLING

Because *dramatic* storytelling often refers more specifically to character-driven stories, it's worth looking at some of the basic elements that make these stories work. As set out by authors David Howard and Edward Mabley in their book, *The Tools of Screenwriting*, these are:

- The story is about *somebody* with whom we have some empathy.
- This somebody wants *something* very badly.
- This something is *difficult*, but possible to do, get, or achieve.
- The story is told for maximum *emotional impact* and *audience participation* in the proceedings.
- The story must come to a *satisfactory ending* (which does not necessarily mean a happy ending).

While their book is directed at dramatic screenwriters, the list is useful for documentary storytellers as well. Your particular film subject or situation might not fit neatly within these parameters, so further explanation follows:

Who (or What) the Story is About

The *somebody* is your protagonist, your hero, the entity whose story is being told. Note that your hero can, in fact, be very "unheroic," and the audience might struggle to empathize with him or her. But the character and/or character's mission must be compelling enough for them to try. In *The Execution of Wanda Jean*, for example, Liz Garbush offers a sympathetic but unsparing portrait of a woman on death row for murder.

The central character doesn't need to be a person. In Ric Burns's New York, for example, a seven-episode history, the city itself is the protagonist, whose fortunes rise and fall and rise over the course of the series. But often, finding a central character through which to tell your story can make an otherwise complex topic more manageable and accessible to viewers. We used this strategy in I'll Make Me a World, a history of African-American arts in the 20th century. For example, producer Denise Green explored the Black Arts Movement of the 1960s by viewing it through the eyes and experience of Pulitzer Prize–winning poet Gwendolyn Brooks, an established, middle-aged author whose life and work were transformed by her interactions with younger artists who'd been influenced by the call for Black Power.

What the Protagonist Wants

The *something* that somebody wants is also referred to as a goal or an objective. In *Blue Vinyl*, filmmaker Judith Helfand sets out, on camera, to convince her parents to remove the new siding from their home. Note that a filmmaker's on-screen presence doesn't necessarily make him or her the protagonist. In Jeanne Jordan and Steve Ascher's *Troublesome Creek: A Midwestern*, the filmmakers travel to Iowa, where Jeanne's family is working to save their farm from foreclosure. Jeanne is the film's narrator, but the protagonists are her parents, Russel and Mary Jane Jordan. It's their goal—to pay off their debt by auctioning off their belongings—that drives the film's story.

Active Versus Passive

Storytellers speak of active versus passive goals and active versus passive heroes. In general, you want a story's goals and heroes to be active, which means that you want your story's protagonist to be in charge of his or her own life: to set a goal and then to go about doing what needs to be done to achieve it. A passive goal is something like this: A secretary wants a raise in order to pay for breast enhancement surgery. She is *passively* waiting for the raise, hoping someone will notice that her work merits reward. To be active, she would have to do something to ensure that she gets that raise, or she would have to wage a campaign to raise the extra money she needs for the surgery, such as taking a second job. Not all passivity is bad, however. Randall Adams, locked up on death row, is a passive protagonist because he *can't* do anything, which is part of what makes the story so compelling.

In general, though, you want your protagonist to be active, and you want him or her to have a goal that's *worthy*. In the example of the secretary, will an audience really care whether or not she gets larger breasts? Probably not. If we had a reason to be sympathetic—she had been disfigured in an accident, for example—maybe we would care. But it's not a very strong goal. Worthy does not mean a goal has to be noble—it doesn't all have to be about ending world hunger or ensuring world peace. It *does* have to matter enough to be worth committing significant time and resources to. If you only care a little about your protagonists and what they want, your financiers and audience are likely to care not at all.

Difficulty and Tangibility

The something that is wanted—the goal—must be *difficult* to do or achieve. If something is easy, there's no tension, and without tension, there's little incentive for an audience to keep watching.

Tension is the feeling we get when issues or events are unresolved, especially when we want them to be resolved. It's what motivates us to demand, "And then what happens? And what happens after *that*?" We need to know, because it makes us uncomfortable *not* to know. Think of a movie thriller in which you're aware—but the heroine is not—that danger lurks in the cellar. As she heads toward the cellar, you feel escalating tension because she is walking *toward* danger. If you didn't know that the bad guy was in the basement, she would just be a girl heading down some stairs. Without tension, a story feels flat; you don't care one way or the other about the outcome.

So where do you find the tension? One solution is through conflict, defined as a struggle between opposing forces. In other words, your protagonist is up against someone (often referred to as the *antagonist* or *opponent*) or something (the *opposition*). In Barbara Kopple's *Harlan County, U.S.A.*, for example, striking miners are in conflict with mine owners. In *James Cameron's Expedition: Bismarck*, the director faced the tremendous logistical challenge, and dangers, of underwater excavation.

Note that conflict can also mean a direct argument between two sides, pro and con (or he said, she said). This can actually weaken tension, however, especially if each side is talking past the other or if the individuals in conflict have not been properly established. But if the audience goes into an argument caring about the individuals involved, it can lead to powerful emotional storytelling. Near the end of *Daughter From Danang*, the joyful reunion between the American adoptee and her Vietnamese family gives way to feelings of anger and betrayal brought on by the family's request for money. The palpable tension the audience feels stems not from taking one side or another in the argument, but from empathy for *both* sides.

Weather, illness, war, self-doubt, inexperience, hubris—all of these can pose obstacles as your protagonist strives to achieve his or her goal. But just as it can be useful to find an individual (or individuals) through whom to tell a complex story, it can be useful to personify the opposition. As the national news media discovered in the 1960s, it was far easier to make northern viewers understand the injustices of southern segregation when they could focus on Birmingham, Alabama police chief Bull Connor as he turned police dogs and fire hoses on young African-American protesters.

Worthy Opponent

Just as you want your protagonist to have a worthy goal, you want him or her to have a worthy opponent. A problem common for many filmmakers is that they create one-dimensional opponents; if their hero is good, the opponent must be bad. In fact, your most memorable opponent is often not the opposite of your hero, but a complement to him or her. In the film *Sound and Fury*, young Heather's parents oppose her wishes for a Cochlear implant not out of malice but out of their deep love for her and their strong commitment to the deaf culture into which they and their daughter were born. Chicago Mayor Richard Daley was a challenging opponent for Dr. Martin Luther King, Jr. in EYES ON THE PRIZE specifically because he *wasn't* Bull Connor; Daley was a savvy northern politician with close ties to the national Democratic Party and a supporter of the southern-based civil rights movement. The story of his efforts to impede Dr. King's campaign for open housing in Chicago in 1966 proved effective at underscoring the significant differences between using nonviolence as a strategy against *de jure* segregation in the South and using it against *de facto* segregation in the North.

Tangible Goal

Although difficult, the goal should be *possible* to do or achieve, which means that it's best if it's both concrete and realistic. "Fighting racism" or "curing cancer" or "raising awareness" may all be worthwhile, but none is specific enough to serve as a story objective. In fact, a nonspecific goal is often a good indicator that your story lacks focus. If your goal is too vague, try asking *how* your character wants to achieve that goal. Civil rights workers in Mississippi in 1964 wanted to end racism by registering black voters. That's a tangible goal. Your character's efforts to find a cure for cancer may take the form of committing a hundred co-workers to join a walkathon. That's a manageable approach to a complex issue.

Note also that the goal is not necessarily the most "dramatic" or obvious one. In Kate Davis's *Southern Comfort*, a film about a transgendered male dying of ovarian cancer, Robert Eads' goal is not to find a cure; it's to survive long enough to attend the Southern Comfort Conference in Atlanta, a national gathering of transgendered people, with his girlfriend, Lola, who is also transgendered.

Emotional Impact and Audience Participation

The concept of telling a story for greatest *emotional impact* and *audience participation* is perhaps the most difficult. It's often described as "show, don't tell," which means that you want to present the evidence or information that allows viewers to experience the story for themselves, anticipating twists and turns and following the story line in a way that's active rather than passive. Too often, films *tell* us what we're supposed to think through the use of heavy-handed narration, loaded graphics, or a stacked deck of interviews.

Think about the experience of being completely held by a film. You aren't *watching* characters on screen; you're right there with them, bringing the clues you've seen so far to the story as it unfolds. You lose track of time as you try to anticipate what happens next, who will do what, and what will be learned. It's human nature to try to make sense of the events we're confronted with, and it's human nature to enjoy being stumped or surprised. *Bowling for Columbine* did this well. Just when you're certain you've figured out what caused the violence in Colorado—too many guns, too much violence in entertainment, too much poverty or racism—Moore confounds you with a contradiction. Other countries have guns. Other countries have violent entertainment. Other countries have violent histories, alienated youth, poverty, racism. So what led two teenage boys to go on a rampage one April day in 1999? You keep watching to find out.

Telling a story for emotional impact means that the filmmaker is structuring the story so that the moments of conflict, climax, and resolution—moments of achievement, loss, reversal, etc.—adhere as well as possible to the internal rhythms of storytelling. Audiences expect that the tension in a story will escalate as the story moves toward its conclusion; scenes tend to get shorter, action tighter, the stakes higher. As we get to know the characters and understand their wants and needs, we care more about what happens to them; we become invested in their stories.

You want to avoid creating unnecessary drama, however—turning a perfectly good story into a soap opera. There's no reason to pull in additional details, however sad or frightening, when they aren't relevant. If you're telling the story of a scientist unlocking the genetic code to a certain mental illness, for example, it's not necessarily important that she's also engaged in a custody battle with her former husband, even if this detail seems to spice up the drama or, you hope, make the character more "sympathetic." If the custody battle is influenced by her husband's mental illness and her concerns that the children may have inherited the disease, there is a link that could serve the film well. Otherwise, you risk adding a layer of detail that detracts, rather than adds.

False emotion—hyped-up music and sound effects and narration that warns of danger around every corner—is a common problem, especially on television. As in the story of the boy who cried wolf, at some point it all washes over the viewer like so much noise. If the danger is real, it will have the greatest storytelling impact if it emerges organically from the material.

Raising the Stakes

Another tool of emotional storytelling is to raise the stakes. This can mean that (genuine) danger is increasing, or time is running out, or that a problem that was local is threatening to become widespread. In *Sound and Fury*, the stakes rise as time passes because for a child born deaf, the cochlear implant is most effective if implanted while language skills are being developed. We see Heather's much younger cousin get the implant and begin to acquire spoken language skills; we also learn that her mother, born deaf, would get little benefit from a transplant done now. As Heather enrolls in a school for the deaf without getting an implant, we understand that the decision has lifelong implications.

A Satisfactory Ending

A satisfactory ending, or *resolution*, is often one that feels both unexpected and inevitable. It must resolve the one story you set out to tell. Say you start the film with a problem. A little girl has a life-threatening heart condition for which there is no known surgical treatment. Your film then goes into the world of experimental surgery, where you find a charismatic doctor whose efforts to solve a very different medical problem have led him to create a surgical solution that might work on the little girl's situation. The ending of the film will not be satisfactory unless it is the outcome of the story you began the film with the story of a little girl with a life-threatening heart condition.

Note that there is never just one correct ending. Suppose, for example, that your film is due to be aired months before the approval is granted that will allow the doctors to try the experimental surgery on the girl. Make *that* your ending, and leave the audience with the knowledge that everyone is praying and hoping that she will survive until then. Or perhaps the surgery is possible, but at the last minute the parents decide it's too risky. Or they take that risk, and the outcome is positive. Or negative. Or perhaps the doctor's breakthrough simply comes too late for this one child but may make a difference for hundreds of others. Any of these would be a satisfactory ending, provided it is factual. It would be unethical to manipulate the facts to imply a "stronger" or more emotional ending that misrepresents what you know the outcome to be. Suppose, for example, that the parents have already decided that no matter how much success the experimental work is having, they will not allow their daughter to undergo any further operations. You cannot imply that this remains an open question, (e.g., with a teaser such as "Whether the operation will save the life of little Candy is yet to be seen.").

Ending a film in a way that's satisfying does not necessitate wrapping up all loose ends or resolving things in a way that's upbeat. The end of *Daughter From Danang* is powerful precisely because things remain unsettled; Heidi Bub has achieved the goal of meeting her birth mother, but even two years after her visit, she remains deeply ambivalent about continued contact. At the end of *The Thin Blue Line*, Randall Adams remains a convicted murderer on death row, even as filmmaker Errol Morris erases any lingering doubts the audience might have as to his innocence.

3

Documentary Storytelling

Armed with an understanding of story, how do you apply it to an idea you have for a documentary? Suppose, for example, that you're thinking of doing a film about Elvis Presley, a diner in your home town, or images of Islam in American popular culture. Something about the topic has caught your interest, and you think you want to take it to the next level.

First, ask yourself what it is about the topic that grabs you. As the initial audience for your film, your gut reaction to the subject is important. Chances are it wasn't a sweeping notion of Elvis Presley that caught your attention, but an account, perhaps, of his time in the military. It's not the fact that there's a diner in your home town, but that rising taxes and a dwindling customer base have left the owners open to offers from developers looking to build a mall despite significant local opposition. You hadn't thought much about images of Islam in America until you watched a couple of newly-arrived students from Iraq and the Sudan trying to make their way through a pep rally at your son's school, and you found yourself seeing American culture—high school culture—through their eyes.

We're surrounded by subjects that offer potential for documentary storytelling. Current events may trigger ideas or an afternoon spent browsing the shelves at a local library or bookstore. Some filmmakers find stories within their own families. Alan Berliner made *Nobody's Business* about his father, Oscar; Deborah Hoffman made *Confessions of a Dutiful Daughter* about her mother's battle with Alzheimer's. Even when you're very close to a subject, however, you'll need to take an impartial view as you determine whether or not it would make a film that audiences will want to see. This is also true when you adapt documentaries from printed sources; a story may read well on paper, but not play as well on screen.) In making CADILLAC DESERT, drawn from Marc Reisner's book of the same name, producer Jon Else chose three of the roughly 40 stories in Reisner's book; Else and his team then conducted their own research and determined the best way to tell those stories on film.

Story Rights

In general, if you're using books and magazines solely for research purposes, you don't need to obtain any of the underlying rights When the film is indelibly linked to a book, however, as was the case with CADILLAC DESERT, *A Brief History of Time* (Errol Morris' film built on Stephen Hawking's book), or *A Midwife's Tale* (Laurie Kahn-Leavitt's film built on Laurel Ulrich's book), you will need to come to a legal arrangement with the author or copyright holder. Consult with a good entertainment lawyer if you have questions about legality, or if you need or want exclusive access to material (or an event). Better to be safe than to waste precious time and money on a subject you can't legally pursue.

Note that when you are negotiating for the rights to a story, you will want to retain creative control over your film. The author may be an expert on the subject, but you are an expert on translating it on film to a general audience. You don't need a degree in science to make an extraordinary science documentary or a degree in social work to create a compelling portrait of runaway teens. What you need are intelligence, curiosity, an ability to learn fast, and a readiness to consult with people who *are* experts in those fields. Ideally, there is a positive collaboration between expert and filmmaker that serves to enrich the film.

"Finding" the Story During Production

It's fairly common to hear filmmakers talk about "finding" the story, or the story revealing itself, over the course of the production or even in the editing room. With experienced filmmakers, this tends to mean *not* that a filmmaker has simply shot material without any story in mind, but that he or she alters the story's focus or, more likely, its *structure* during production and post-production. Even vérité projects, which are significantly crafted in the editing room, are generally begun with a sense of the story and its potential development. You can't know where real life will take you, but you can certainly anticipate a range of outcomes and determine whether or not the story holds sufficient promise. Filmmaker Susan Froemke spent months conducting research before she was confident that she had the right characters and story through which to explore the issue of poverty in *Lalee's Kin*.

Sometimes an opportunity comes along that precludes extensive planning. Filmmakers Gail Dolgin and Vicente Franco had just days to decide whether or not to travel to Vietnam after they learned about an upcoming reunion between Heidi Bub and the birth mother who'd given her up during "Operation Babylift" in 1975. "We all really believed that we were going into a happy reunion, and we had no idea whether we would come back with anything more than that," Dolgin says. "It just grabbed us with the possibilities of raw emotion and passion, and those are great elements for a documentary. And we're also drawn to films where we don't know what's going to happen—we have a concept and we go with it." At a minimum, the filmmakers had a basic, straightforward narrative of an adoptee returning to her homeland, although whether or not that could be turned into a documentary remained to be seen. "Maybe there would be a film that would explore what happens when you lose your birthplace identity," Dolgin says. "Heidi grew up in southern Tennessee, and we imagined going back with her and having her rediscover her roots in some way. But we had no idea, truly. We just went. And of course as soon as we got there it became clear that what we had anticipated was going to go in a different direction." In Vietnam, the filmmakers found themselves immersed in the complex story they told in *Daughter From Danang*.

Frederick Wiseman, renowned for his exploration of American institutions (*Hospital, Basic Training, Welfare, Public Housing, Domestic Violence*) has told interviewers that once he is given permission to film, he moves quickly, spending weeks shooting and then finding his themes and point of view over the course of several months of editing. But note that there is an inherent structure to Wiseman's work—the rhythms of daily life and of the individual stories he picks up over the course of filming—and a distinctive style that he brings to his films. For a 1998 interview (published in *The Boston Phoenix*) about the film *Public Housing*, writer and filmmaker Gerald Peary asked Wiseman if he looked for "drama" while shooting. "The first thought: I'm trying to make a movie,"

Wiseman responded. "A movie has to have dramatic sequences and structure . . . So yes, I am looking for drama, though I'm not necessarily looking for people beating each other up, shooting each other. There's a lot of drama in ordinary experiences." It's also worth noting that Wiseman's style of shooting almost invariably necessitates a high shooting ratio (footage filmed versus footage that ends up on screen) and a lengthy editing period.

Serendipity

It's not unusual for filmmakers to begin one project, only to be drawn by the characters and situations they encounter toward a film that is both different and stronger than they anticipated. In publicity material for the film *Sound and Fury*, director Josh Aronson says that he initially intended to film five deaf individuals whose experience covered a range of viewpoints on deafness. But in his research, he discovered the Artinians, a family in which two brothers—one hearing, one not—each had a deaf child. This created an opportunity to explore conflict within an extended family over how to raise deaf children. In another example, filmmaker Andrew Jarecki was making a film about birthday party clowns when he discovered, through one of his characters, the story that he eventually told in his documentary, *Capturing the Friedmans*—that of a family caught up in a devastating child abuse case.

Knowing that this may happen, or is even *likely* to happen, doesn't mean that you shouldn't approach a general idea by looking first for the best story you can given the subject as you then understand it. Knowing at least your baseline story helps you to anticipate, at minimum, what you'll need to make the film, including characters and location setups. In his work with emerging filmmakers at the University of California, Berkeley, Jon Else requires that they head out "with some bomb-proof fall-back plan," so that even if everything on the shoot goes wrong, they still come back with something.

EVALUATING STORY IDEAS

Beyond the conviction that a story you're developing will work well on film, the following important practical considerations may be helpful to consider.

Access and Feasibility

Does your film provide entré into new or interesting worlds, and can you obtain access to those worlds? Whether it's the changing world of the people of Namibia (*N!ai, The Story of a K!ung Woman*), a New York psychiatric institution (*Bellevue Inside Out*), or the lives of would-be basketball stars (*Hoop Dreams*), a film that takes viewers inside experiences beyond their own is often well-received. Aside from exclusive or extraordinary access, any film, even one shot in your grandmother's kitchen, depends on some kind of access being granted, whether it be personal (your grand-mother), location (permission to bring your equipment into her home), or archival (access to her photo album or those poems she's been writing all these years). In some cases, *lack* of access may become part of the story, as with Michael Moore's pursuit of General Motors chairman Roger Smith, in *Roger & Me*. In others, extraordinary access leads to unique films: news producer Alexandra Pelosi's proximity to George W. Bush as he campaigned for the presidency in *Journeys with George*, for example, or director James Cameron's filmed journeys deep into the wrecks of the Bismarck and Titanic.

As you develop your idea, you need to determine if what you need for production is really possible. Can you get inside a cyclo-tron to film? Will that Pulitzer Prize–winning author grant you an interview? Will you be allowed to follow a third-grade student during that spelling bee? Several years ago, I worked on a science documentary for which we wanted to film cyclists in the Tour de France to illustrate the conservation of mass and energy. The success of a good portion of that film depended on access to the Tour and to exclusive CBS Sports coverage of it. Had we not been able to arrange these, we would have had to find a different illustration.

As an additional note, gaining access usually means establish-ing a relationship and building trust with the people who can grant it. This is a professional relationship, although filmmakers often grow very close to their subjects. It's important to respect that trust, so be truthful about yourself and your project from the start. You can generally get people to talk to you even if they know that you don't agree with their position, as long as you make it very clear that they will be given a fair hearing and that you value their point of view. (Again, there are exceptions. Filmmakers such as Nick

Broomfield *[Kurt & Courtney]* and Michael Moore may push the boundaries of access as a matter of style; they may show up with the cameras rolling deliberately to put their subjects on edge.)

Affordability

In terms of budget and schedule, is it realistic to think that you can afford to tell the story you want to tell, in the way you want to tell it? Even if digital technology can put a relatively inexpensive camera in your hands, getting your film shot, edited, and technically ready for broadcast or theatrical release will still be very expensive. Even celebrated filmmakers have trouble raising money these days. Have you set your sights too high? Don't think small, just realistically. Know that some types of documentaries are costlier to produce than others, and that "extras," such as the rights to use a single clip of archival film from a private library or a short piece of music from your favorite album, could set you back thousands of dollars.

Passion and Curiosity

Do you care deeply about the subject? Passion is going to be your best weapon against discouragement, boredom, frustration, and confusion. Passion is not the unwavering conviction that you are right and the whole world must be made to agree with you. Instead, it is the commitment to the notion that this idea is exciting, relevant, and meaningful, and perhaps more importantly, that it's something you can look forward to exploring in the months or even years to come.

Audience

Who is your intended audience? Many documentaries, whether produced independently or in-house, are created with an audience in mind. It's always possible that the film you thought would only reach your immediate geographic region will be a break-out hit, but in general, you should have some idea who you *want* it to reach: age, geographic area, educational level, etc. This doesn't mean that you shouldn't try to also reach a wider audience, just that you're likely to approach MTV's audience differently, for example, than Lifetime's or PBS's. Is your film not intended for broadcast, but for use by community or educational groups? Do you want to try to release your film theatrically? Does it have the potential to be the next *Roger & Me* or *The Kid Stays in the Picture*? These questions are worth thinking about early on.

On the other hand, plenty of filmmakers simply get to work, especially when fundraising is not as big an issue. They show their films (often at the rough cut stage or later) to invited audiences or submit them to "open calls" for program slots or festivals, and in that way they gradually find an audience. If there's a story in you that has to get made, and you have the resources to go ahead and make it, this route gives you freedom that others don't. Keep in mind, though, that in the end, you still want to reach people with a subject and story that grab them, hold them, and—ideally—stay with them long after the lights are back on.

Relevance

Will anybody care about your film, or can you make them care? This can be a tough one. You may be passionate about 14th-century Chinese art or the use of mushrooms in gourmet cuisine, but can you really find a compelling story that will be worth others not only funding but watching? It's possible to make people care about all sorts of things, but it usually takes the right approach—and a solid story.

By rising beyond its specifics, a story may gain greater relevance for a wider audience. According to information on his website, Alan Berliner's *The Sweetest Sound* started out as a documentary about names, and gradually became a documentary about the filmmaker's name, one that he discovered he shared with about a dozen other people worldwide. In Berliner's hands, the film becomes a humorous and thought-provoking essay about identity and the perception of self, both internal and external—a film that has appeal far beyond people named Alan Berliner. *Daughter From Danang* has layers of story that each add relevance—the reunion of an adopted daughter and her birth mother, the cultural dissonance felt by an American woman returning to the Vietnamese homeland she barely remembers, the changes that have occurred in both countries in the years since 1975, and questions about expectation and need, both emotional and material, that are made all the more difficult by barriers of language and culture.

Timeliness

One aspect of relevance, though not always the most important one, is timeliness. Television executives may plan documentary programming to coincide with major events, anniversaries, or even high-profile motion picture releases—anything to capitalize on public and press interest. In other cases, filmmakers may argue for audience interest in a subject because it expands on current topics in the news or on television, or it's a story from the past that has particular relevance in the present time. The fact that a subject is topical, however, is not by itself a reason to pursue it, because by the time you finish the film, interest in that issue may have passed.

In fact, the quality of being "evergreen," meaning the film will have a shelf-life of many years as opposed to many months, can be a positive selling point. A film on elephant behavior or the American electoral process in general may be evergreen, whereas a film that specifically explores a particular environmental campaign or issues in the presidential campaign of 2004 probably will not be.

Visualization

Is the story visual, and if not, can you make it visual? This is an important question whether you're telling a modern-day story that involves a lot of technology or bureaucracy, or you're drawn to a historical story that predates the invention of still or motion picture photography. A film subject that doesn't have obvious visuals requires additional foresight on the part of the filmmaker; you'll need to anticipate exactly *how* you plan to tell the story on film. The opposite may also be true: a subject can be inherently visual—it takes place in a spectacular location or involves state-of-the-art microscopic photography, for example—without containing an obvious narrative thread. One trend in nature and wildlife programming, for example, is to tell stories about the natural world by focusing on human subjects, as when the PBS series IN THE WILD sent celebrities on journeys of discovery. The actress Goldie Hawn, for example, traveled through India in search of a partially blind female elephant she'd encountered seven years earlier (*The Elephants of India*, with Goldie Hawn). Programming that builds stories around the natural world still exists, of course; a recent example is BLUE PLANET: SEAS OF LIFE, a series jointly produced by the BBC and the Discovery Channel.

Hook

Another question to ask as you evaluate the story is, does it have a hook? In its simplest form, the hook is what got you interested in the subject in the first place. It's that bit of information that reveals the essence of the story and its characters, encapsulating the drama that's about to unfold. *Sound and Fury*, for example, is the story of the little girl who wants a cochlear implant. The hook is not that she wants this operation, nor that the implant is a major feat of medical technology. The hook is that the little girl's parents, contrary to what many in the audience might expect, aren't sure they want her to have the operation. It's the part of the story that makes people want to know more.

Existing Projects

What else has been done on the topic? It's useful, before you get too far, to explore what other films have been made on a subject and when. In part, this may simply inform your own storytelling. What worked or didn't work about what a previous filmmaker did? How will your project be different and/or add to the subject? It's not that you can't tackle a subject that's been covered; look at the range of projects on the civil rights movement, George Washington, or dinosaurs. Just because HBO broadcast a film on the 1963 church bombing in Birmingham (*4 Little Girls*) doesn't mean there isn't a different angle you could take in telling the story for the History Channel. But knowing as much as you can about your subject also means knowing how else it's been treated on film.

DEVELOPING THE STORY

Once you've decided that your idea is worth pursuing, you'll need to start refining the story and planning how you'll tell it. There's no single way to do this, and furthermore, it's a process that tends to continue from the moment an idea strikes you until the final moments of post-production. In general, though, depending on the needs of the project, the budget, and the schedule, you are likely to write some form of outline, treatment, and script, and/or several drafts of one or all of them. Many producers create what's known as a "shooting treatment" or a "shooting script" prior to

Jeanne Jordan and family in 1960, from *Troublesome Creek: A Midwestern.*
Photo courtesy of the filmmakers.

filming, which is used as a blueprint for the work ahead (for examples, see Chapter 9). A small minority of projects are fully scripted in advance, with material shot to accompany narration or scripted "scenarios" (as in recreation docudramas). Some projects are never scripted. The direct cinema film, *Lalee's Kin*, existed on the page only in terms of a basic description for the commissioning network (HBO) and an outline from which the editor could work.

IF YOU ALREADY KNOW YOUR STORY, WON'T YOUR PRESENTATION BE BIASED?

Knowing your story (or at least the germ of it) at the start of a project is not the same thing as knowing exactly what you want to say and how. It simply means having an idea of the narrative spine on which you could hang your subject and having at least some idea of themes you want to explore. From there, you need to research, develop, and shoot your story with an open mind. Give the "opposition" a fair hearing. Building on an earlier example, as sympathetic to the diner owners as you may feel at the start of your project, you might come to find yourself sympathizing with the developers, or discovering that a third solution, while meaning the end of the diner, is best for the town.

Suppose you've decided to explore the story of Thomas Jefferson and his relationship with a slave, Sally Hemings. That's a complex story that can be tackled from many points of view, past and present. If you start that project having already decided to paint Jefferson solely as exploiter and Hemings as victim, you probably shouldn't make the film. Having an axe to grind or a point to make is not the same thing as having the germ of a story to explore. The film that ensues is almost guaranteed to be a one-sided rant that is neither engaging nor informative. Besides, if you already know everything, why make the film? It's a long, hard, and often thankless process, and if there's nothing in it for you as the filmmaker—nothing to learn, to discover, to be surprised or confused or challenged by—why expend the energy?

Films that end up advocating a position or idea—that these chemicals shouldn't have been dumped, that law enforcement used too much force, that laws are being broken—can be as hard-hitting or irreverent or personal as you want. But as you make them, you want to remain open to new and even conflicting information, whether or not it ends up on screen. The more effectively you can present your case, and the better the film will stand up to scrutiny.

TELLING AN ACTIVE STORY

A significant percentage of the documentaries on television these days are about events that are over and done with. You still need a narrative to unfold over the course of the film; one solution is to keep the storytelling (and interviews) in the moment. You build the story and tell it in ways that leave the outcome uncertain. Witnesses, for example, do not say: "I found out later he was fine but at this point I got a call from somebody, Andy I think it was, he later became mayor, and Andy told me that my boy Jimmy was down the well." They stick to what is known at this point in your story, such as, "I got a call that Jimmy was in the well. I ran screaming for help." By doing this, you build tension. Starting with, "I found out later he was fine," lets all of the suspense out of your story. Surprisingly, this is a common mistake, not only in interviews but in scripted narration, such as, "Although he wasn't badly hurt, Jimmy had fallen down a deep well." Note that your adherence to present tense does not mean that you can't offer interpretations of the past. For example, "People complain about over-regulation, that there's too much of it. But there are laws that should have made the contractors responsible for sealing that well up. Instead, they left it open, and a little boy fell in." The expert hasn't yet said when or how the boy got out.

When considering a topic or story that's in the past, whether recent or distant, you'll need to consider how you're going to bring that story to life on screen. For example, suppose that members of the local historical society want you to make a film about their town's founding in 1727, and they want to fold in some material about the origins of some of the wonderful old architecture that still survives. They're excited by the fact that many of the local families are descended from early residents, so they have access to a decent collection of old oil portraits as well as photographs and even some letters. What does it add up to? Not much that will interest anyone who's not a direct relative of the folks on camera because there's no story being told on screen—yet. When Ken Burns, Ric Burns, and Geoffrey Ward used artifacts and images from the 19th century in THE CIVIL WAR, they used them in the service of a powerful story— the North against the South. What's the *story* of this town's history? Or if there is none, can a present-day story be told that would motivate a look back?

In the search for narrative, some filmmakers find a "guide" to the past—for example, the town's mayor says, "Let's set out to see where this great city came from," and off he or she goes. But there are often more creative devices. What if students from the local middle school are researching the town's history in order to write a play that they will perform later that year? That's a possible framework. What if a local builder is trying to restore the town's oldest house, which has been renovated repeatedly over the years? In order to do so he's got to peel back the layers one by one, offering a reason to explore the town's architectural history while also giving us a chance to follow the kind of THIS OLD HOUSE renovation that audiences enjoy. These aren't earth-shattering ideas, but they demonstrate ways to consider a subject that might not seem, at first glance, to have much potential as a film. A more detailed discussion about approaching subjects and about moving film stories forward in time can be found in later chapters.

4

Structure

We've all sat through documentaries that seemed pointless and meandering. Maybe they had great beginnings, but then they seemed to start again, and again, and again. The film seemed to be about one thing, but the rousing conclusion was about something altogether different. The story started in the present, and then quickly plunged into background and never resurfaced. Or the situation and characters were so weakly developed that we found ourselves caring little about the outcome.

Mai Thi Kim and her daughter, Heidi Bub, in *Daughter From Danang*. Photo courtesy of the filmmakers.

These are often problems of structure. Structure is the foundation on which story is built, whether that story is being told in person, in a book, or on screen. It's the narrative spine that determines where you start the story, where you end it, and how you parcel out information along the way. Structure works in response to the audience's built-in expectations; it's human nature to try to make sense of patterns and arrangements, to work at filling in the blanks and guess what happens next. Filmmakers can work to heighten that anticipation or to meet or confound those expectations, thereby increasing the viewer's involvement in a story and investment in its outcome. There's no such thing as a lack of structure; even in an experimental film, *something's* stringing those images together. That something—for better or worse—is structure.

ELEMENTS OF STRUCTURE

The building blocks of a film are shots, scenes, sequences, and, in some but not all cases, acts. Since these are commonly used words that at times have conflicting meanings, the following definitions clarify how they're being used here.

Shot

A shot is a single "take" on an image. There may be movement within the shot, or it may be static. It may be a close-up, a wide shot, a pan, or a tilt. But it begins and ends with the action of the cinematographer turning on and off the camera; later, the editor will further refine the shot by selecting from within it, giving it a new beginning and end point. Individual shots can convey a great deal of storytelling information: point of view, time of day, mood, emotion, character, rhythm, theme. A single shot may also include a "reversal," which is a twist in the plot, sometimes described as a change in values from one state to another. An example of a shot that contains a reversal can be found in *Yosemite: The Fate of Heaven*; we follow a cascading waterfall down through what appears to be pristine wilderness—until we land in a crowded tram full of noisy tourists. The reversal is from isolation to crowds, from nature to humankind, from pristine to polluted.

Scene

A scene is a consecutive group of shots within a single location. You might have a "scene at the courthouse" or a "scene on the boat." A scene is usually more than simply a snapshot of a location, however; it's a subset of the overall action.

A scene is made up of beats. In *Bowling for Columbine*, the scene "Michael Moore interviews Charlton Heston" might be broken down like this:

- Moore outside gate, buzzes, Heston answers, they arrange a meeting;
- Title card reads, "The Next Morning";
- Moore again outside gate, this time it's opened, Moore walks up, Heston meets him in driveway;
- Moore and Heston together walk up the steps to the pool and tennis house;
- The interview setup with Moore, both men seated, which ends with Heston walking away;
- Outside, Moore pursues Heston with a photo of a little girl killed by a classmate;
- Moore leaves the photo behind; the camera lingers on the photo;
- Moore walks along the driveway toward the street.

Scenes, too, contain reversals. Here, when the filmmaker shows up at Charlton Heston's home and pushes on the intercom, Heston unexpectedly answers, and furthermore he agrees to be interviewed. These are reversals because the audience is likely to think that Moore will get either no response or a negative one.

Scenes are strongest when they begin at one emotional or informational point and end at another; in other words, each scene has its own beginning, middle, and end. This means shooting with an eye toward storytelling, being sure that the scene has been sufficiently covered. "I've got to get cutaways, I've got to get an end point of the scene, and I've got to get into the scene some way," says director Susan Froemke. Filmmaker Steven Ascher notes that a scene must be filmed in a way that will allow its essence to be conveyed in significantly less than actual time. "Filming real life is a constant struggle to distill reality into a meaningful subset of itself . . . the telling moments, the telling gestures, the lines of dialogue that will suggest the rest of the scene without actually having to see the rest of the scene."

Scenes (alone or grouped in sequences) often culminate in reversals, called *turning points*, that motivate a shift in action of the overall story. For example, investigators analyzing the skeleton of a body believed to be that of an old man discover, instead, that they're the bones of a young woman. *Because* the body turned out to be that of a girl, investigators must release the suspect they brought in earlier. Or, fighting to get their ship across the Antarctic, Ernest Shackleton and his men become trapped by ice. *Because* Shackleton's ship is trapped, he and the men must set out on foot.

Sequence

A sequence is a collection of shots and scenes that together tell a more or less continuous story of an event that is a piece of your bigger story. Something like a book's chapter, a sequence in itself usually has a beginning, middle, and end. Note that a turning point at the end of a sequence will be bigger than one at the end of a scene or a shot. Story expert Robert McKee says that ideally, each scene creates a shift or reversal that is at least *minor*; each sequence, a change that is *moderate*; and each act, a change that is *major*.

Sequences can generally be summarized by the job they do in the overall storytelling. They're different from scenes in that they may cover a series of locations. *Frankie goes to the prom*, for example, is a sequence that might begin with Frankie rushing home from her job at the mall and might continue with her emerging from her bedroom in a long white gown, dancing with her boyfriend, crying in the ladies' room because she's been dumped, and then arriving home, where she collapses into her mother's arms.

It's important that the overall sequence advance the larger story you're telling. If, for example, you're doing a film about Frankie working doggedly to earn a college scholarship, you might not have as much use for a sequence about Frankie going to the prom as you would for one such as *Frankie gets an internship* or *Frankie retakes her SATs*. (The latter might begin with Frankie hiring a private tutor and continue with a montage of her studying late at night and on Saturdays, getting ready to take the test, entering the test room, and end with her nervously taking the envelope, with her results, out of the mailbox.) If Frankie going to the prom is just a pleasant distraction from her real task at hand—and your story—it's probably not worth the time and effort to film.

In *Bowling for Columbine*, Moore builds a sequence around two of the boys who were injured in Littleton, one of whom is partially paralyzed and both of whom are still suffering from the effects of what Moore describes as "17-cent bullets" from K-Mart. The sequence includes roughly four scenes (arguably, the different locations in the first scene could be counted separately, but it's not an exact science):

- In separate locations, each of the boys is interviewed and shows his wounds;
- Moore brings the boys to Troy, Michigan, where they go to K-Mart's headquarters and complain about the sale of bullets, but get little satisfaction;
- One of the boys goes to a nearby K-Mart and buys out its supply of bullets;
- Moore and the boys bring the K-Mart bullets, and the local press, back to K-Mart's headquarters, and this time get satisfaction—the company agrees to phase out its sale of ammunition.

These four scenes add up to a sequence that advances the story and, as Moore narrates it, motivates his decision to confront Charlton Heston.

Act

An act is a series of sequences that drives to a major turning point – a climactic moment that springs directly from the story and makes necessary the next series of sequences in the act that follows. Each act plays a role in the overall storytelling, and the tension and momentum within each should be increasing. In traditional three-act (also known as dramatic) structure, the first act covers the bulk of the story's exposition and, to paraphrase the late showman and writer George M. Cohan, gets your hero up a tree. In the second act, you throw rocks at him, forcing him higher up in the tree. In the third act, you force him to the edge of a branch that looks as if it might break at any moment . . . and then you turn the corner to your story's resolution, and let your hero climb down.

There are three important things to know about acts. The first is that there is something about dramatic structure that seems built into the way we receive and enjoy stories. The second is that many documentaries do not fit neatly into this structure, but an approximation of it. And third, there are many ways to create a compelling structural throughline—what fiction writer Madison Smartt Bell describes as "narrative design"—in a documentary without going anywhere near dramatic three-act structure. The film still needs to have compelling characters and rising tension, each scene should move the narrative forward, and the film should satisfactorily conclude the story (or mission, essay, journey, etc.) with which it began. But it doesn't have to do it in three acts.

Before we move into some specifics of act structure, here are a few other useful terms.

Inciting Incident

The inciting incident is the event that sets the action of the story into motion. It may be something that's occurred before you start filming. In *Lalee's Kin*, the slavery and sharecropping that have left a devastating legacy of poverty and illiteracy in the Mississippi Delta can be viewed as "inciting" the situation facing Lalee and her family. More tangibly, however, the film's story is incited when the Tallahatchie School District, where some of Lalee's grandchildren and great-grandchildren are enrolled, is put on probation. This sets in motion Superintendent Reggie Barnes's efforts to raise student achievement on the statewide standardized tests enough to get the schools off of probation.

In *Troublesome Creek*, the inciting incident also takes place before the filmmakers show up. That spring, when the Jordans got their yearly $150,000 operating loan from the bank, they learned that the local loan officer had been replaced by someone from corporate headquarters who would oversee their account, which—with an accumulated back debt of $70,000—was considered "troubled." Fearing that they were on the road to foreclosure, the Jordans decided to farm for one more year before auctioning off everything but their land to pay off their debt. It's this decision that sets the story of the film in motion.

Point of Attack

Not to be confused with the inciting incident, the point of attack is where *you*, as the filmmaker, enter the story. It's generally agreed that this is one of the hardest decisions to make over the course of production. In fact, it's often made and unmade many times before the right point of attack is found, and you can't imagine why you ever tried anything else. The point of attack ushers the viewer into the world of your film and its themes and characters. Discussing the opening visuals of his film *The City and the World*, episode seven of New York (1945–present), Ric Burns says, "It wasn't until fairly late in the editing process that we realized the beginning of the film was a moment in 1944 when Helen Leavitt borrows a 16mm movie camera and takes it up to the streets of East Harlem, and with a couple of friends, including James Agee, begins to shoot the footage that becomes her extraordinary film, *In the Streets*. That scene is absolutely, in my view, the best way to start that film, and it seems so completely inevitable—but it wasn't inevitable in the sense that we knew it from the beginning."

4 Little Girls, directed by Spike Lee and produced by Lee and Sam Pollard, begins in a cemetery, as on the soundtrack Joan Baez sings the haunting "Ballad of Birmingham," which recounts the deaths of four children in a church bombing in 1963. At one time, though, the film opened with Reggie Smith and other members of the Green Bay Packers running out onto a football field, according to Pollard, who edited the film. Smith, who is also a minister, linked the violence in Birmingham with more recent racially-motivated church burnings in the South. Executives at HBO didn't like the emphasis on sports, however, so the filmmakers created the current opening.

Your point of attack is almost guaranteed to change as you grow closer to your material and see which themes best serve the story you want to tell. You simply start with the best opening you have at that time and let it evolve from there.

Backstory

Backstory is a form of exposition, but the two terms are not always synonymous. The backstory includes the events that happened before the main story being told; it often includes material a filmmaker thinks is critical for the audiences to understand in order to "get" the story.

Backstory can be conveyed in a number of ways, including title cards (text on screen), interviews, and narration. Frequently, and sometimes painfully, it's the information that gets dropped in the cutting room because the story itself becomes so compelling and the themes so evident that the backstory is more of an interruption than a necessity. But when use of the backstory is motivated, it enhances and enriches the story unfolding on screen, adding depth to a character's motivation, illuminating themes and issues, or underscoring irony or historical continuity. A little goes a long way, however. If the backstory starts taking over your film, you might need to rethink which story, past or present, you really want to tell.

THREE-ACT STRUCTURE

For those who want to tread into the world of three-act structure, the following is a basic introduction. Three-act or dramatic structure is a staple of the Hollywood system, so one of the best ways to study it is to rent some current films (it's easiest to do this with popular dramatic films such as *My Cousin Vinny* or *Something to Talk About*, which are more likely to be built around a traditional three-act formula) and map them out, scene by scene, using a stopwatch or the video counter on your screen. You may not be able to really "see" the act structure until you're all the way through the film, but what you'll tend to find is that it *roughly* divides as follows:

Act One

The first act generally runs about one-quarter the length of the story. In this act, you introduce your characters and the problem or conflict (in other words, this act will contain most of your important exposition). Act One often contains the "inciting incident"—the event that gets everything rolling—although this event sometimes has already occurred when the story begins. There tends to be a "first turning point," which is somewhat smaller than the turning point that ends the act. By the end of Act One, the audience knows who and what your story is about and, at least initially, what's at stake. The first act drives to an emotional peak, the highest in the film so far, necessitating the action that launches the second act.

Act Two

The second act is the longest in the film, about one-half the length of the story. The stage has been set in Act One and the conflict introduced. In the second act, the story's pace increases as complications emerge, unexpected twists and reversals take place, and the stakes continue to rise. The second act can be difficult, because there is a risk that the story will bog down or become a succession of "and then this happened, and then this." You need your second act to continue to build as new information and new stakes are woven into your story. The second act drives to an emotional peak even greater than at the end of Act One, necessitating the action that launches the third act.

Act Three

The third act is usually slightly less than one-quarter the length of the story. As this act unfolds, the character is approaching defeat; he or she will reach the darkest moment just as the third act comes to a close. It's a common misperception that your third act resolves the story, but it doesn't. It intensifies it; the tension at the end of the third act should be even greater than the tension at the end of Act Two. That tension then pushes you into the *resolution*, those last moments where you resolve the story, tie up loose ends as necessary, and let your hero out of the tree.

Structuring Multiple Storylines

Although you can only tell one primary story, it's possible to follow two or even three storylines within that story. In Hollywood terms, these are "A" stories, "B" stories, and possibly even a "C" story. The "A" story carries the primary weight and is the story around which the piece is structured, but the other stories should also have emotional peaks and valleys.

Most importantly, the stories should inform each other, meaning that at some point they should connect to a coherent whole and advance a single overall storyline. With *Lalee's Kin*, matriarch

Lalee Wallace and school superintendent Reggie Barnes are the protagonists of separate but related stories. Both want what's best for the children in their care and both see education as the route to getting it. Lalee's grandchildren and great-grandchildren attend the schools that Barnes oversees; they embody the difficulty and hope of Barnes' work.

When she was filming *Lalee's Kin*, Susan Froemke also began pursuing a third storyline, about a man who taught literacy to young fathers in prison. It fit the program's themes, but there was no direct overlap and eventually the story was dropped. "In terms of storytelling and in terms of a budget it became almost overwhelming," Froemke says. "We found that the more questions we had and the more questions we answered we still had to keep simplifying." (About a year after the filming was complete, she adds, the stories did unexpectedly intersect, through the imprisonment of Lalee's son, Eddie Reed.)

Yosemite: The Fate of Heaven contrasts the primeval Yosemite that survived until the 19th century with the national park that today accommodates several million visitors a year. The filmmakers interweave two stories, one more clearly narrative than the other. The first is built around an 1854 diary kept by Lafayette Bunnell, who was part of a battalion that entered Yosemite on an Indian raid. "It was a search and destroy story, eerily reminiscent of Vietnam," says filmmaker Jon Else, "an old-fashioned war story of a bunch of soldiers looking for a bunch of Indians, and going out and driving the Indians from their home." The second is a more impressionistic look at the ongoing, day-to-day struggle to balance use of the park by those who love it with the needs of those who maintain it and are working to preserve it for the future.

The use of multiple storylines often enables filmmakers to create films that are more complex than would be possible with a strictly linear approach. Rather than tell everything in the order in which it occurred, they select an event *within* a life and use that to focus the primary film narrative, which frees them to look back into the past or even ahead into the future as needed. This format can be seen in the upcoming case study of *Daughter From Danang*.

What Three-Act Structure is Not

Three-act structure does not mean taking a film and dividing it into three parts and calling each part an act. An act can only be considered as such if it advances the one overall story (or essay) that you set out to tell. For example, a film that looks at early settlements in America cannot be structured, "Act One, Plymouth, MA; Act Two, Jamestown, VA; Act Three, New York, NY." There is no common story there; there may be common themes and this may work as an organizational construct for a film, but these aren't acts. On the other hand, you could tell three individual dramatic stories within that structure, one within each location that you then combine into a film.

Three Acts in Five or One or Two

Whether your film is described as having five acts or one, it can still follow dramatic (three-act) structure. There are many practical reasons to divide a story, including breaks for commercials (television) or audience intermission (theater). But "one-act" plays and "five-act" television specials can often still be divided into three acts. For example, while David Auburn wrote *Proof* as a fictional, two-act stage play, the action can easily be broken into three-act dramatic structure. Auburn's "first act" actually contains all of Act One and the first half of Act Two; his "second act" contains the balance of Act Two and all of Act Three. Where you break a story for reasons like commercials or intermissions is part of the structural discussion, but does not necessarily interfere with your use of dramatic three-act structure. With stakes rising throughout, there are natural places in most stories (e.g., the first turning point in the first act, the midpoint of the second act) that lend themselves to breaks.

Conversely, simply because a story is divided up for commercial breaks doesn't mean it's divided into acts; many biographical films, for example, are shaped more by chronology than a story being told, so that breaks come at dramatic moments but do not generally represent an underlying three-act structure.

Case Study: *Daughter From Danang*

Daughter From Danang, nominated for an Academy Award in 2003 and broadcast on PBS's THE AMERICAN EXPERIENCE, is roughly 78 minutes in length. As discussed, the film tells the story of Heidi Bub, an Amerasian woman raised in Tennessee who travels to Vietnam to meet the birth mother who gave her up for adoption.

Elements of the film include live-action shooting, archival footage and stills (including personal archival material), and interviews.

Filmmakers Gail Dolgin and Vicente Franco shot in Vietnam for about a week with Bub and did additional shooting in Vietnam after she went home. After they returned to the United States, they conducted a follow-up interview with her. "Everything happened quickly, and we were really just gathering material," Dolgin says. "We came back with the story we had and then started doing research for the backstory of Bub's experience in the U.S., the babylift, and what the mother's experience might be, and it wasn't until after we accumulated all of that and started looking at it that we said, "Wow, we've got a lot of material here, what do we do with it?"

At that point, they began approaching financiers, who wanted to know how the film would be structured. "They weren't asking for a script," she says, "but they wanted a clear sense of how we were going to tell the story." The filmmakers didn't want to tell a strictly chronological story, one that would begin with Bub's Vietnamese mother giving her up and move forward to the reunion. "We were playing with the concept of memory; it's so capricious," Dolgin says. "Heidi's memories of her past with her mother—she says at different times in the film, 'I had such great memories,' and 'The memories are so painful, they're all going to heal when I go to Vietnam.' " Because of this, they decided to structure the film around Bub's trip to Vietnam, using moments within the trip to motivate her memories of the past. "Working with that structure allowed us to figure out what story to craft out of this very complicated journey that we had all been on," she says.

The film took about a year to edit (Kim Roberts edited), and the final version offers an excellent example of three-act dramatic structure as applied to a documentary film. Note, however, that the timings and outline that follow are an analysis done by me, not the filmmakers. Dolgin says that the process of structuring their film was more organic, and that although they tried outlining material on the computer, "ultimately, having an Avid or any of the non-linear (digital editing) systems, you can do so much of that trial-and-error with the actual material that it just made more sense to work that way."

Zeroing the counter (00:00) at the first frame of action, Act One begins with text on screen that sets up basic information, that in 1975, the U.S. government launched "Operation Babylift," through which over 2,000 Amerasian children were brought to the United States for adoption. We then meet a Vietnamese woman (Bub's mother) who has sent her child away ("If I didn't send my child away," she says, "both she and I would die"), and an Amerasian woman (Heidi Bub) who remembers being torn from her family ("How could she do this to me? How could you just give up a child like that?"). Briefly, then, we have the inciting incident (the separation), the protagonist and opponent (daughter and mother), and a foreshadowing of the conflict that will emerge between them.

Act One continues with Bub and her mother, interviewed separately, anticipating their first meeting in 22 years. Finally, Bub's on a plane, "going home," which she says brings back memories: "I was born in Danang, in 1968." The filmmakers use this opening to motivate a return to the past: we learn more about Bub's birth (her mother says Bub "had no father"), the war, and why Bub's mother decided to send her away. (Note that the filmmakers tell us only what we need to know. Only later, for example, will we learn important details about Bub's father.)

Bub's mother brings her to the orphanage, telling her she "must never forget" (6:02). This is the first big turning point; it also provides motivation for the filmmakers to explore the historic issues of Operation Babylift and what it meant in terms of United States policy. Among the storytellers in this section is Tran Tuog (T.T.) Nhu. Identified as a journalist. She and her husband talk about their awareness, even then, that some of these "orphans" had families in Vietnam; through archival footage we see American social workers pressuring Vietnamese mothers to give up their children, a detail that adds complexity to the specific story of Bub and her mother.

A little more than 10 minutes into the film, Bub describes meeting her adoptive mother, with whom she moves to Tennessee, assuming an American identity. The sequence culminates with Bub being told, "If anybody asks where you were born, you tell 'em Columbia, South Carolina" (16:27).

But Bub's birth mother has begun searching for her daughter, and by coincidence gives a letter to an American who knows T.T. Nhu. Through her, the mother's letter reaches the Holt Adoption Agency. In the meantime, Bub, at the age of 20 or 21, started looking for her birth mother, and she, too, ends up at Holt. She contacts T.T. Nhu, and together they make plans to go to Vietnam for the reunion. This is the end of Act One, roughly a quarter of the way into the film.

Act Two begins on the plane, as T.T. Nhu and Bub head to Vietnam. Bub begins to worry; she's been "101% Americanized" and has "no earthly idea" of her family's expectations. In this act, the filmmakers show how out of place Bub is in her native Vietnam; they set up her nervousness about meeting her mother, and her high hopes for what this meeting will mean. "It's going to be so healing for both of us to see each other," Bub says. "It's going to make all of those bad memories go away, and all of those last years not matter anymore."

At around 24:00, Bub and the filmmakers meet Bub's mother and other members of her family in Vietnam. Had this moment come earlier, the audience would not have been as prepared as they are, by this point in the film, to *experience* it. We are emotionally invested in the reunion because we've gotten to know something about Bub and her mother, and we're curious about the growing number of questions that remain unanswered: Where is Bub's adoptive mother? Who was her father? Are Bub's expectations realistic?

The reunion plays on screen for a while before the filmmakers use another interview statement to again motivate a return to the past. "I always wanted the feeling that someone would love me no matter what," Bub says. "And I never had that with Ann [her adoptive mother]." This time, the filmmakers' exploration of the past drives to a painful revelation: escalating tension between Bub and her adoptive mother led to a severing of their relationship when Bub was still in college. By presenting this information here, the filmmakers have raised the stakes on the reunion currently under-way in Vietnam. Bub has felt rejected by two mothers; the reunion with the first now has added significance. We carry this new infor-mation with us as we return to Vietnam, and the visit continues.

Act Two continues in this fashion, balancing the story on screen with events that have led to these moments. We learn more about Bub's own family, her husband and two children, and her birth father, an American soldier. We also see a new complexity in the visit. Bub is getting homesick; she is over-whelmed by the poverty and lack of opportunity she encounters in Vietnam and newly appreciative of what her life in the United States has afforded her.

At this point, events themselves raise the stakes on Bub's story, as her Vietnamese family begins asking her for money. T.T. Nhu, serving as cultural interpreter for the viewer as well as for Bub, explains that having a relative overseas can be an important lifeline to those in Vietnam. But Bub says she doesn't want to be anybody's salvation; she came here to be reunited (50:00). Tension continues to build as we realize Bub and her family each have a very different understanding of what this visit might lead to. Increasingly critical of her mother and feeling smothered by her family's attention, Bub finally says, "I can't wait to get out of here."

But the worst is yet to come, which is part of what makes the third act so strong. T.T. Nhu has to leave, so a new translator is brought in to help Bub through a lengthy and painful family meeting in which all of the misunderstandings come to a head. Bub's brothers ask her to bring their mother to the United States; then they suggest that she assume her "filial responsibility" by sending a monthly stipend. Bub is hurt, then outraged, even refusing to allow her mother to comfort her (63:36). Speaking to the filmmakers, Bub takes a position almost opposite to the one with which she began the journey: "I wish I could have just kept the memories I had—they were so happy. I wish this trip never happened now." She leaves Vietnam, and when the filmmakers visit her at her home in Rhode Island shortly afterward, she's not even sure she wants to write to her mother; "I wouldn't know what to say." Arguably, Act Three ends either when Bub leaves Vietnam (off screen), or here, at around 75:00. Although she's achieved her initial goal, to reunite with her birth mother, Bub has not succeeded in forming a bond with her or "erasing" bad memories. In some ways, the two women seem farther apart than they were before the story began, because their hopes for the reunion are gone.

The resolution comes in the form of a brief epilogue, which begins with a caption that reads: "Two Years Later." Bub and her children are seen visiting her adoptive grandmother. In an interview, Bub summarizes her current feelings about her Vietnamese family. "I guess I have closed the door on them," she says, adding, "but I didn't lock the door. It's closed, but it's not locked." The ending, in part because of this ambiguity, is a satisfying resolution to the story that began the film.

Case study: *Bowling for Columbine*

Most documentaries don't follow three-act structure or don't follow it neatly. It's worth renting several films that you like and mapping them out as a way of decoding their structure. Briefly, here's a look at the Academy Award winner for 2003, Michael Moore's *Bowling for Columbine,* which has an essay-like structure that draws the viewer in through a series of escalating questions, as well as an interesting mix of humor and tragedy. Roughly 120 minutes long, the film's elements include archival footage from a wide variety of sources (home movies, informational films, advertisements, news coverage, etc.), interviews, and sequences set up by the filmmaker for the purpose of advancing his essay (such as the sequence in which he opens a bank account in order to qualify for the bank's offer of a free gun).

Interestingly, while the film does not tell a traditional character-driven story, the essay Moore crafts is, in many ways, built in three acts. Again, it's unlikely that this was plotted out in advance; the analysis is a construct used after the fact to better understand the very successful pacing of this film.

Zeroing the counter at the first frame of action, the film opens with old footage from the National Rifle Association, setting a tone of irreverence and setting the NRA up as something of a target in the film. "The NRA has produced a film, which you are sure to find of great interest," says the host on the clip. "Let's look at it." Moore's narration (in voice-over) then begins the essay: "It was the morning of April 20, 1999, and it was pretty much like any other morning in America . . . ." He continues through a range of images, and then adds, "and out in a little town in Colorado, two boys went bowling at six in the morning. Yes, it was a typical day in the United States of America." Note that the film assumes the viewer knows that this documentary is about a school shooting that took place on that date in 1999; he does not otherwise mention the shooting or tease it, because that's not, ultimately, what this film is about. Instead, Moore is exploring what, in his view, passes for "typical" in America. To demonstrate, he goes into a bank, opens an account, and walks out with a gun. "Here's my first question," he says, when the transaction is over and done with. "Do you think it's a little dangerous, handing out guns at a bank?"

The title sequence is followed by Moore bringing us up to speed on himself (the protagonist, who narrates the film first person) and the individual who embodies the opposition, Charlton Heston, the actor and president of the NRA. (Note that Heston is not strictly an antagonist, because he does nothing to obstruct Moore.) A series of humorous sequences follow. Moore gets a haircut and some ammo; comedian Chris Rock argues for bullet control, not gun control; Moore visits with the Michigan Militia and spends time with the tightly-wound James Nichols, whose brother, Terry Nichols, was convicted in the 1995 bombing of a federal building in Oklahoma City. Moore then hangs out with two other Michigan residents, Brent and DJ, whose "every kid" innocence evaporates the longer they talk, until we learn that DJ has in fact made bombs and most recently, a five-gallon drum of napalm. The sequence builds to a montage of quirky news stories about guns. Skillfully, Moore is following an old rule of tragedy, which is that you start with comedy. Then, about 19 minutes into the first act, the mood turns dark, as people start to get shot, hurt, and killed.

Moore now turns his attention to Littleton. He visits with a home security consultant whose eyes tear up at the thought of the violence at Columbine as he says "there's something about that kind of . . . indiscriminate killing"—which motivates Moore's transition to the Lockheed Martin factory, where he interviews a public relations official. Moore's premise here (bolstered by a montage of American aggression in such places as Iran and Chile) is that this industrial military complex is in the backyards of the "children of Littleton." At roughly 29 minutes, Moore shows two events that occurred on April 20, 1999, both announced by then-President Bill Clinton: U.S. bombing in Kosovo and, an hour later, a school shooting in Colorado. This ends Act One and drives us into Act Two.

For the next 3½ minutes, we are at Columbine High School, tapped in to the 911 emergency network, watching school security video, and seeing news footage of terrified students and parents. "When the shooting was over," Moore says, "Eric Harris and Dylan Kliebold had killed 12 students and 1 teacher. Dozens of others were wounded by the over 900 rounds of ammo that were fired. It is believed that the guns that they used were all legally purchased at stores and gun shows, and many of the bullets were bought at the Littleton K-Mart, just down the street." This sets up a new opponent, K-Mart, although Moore doesn't yet focus on the company (34:00).

Instead, Moore cuts to a fierce-sounding Charlton Heston. "I have only five words for you," Heston says. "From my cold, dead hands." In narration, Moore says that the NRA came to Littleton for a "big pro-gun rally" just 10 days after the shooting, despite requests that they stay away. This launches a sequence that looks at both the NRA and Columbine, merging the two through Heston's visit to Colorado and an interview with a former Columbine student, Matt Stone, best known for the cartoon *South Park*. Stone helps advance Moore's essay about this all being "normal"; he calls Columbine a "crappy school" and describes it as "painfully, painfully, painfully normal." At 40 minutes, Moore's essay expands on this. "I guess we'll never know why they did it, but one thing adults should never forget—it sucks being a teenager, and it really sucks going to school . . . Yes, and after Columbine it really sucked being a student in America." Fears of another Columbine have escalated school security measures; Moore shows "zero tolerance" policies that send children home for guns made out of paper or fried chicken. "Our children were indeed something to fear," Moore comments, "but who was to blame?"

This question, posed about 44 minutes into the film, motivates Moore's exploration into who or what's at fault. Heavy metal? Broken homes? Television? Shock rocker Marilyn Manson? "Why not blame bowling?" Moore asks, challenging this series of hypotheses as he points out that people all over the world bowl, listen to Goth music, watch violent movies, and play violent video games. Parents get divorced. People are poor. Other countries have violent pasts. But how many people are killed by guns? At 50:58—halfway through the film and halfway through the second act—Moore compares the number of annual gun deaths in the United States (11,127) with the next highest rate, Germany's (371) and wonders, "What is so different about Americans?"

As the second act continues, Moore offers an interpretation of American history (interweaving the stories of the Ku Klux Klan and the NRA) and concluding that everyone "lived happily ever after." But "if you turn on the evening news," Moore says, "America still seems like a pretty scary place." Moore uses television clips to demonstrate that Americans are being pumped with dread by hyped-up news reports and vague warnings from the White

House. He then walks through South Central Los Angles with Barry Glassner, author of *The Culture of Fear*, as he begins to weave a new strand into his argument—race. "The one thing you can always count on," Moore narrates, "is white America's fear of the black man." We're still in the second act, as Moore spends about 10 minutes looking at the media's negative portrayal of black men, in the news and on entertainment programs such as *Cops*. "Anger, hate, and violence do well in the ratings," a former producer of that show tells Moore. The producer turns the next corner in Moore's essay as he adds, "You watch violence on TV in a place like Canada, and you *know* it's not next door. You watch it here, and you know it is happening next door . . . I don't know what the difference is." Moore says he doesn't know either, and he sets out to find out.

So, roughly 71 minutes into the film, Moore is in Canada, opening unlocked doors and interviewing progressive government officials. "Night after night, the Canadians weren't being pumped full of fear," Moore concludes, "and their politicians seemed to talk kind of funny." The latter statement offers a transition for the sequence to come.

Roughly 81 minutes into the film, we hear a 911 call from Flint, Michigan. Moore visits with the principal of an elementary school where a 6-year-old first-grader shot and killed his classmate, a little girl. It's possible to view this transition as the end of Act Two and the beginning of Act Three; the shift escalates Moore's essay considerably and bring new strands into the argument. The filmmaker builds an unflattering portrait of the media pack that gathers in the tragedy's aftermath, and then uses their focus only on the sensationalism of the immediate story to explore the issue they're *not* covering—poverty in Flint.

At the elementary school, Moore is comforting the principal when he brings in his old nemesis; we hear Heston's voice again saying, "From my cold, dead hands." Moore then cuts to Heston on camera (88:14), as Moore says, "Just as he did after the Littleton shooting, Charlton Heston showed up in Flint to have a big pro-gun rally." Reminding us of Heston makes sense in terms of his film's structure, but this particular connection is a leap. Heston reportedly didn't go to Flint for several months. In any event, Moore's focus in the essay now is to connect the tragedy at the elementary school to Michigan's "welfare to work" program, and in turn to link that to "the number one firm states turned to privatize welfare systems—Lockheed Martin."

After traveling to Los Angeles to confront entertainer Dick Clark, owner of one of the restaurants at which the boy's mother worked, Moore abruptly escalates his argument, cutting to an image of President George W. Bush as he posits, "In George Bush's America, the poor were not a priority, and after September 11, 2001, correcting America's social problems took a back seat to fear, panic, and a new set of priorities." We see the president pushing for support of his military budget, followed by news coverage about people arming themselves. "The threat seemed very real," Moore says, adding that "our growing fears were turned into a handsome profit for many." Making it clear who he's referring to, Moore cuts to home security systems companies and leading politicians, before adding, "And what better way to fight box cutter–wielding terrorists than to order a record number of fighter jets from Lockheed?" The strands of Moore's essay are coming together as he adds, about 98 minutes into the 120-minute film, "the greatest benefit of it all, of a terrorized public, is that the corporate and political leaders can get away with just about anything."

Like a good monologist, Moore now brings the threads of the story back to their initial focus—Columbine. "A public that's this out of control with fear should not have a lot of guns or ammo laying around," he says. At about 99:30, he begins the sequence described earlier, in which two victims of Columbine succeed in getting K-Mart to agree to stop selling ammunition. Their victory, Moore says, inspired him to "do something that I knew I had to do"—confront the opponent he identified at the start of the film. His visit to Heston's home (107:15) is more than 8 minutes long. As Moore leaves Heston's estate, Act Three ends, leading to the film's resolution. Moore, the narrator, says that he's returning to the real world, "an America living and breathing in fear . . . where gun sales were now at an all-time high . . . and where in the end, it all comes back to bowling for Columbine. (He cuts to news footage of a triple murder at a Littleton bowling alley.) "Yes," Moore says, "it was a glorious time to be an American." The filmmaker sends a ball down the lanes at a bowling alley—and bowls a strike.

APPLYING FILM STRUCTURE

Some documentary filmmakers think about structure over the course of production but don't focus on it until they're editing. Others play with structure from the start, creating outlines that they return to during production and post-production, revising them and reshaping them as needed. No matter how you anticipate structuring your film or what your process is, structure is a type of grid that allows you to anticipate and critique, the rhythms of your storytelling—not a formula for production.

In terms of actually weighing the relative length of scenes, sequences, and acts, it's safe to say that most filmmakers don't do it; storytelling is usually more intuitive. However, if a film feels like it takes forever to get going, or your test audiences love the opening but lose interest from there, or your audience is thoroughly confused by a terrific ending that seems to have nothing to do with the film you introduced at the beginning, mapping structure can be a good idea.

I do it all the time in my consulting. I try to figure out what the film story is at its most basic, and then I go through the film with a stop watch and sketch out where the story goes and when it reaches its various peaks. Seeing the film on a single piece of paper like that, it's often very easy to see that it began twice, or that the first act is twice as long as it should be, or that the third act drives to a climactic moment that may be emotional but is unsatisfying because it has nothing to do with story that began Act One.

As you do this, keep in mind that if a film is working—even if the charts and stopwatches say it shouldn't be—*leave it alone.* Storytelling is an art, not a science. Go with your gut. If the film's great, who cares what "rules" you broke?

$$5$$

Manipulating Time

Film is a linear medium. People watch it from beginning to end, with one shot following another, one sequence following another, until the film is over. "I've never seen an even vaguely successful documentary film that does not move forward through time," says filmmaker Jon Else, citing a number of disparate examples. "*Night and Fog* has an absolutely traditional, very simple forward chronological motion through the late 1930s to the end of World War II. *Tongues Untied*, Marlon Riggs's film, appears to be a nonlinear rumination about what it means to be young and gay and black in America in the 1980s, but in fact it moves through his life. Even Chris Marker's *Sans Soleil*, which is often described as being nonlinear, moves forward through time. This whole business of a plot moving forward, I think, is just so inextricably embedded in our cultural DNA."

Moving a story forward through time, as evidenced by the above examples, does not mean resorting to a plodding narrative that is strictly a chronological recitation of events in the order they occurred. Often, it involves the interweaving of chronological and nonchronological elements to form a cohesive and satisfying whole; a film that drives forward while being enriched and made complex by elements outside or apart from the chronology. *Daughter From Danang* selects an event within the chronology of Heidi Bub's life—her trip to Vietnam—to explore issues and events that cover the entire span of her life.

But there are other ways to present even a focused chronological story in an order that better satisfies the requirements of good dramatic storytelling. This is done not through the fictionalization of actual events, but through the creative manipulation of time—presenting those events in an order that you, as the filmmaker, can control.

TELLING A CHRONOLOGICAL STORY, BUT NOT CHRONOLOGICALLY

As a documentary storyteller, you decide where to begin and end the story. You can begin in the middle, go back to the beginning, catch up with your story, and then move ahead to the end. You can start at the end before moving to the beginning to ask, "How did we get here?" You can flash forward or back. The only thing you can't do, in a documentary that's driven by a narrative sequence of events, is change the important facts of the main underlying chronology.

Suppose you've unearthed a story in the archives of your local historical society. The following are the events in chronological order:

- A young man becomes engaged;
- His older brother enlists to fight in World War II;
- The young man also enlists;
- Their father dies;
- The young man is shipped overseas;
- He learns that his brother has been killed;
- His fiancée sends a letter, breaking off their engagement.

These events haven't happened in an order that's particularly dramatic, and there's no way to tell, on the surface, which events are linked by cause and effect. It may be that *because* his brother enlisted, the young man also felt obligated, but there could be other reasons. If you can verify your characters' motivations, whether through records or eyewitnesses, you can state them; otherwise, present the facts and let the audience draw its own conclusions. By the same token, you may not rearrange the underlying chronology to imply a more interesting cause and effect. For example, based on the above chronology, you might be tempted to:

- Present the father's death followed by the enlistment of the two sons, to create the impression that they enlisted in his honor;

- Film a recreation in which the young man, already in uniform, proposes marriage;
- Present the fiancée's letter in voice-over as the young man enlists, implying that he's reacting to the breakup.

Each of these might be dramatic, but they all lead the audience to a false understanding of cause and effect. This doesn't mean that you're forced into a straightforward chronological narrative, however; you can tell the story in any order you like, or select from among the characters and events, as long as you do so accurately. Start with the young man's rejection by his fiancée, for example, and then reveal that this is another in a string of losses. Leave the father and fiancée out of the story and focus on the two brothers at war. Tell the story of the young man going to war and then go back to follow the story of his engagement. There's plenty of room for creativity.

An example of a documentary that creates a false impression of chronology, to the detriment of an otherwise powerful argument and film, is Michael Moore's *Roger & Me*. Critic Harlan Jacobson published a detailed review of this film in the November/December 1989 issue of *Film Comment*, outlining some of the problems. The film's present-day narrative begins in late 1986, when, according to Moore, General Motors chairman Roger Smith closes 11 plants in Flint, Michigan, leaving 30,000 people jobless and sending the city on a downward spiral.

Moore then presents a series of events, including these, in this order:

- Eleven GM plants are opened in Mexico, where, Moore says, workers can be paid 70 cents an hour;
- The last vehicle rolls off the assembly line in Flint;
- Ronald Reagan visits Flint; over archival news footage, Moore narrates, "Just when things were beginning to look bleak, Ronald Reagan arrived in Flint . . . " At the end of the scene, Moore says someone "borrowed the cash register on his way out the door";
- A parade is held in Flint, and Moore interviews Miss Michigan shortly before she'll compete to be Miss America;
- Evangelist Robert Schuller comes to Flint to cheer people up;
- As Moore presents an abandoned and decaying Flint, he says, "The city had become the unemployment capitol of

the country. Just when it looked like all was lost, the city fathers came up with one last great idea." This plan includes the building of a Hyatt Regency hotel downtown; the Water Street Pavilion, a new shopping center; and the opening of Auto World.

Remember that the film began with the closing of 11 plants in Flint, late in 1986. From Harlan Jacobson's article, here is the actual chronology of the events:

- In 1980, Ronald Reagan arrives in town as a presidential candidate and buys folks pizza. Two days before his visit, the cash register was stolen;
- In 1982, Reverend Schuller comes to Flint and the Hyatt Regency is opened;
- Auto World opens in mid-1984 and closes in early 1985;
- In 1986, the Water Street Pavilion opens, the result of a plan that may have been underway since the early 1970s. Also in 1986, the number of layoffs at GM do not total 30,000 but about 10,000, according to Jacobson. The real "watershed" of layoffs had occurred much earlier, in 1974. The net loss of jobs since 1974 was about 32,000.
- In the fall of 1988, shortly after the parade, Miss Michigan is crowned Miss America.

In other words, many of the events presented as the efforts of the powers-that-be to staunch the bleeding from the 1986 layoffs actually occurred or were underway long before those layoffs took place. Jacobson's article includes an interview with Moore, in which he asks the filmmaker about these issues. "The movie is about essentially what happened to this town during the 1980s," Moore responded. "As far as I'm concerned, a period of seven or eight years . . . is pretty immediate and pretty devastating" [*ellipses in the original*]. Moore argued that he was trying to "tell a documentary in a way they don't usually get told. The reason why people don't watch documentaries is they are so bogged down with 'Now in 1980 . . . then in '82 five thousand were called back . . . in '84 ten thousand were laid off . . . but then in '86 three thousand were called back . . . but later in '86 ten thousand more were laid off.' "

In fact, telling an accurate story doesn't have to mean getting bogged down in detail or needing to tell the story sequentially.

Arguably, you could leave the edit of *Roger & Me* exactly as it is and simply rewrite Moore's narration. For example, there's nothing to stop your use of footage of candidate Reagan stumping through Flint years before the plant closings; you simply write into it in a way that acknowledges the time shift. Here's Moore's narration, building on the aftermath of the 1986 layoff: "Just when things were beginning to look bleak, Ronald Reagan arrived in Flint and took a dozen unemployed workers out for a pizza. He told them he had come up with a great idea, and if they tried it they'd all be working again." (In archival footage, a woman then explains that Reagan suggested they move to another state to find work.)

Alternative narration: *People had been trying to help the unemployed in Flint for years. As a candidate in 1980, future president Ronald Reagan took a dozen workers out for some pizza and inspiration.*

The narration needs to keep track of where you are in the film's present—in this case, somewhere between 1986 and 1988—while letting us know that what we're seeing is from the past, and how it informs the present. What to do about the cash register theft? This sounds like one of those facts that are "too good to check," but it must be done. If you know that the theft occurred two days before Reagan's visit, and you really want to use it, you have to be a bit creative.

Moore's words: "None of Reagan's luncheon guests got back into the factories in the ensuing years, and the only bright spot to come out of the whole affair was the individual who borrowed the cash register on his way out the door."

It's unclear whether these luncheon guests were already laid off before Reagan arrived (and stayed that way) or if they were employed between Reagan's visit and the layoffs later in the 1980s. In any case (or if you can't find out the specifics about the individuals in this footage), you could say something more general, such as: *In the years to come, Reagan's luncheon guests may have wished that instead of listening to the candidate, they'd taken a cue from the guy who'd robbed the pizza parlor two days earlier and made off with the cash register.*

While mine is not brilliant voice-over, it's a quick example of how you can tell a story out of order, with as much irreverence as you want, without building a case that has a weak or inaccurate foundation. To imply that the visits of Reverend Schuller and Ronald Reagan and the opening of the Hyatt Regency and Auto

World occurred both after and because of a plant closing in 1986 is simply inaccurate. In his defense, Moore told Jacobson that *Roger & Me* isn't a documentary but "an entertaining movie that hopefully will get people to think a little bit about what is going on." However, audiences and critics received the film as a documentary, and it's highly regarded as such. The power of doumentaries comes from their veracity, and it's undermined if people discover that in the interest of a compelling argument, they've been misled.

Not all documentaries or sequences within them need to adhere to a strict chronology; filmmakers may rearrange filmed sequences if they are typical but not necessarily specific to a timeline, such as routine events (skateboard practice, Sunday church, an annual holiday). Where you place this material in the film, regardless of when it was shot, is generally up to you. If you're following a group of people—residents in an assisted living center, for example—your choice of which scenes and stories to present and when may be driven by the emotional argument you're building, rather than any specific chronology or the order in which stories were filmed. (Within each story, however, rules of cause and effect still apply. If a woman suffers a heart attack, recovers, and then dances with her husband at a formal dinner, it would be dishonest to edit the sequence to imply that the dancing led to the heart attack.)

Material filmed for thematic reasons may also stand apart from the chronological sequence. An example of this can be found in the Academy Award–winning documentary *Troublesome Creek: A Midwestern*, in which filmmakers Jeanne Jordan and Steven Ascher follow the efforts of Jordan's parents to save their family's farm from foreclosure. The chronology is built on the Jordans' efforts to pay off a bank debt by auctioning off their belongings. For thematic reasons, the filmmakers asked the Jordans to return to a farm they'd rented for many years before moving to the farm they're now at risk of losing. The scene's exact placement in the film, other than sometime before the auction, isn't specific. Jordan's voice-over simply says, "Early one morning we took a trip to Rolfe to visit . . . the farm I grew up on." Jordan's parents are upset to discover that the old place is abandoned, but their visit doesn't motivate any action. Instead, it serves a filmmaking purpose— shedding light on the historical context of the overall film and on themes of change and loss.

COLLAPSING AND EXPANDING TIME

Filmmaking, from shooting through editing, is a process of expanding and/or collapsing real time. "Filming real life is a constant struggle to distill reality into a meaningful subset of itself, into the telling moments, the telling gestures, the lines of dialogue that will suggest the rest of the scene without actually having to see the rest of the scene," says Steven Ascher. The event needs to be covered with the editor in mind, so that there is enough variety of shots, cutaways, and transitional material to make a creative edit possible.

For the most part, simple editing can imply a passage of time. Your characters are at home, seated around the breakfast table, and then they're on the school basketball court; or your character is trying on a tux for the prom, and then he's at the prom. If the story has been taking place in the summertime, and you cut to children playing in the snow, the season has changed. Sometimes, filmmakers emphasize passage of time with dissolves, time-lapse photography, an interlude with music, or a montage. If the passage of time is part of the story, the filmmaker might comment on that by showing a clock, as Errol Morris did to mark the hours that passed while Randall Adams was being pressured to confess in *The Thin Blue Line*.

The amount of time you give to a scene is important; some scenes may be granted greater or less emotional weight than others through the length of time you devote to them. For example, you might spend 2 minutes of screen time bringing the audience up to date on 10 years of history prior to a candidate's decision to run for office, and then spend the next 45 minutes on an 8-month campaign. You've collapsed the first part of the chronological story in order to focus more time on the campaign itself. And sometimes you expand time because you've built to an emotional moment and you need to let it play, as was true in at the end of *Bridge to Freedom*, the last hour of the first season of Eyes on the Prize.

CONDENSING INTERVIEWS

There are two primary reasons to edit an interview: to focus information for placement in the best possible location in your film's story and to shorten it. A person will talk to you for 10 minutes, an hour, maybe two or three hours, and you'll end up using only a few bites at most, unless the entire film is "a conversation with." In any case, you must condense the interview material in a way that does not alter its initial meaning, no matter how "close" it might be or how accurate it remains. You have to remain true to the intent of the speaker, not the story. For example, here's the raw transcript of a witness describing your character, Sanders:

> *CHARLIE: Sanders wasn't a bad man, in fact I'd have to say he was a pretty good guy, overall, which is why nobody could figure out—at least I couldn't figure out—uh, what the, what he was doing even thinking about embezzlement. I don't know, but I think, I mean, who knows, but in my opinion, he was just panicked about money. I mean for crying out loud, this guy's got three, uh, three, uh, you know, he's got three kids and another one on the uh, on the way—maybe it got to him, I don't know, maybe he just couldn't figure out how he was going to support all these little ones or whatever, you know? He was selling auto parts, used auto parts. Besides, embezzlement's a white collar crime, he's a blue collar guy—well, not really, he's not working with the auto parts, he's more the manager of the store, driving to work in his, oh, what was it, Tercel, his blue Tercel, shirt and tie and all the while I guess he's thinking nobody above him would miss that thirty thou. Arrogance, I guess. Yeah. Arrogance.*

What can't you use? No matter how catchy it sounds, I wouldn't use, "embezzlement's a white collar crime, he's a blue collar guy" for two reasons. Sanders is not, in fact, blue collar, and furthermore, the witness *himself* corrects this statement.

In terms of editing for time, however, condensing the *essence* of this paragraph, you could do any number of cuts depending on the point you want Charlie to make and where it will be used in the film. What material is the interview bite following? What will it precede? One of the ways to see this before trying it in the editing room is to make the cut on paper, which you can then give to the editor. Two things to remember. First, don't make the editor crazy by cutting out every third word and expecting her to construct a sentence or a paragraph out of the bits and pieces. This is very difficult and very time-consuming, and furthermore, any interview material that's hacked to bits will have to be used as a voice-over. In any case, if you're hacking an interview to bits, chances are good that either you've interviewed the wrong person or you're asking this interview to do a job in the film it wasn't meant to do, and you should probably look for other solutions.

The second thing to remember is that a cut on paper may not work on film. The way people speak often reads different than it sounds. People end sentences with a question, or they run two sentences together, or they burp or sigh or a plane flies overhead or their energy level shifts so much that you can't cut between two bites. You do the best you can to note the big issues when you're watching rushes (the raw footage) with the transcripts in hand, but there will still be times when something that should work just doesn't.

With that said, there are a few tricks to increasing the odds that your paper cut will work. It's generally easier to cut into a hard consonant, such as b, t, or v. Words that begin with soft consonants, such as s or h, can be more difficult. Note that just because you cut the "Well" from "Well, I think it started" doesn't mean that the editor can make the excision. Usually, though, if one bite or cut doesn't work, there will be something else available that's close enough. Finally, there is a rhythm to how long a person needs to be on camera before you can cut away from him, depending in part on whether you've seen the person on camera before. While this is something you can anticipate in a paper cut, it can't really be decided until the editor is working with the material. (And as will be discussed in Chapter 12, another common problem is that as the schedule wears on, the production crew gets tired of interview bites they once found exciting and cuts them too close.)

Covering the edits is a matter of style—whether you want to use cutaways, or jump cuts; how long you want to cut away from someone; how long before you need to see that person again on camera. Sometimes, you let an interview play simply because you don't want to interrupt the answer; conducting the interview with this in mind, requesting more condensed versions of answers if possible, will help with this. And sometimes, the entire interview will be "voice under," especially if the footage is all of one person and/or it's very obvious who is speaking. Effective portraits of people at work—a zookeeper, an underwater explorer—have been done this way.

Of course, editing *within* an interview is only one solution. You can also synthesize a story by using multiple storytellers and cutting between them, or using narration to reduce the amount of interview needed or to state concisely something with which the interviewee struggled. For this discussion, the focus is on reducing the length of the interview in a way that is consistent with generally accepted principles of documentary ethics. For example, here are some ways to shorten the interview in which Charlie discusses his friend, Sanders:

- CHARLIE: Sanders wasn't a bad man, in fact I'd have to say he was a pretty good guy, overall, which is why nobody could figure out . . . what he was doing even thinking about embezzlement. . . . Arrogance, I guess. Yeah. Arrogance.

- CHARLIE: *(beginning v/o)* . . . he was just panicked about money . . . *(possibly on camera)* he's got three kids and another one on the uh, on the way—maybe it got to him, I don't know, maybe he just couldn't figure out how he was going to support all these little ones or whatever, you know?

- CHARLIE: He was selling auto parts, used auto parts . . . driving to work in his, oh, what was it, Tercel, his blue Tercel, shirt and tie and all the while I guess he's thinking nobody above him would miss that thirty thou.

Depending on what your story is and where you're going with it, each of these edits might work. The first gets to the root of *why* Sanders did it, at least in Charlie's opinion—arrogance. The second explores a more sympathetic reason behind the crime. And the third paints a picture and gives some specific information about Sanders and his job. If you already have Sanders' wife describing him staying up late at night panicked by bills, you might not want to use version #2. If in fact he was not at all arrogant, just blindly panicked, you might not use #1. And if you find out that he drove a used BMW, you can't use #3 because it's not accurate. Your talking heads must be fact-checked, and errors can't be left in simply because you, the filmmaker, didn't say it. By leaving it in, you *are* saying it. Note that a significant exception is when the falsehood is part of the story, as was the case with the "eyewitnesses" rounded up by law enforcement personnel in *The Thin Blue Line*.

Another problem to watch out for when condensing interview material (or any sync material, which includes footage of people talking to others on camera) is that out of context, something may honestly seem to mean one thing, but those who were on the shoot know that it meant something else. This is why I think it's essential that someone connected with the original shooting be involved in the edit, or at least given a chance to sign off on it. (Usually, the director maintains this oversight, and/or the producer, but cost-cutting has led some venues to use "field crews" that are relatively separate from the process of editing.) Without a direct link to production, it's easy for well-meaning people to misconstrue an interview's meaning. (For the same reason, a writer or consultant who begins work on a film in progress should refer back to original transcripts and unedited footage.)

The shades of gray when collapsing interviews put the onus on the filmmakers to watch out for solutions that might prove less than accurate. Something as simple as taking a sentence from late in the interview and putting it at the beginning might make sense for the overall film, but if it distorts the interview, you can't do it. "You've always got to try to know when to back away from that stuff," says filmmaker Sam Pollard, "not to manipulate it to such a degree that it's like a lie."

6

Approach

If you gave any group of filmmakers some gear and the general topic, "the minimum wage," you'd end up with very different films and film stories. One filmmaker might look at the historical roots of the federal minimum wage, the efforts to establish it in the 1930s, and the various raises in the wage prior to the current level. Another might look at the controversial issues concerning the impact of minimum wage on employment—does raising minimum wage help or hurt workers at the low end of the job market? A third filmmaker might decide to film only those people who are "making it"—or not—on $5.15 an hour. And a fourth might compare two workers doing the same job for the same company, one for minimum wage in the United States, another for a minimum wage set overseas. In addition, the four films will be made using vastly different film styles, points of view, and tones. In fact, two films could be made that looked only at minimum wage workers in the United States, and they're likely to hardly resemble each other, even if the filmmakers are working with the same raw material.

These differences are in what's known as approach—how you present your story on screen. Do you intend to create a half-hour special or a 10-hour series? Is your tone humorous? What production elements will you use, such as live shooting, recreations, a narrator, time-lapse photography, or animation?

It's helpful to begin thinking about your approach almost as soon as you come up with a subject or story that interests you. If you've become passionately interested in the War of 1812, for example, you'll need to think about how you might make a film about this event that occurred before the invention of photography. If you want to film a local daycare center, it would be good to know early on what kind of access you'll want and what sort of filming schedule you'll need. Following the residents of a group home on a field trip to Washington is very different than filming them over the course of a year as neighbors seek their eviction. Your approach will evolve as your knowledge of the material increases and you have a better sense of what's practical, but it's good to start off with some ideas.

Main and Redman, from *Lalee's Kin: The Legacy of Cotton*. Photo courtersy of the filmmakers.

One way to begin the process is to screen many films and talk with your collaborators about which elements you like or don't like, and which might best serve the project at hand. Do you want to create an intimate portrait or a stylized whodunit? An historical film using archival footage or recreations, or both? Watching several films by the same filmmaker can also help you to get a sense of how style and approach change depending on the project. Conversely, see how some filmmakers bring a fairly established style to subjects chosen, in part, because they are *suited* to that style.

Approach involves the essence of the film itself. Suppose, for example, that you're drawn to the issues of abused, abandoned, and stray pets and what happens to them in shelters. You might decide to:

- Create a journalistic piece on animal welfare that uses experts and news-style footage to explore controversial issues such as unethical breeding, the culture of "fight dogs," and the issue of euthanasia;
- Create a cinéma vérité portrait of one shelter and its staff for whom these issues are part of a day-to-day struggle, as Cynthia Wade and Heidi Reinberg did in the feature-length documentary, *Shelter Dogs*;
- Script and narrate a film that involves a family re-enacting its search in local shelters for a dog to bring into their home, and then film the process by which experts can rebuild trust and calm aggression in dogs that have been abused.

As another example, suppose you know what elements you want to use for an historical film, but not how to use them. You have a collection of diaries, letters, and newspaper clips pertaining to your story, which is set in the past. You might do the following:

- Have actors read this material in voice-over, as in Ken Burns's work;
- Have actors portray the authors of this archival material and appear, in period costume, on camera; this was the style used by the producers at Middlemarch Films for their series LIBERTY! THE AMERICAN REVOLUTION;
- Have actors perform this archival material on camera but without costumes or make-up, as was done by actors portraying the elderly former slaves documented by workers for the Works Progress Administration, in the HBO film *Unchained Memories*.

A final example: Who will tell the stories in your film? What will drive the narrative?

- In *Lalee's Kin*, an observational film, title cards (text on screen) are used to convey introductory exposition, location identification, and occasional details that ground the viewer in the scenes to follow; note that the use of this is very

different than the "chapter titles" seen in some of Ken
Burns's work;

- In *Brother Outsider: The Life of Bayard Rustin*, a historical
  film about a key figure in the civil rights movement, filmmakers Bennett Singer and Nancy Kates also eschew narration in favor of narrative conveyed through on-screen
  storytellers, headlines, surveillance reports, and excerpts
  of various writings by Bayard Rustin, read in voice-over
  by an actor;
- In Nick Broomfield's *Kurt & Courtney*, a film about the death
  of rock star Kurt Cobain that paints an unflattering portrait
  of his widow, Courtney Love, Broomfield makes himself
  and his quest to make the film the story of the film.
- In some of the more popular biography series on television,
  the focus is less on storytelling and more on a sort of narrated "scrapbook" approach to a celebrity's life, telling the
  key events in chronological order and building to emotional
  highs and lows, such as illness, marriage, or scandal.

In discussing your approach, think about whether you want some
or all of your film to be observational (*Lalee's Kin* is an example of a
film that's almost entirely observational; many, many films include
some observational sequences); whether you want to set up sequences (such as Michael Moore bringing two Columbine victims
to K-Mart headquarters, or Alan Berliner inviting a dozen other
real-life Alan Berliners to his New York City apartment); or
whether you want to direct a demonstration of some sort. For a
series called THE RING OF TRUTH, I was involved in arranging a
sequence in which we drove a yellow rental van 183 miles due
south and charted the path of Antares at each location, in order to
do a modern-day version of an ancient measurement of the Earth's
circumference. The entire demonstration, involving the series'
hosts, Professor Philip Morrison and his wife, Phylis, had to be
planned well in advance.

There is an approach to consider for almost every aspect of
your filmmaking. Will you interview people alone, together, inside,
outside, informally? Will the interviewer be on camera or off
screen? If off screen, will the questions be heard at all by the
viewers? Not every detail needs to be considered right up front,
but, for example, if you're telling the story of a particular military
unit, rather than interview members separately, there might be

value added to bringing them together and filming their inter-action. (What you want, however, is for this interaction to be genuine. You almost never want to ask non-actors to recreate the past, especially if it includes dialogue, and you don't want to set up scenes in which people tell each other information that they already know, as in "Well, Jim, wasn't it a good thing that we invented that breathing apparatus?" "Yes, Pete, without it many more lives might have been lost.")

ARCHIVAL FILMMAKING

Say "archival films" and most people think of Ken Burns and THE CIVIL WAR. While this is a great example of archival filmmaking, there are plenty of other films that use archival footage. Films on science and technology, biographies, personal essays, and diary films all may use archival material. The material might have originated as news footage, a training film, an advertising piece, footage to promote a company or product, or even another docu-mentary.

In fact, "archival" is a term often used to describe any footage that is not filmed specifically for the purposes of the docu-mentary in question, and can therefore refer to all sorts of found or acquired material. In *Bowling for Columbine*, for example, Michael Moore fancifully uses archival material from diverse sources, in-cluding promotional material for the National Rifle Association, 1950s footage of people bowling, news footage of hunters, and home movies of Moore himself as a kid growing up in Michigan. These create an overall portrait that is at once very American, very normal, and not a little disturbing.

Alan Berliner has been collecting others' family photos and home movies for years, the visual history of people whose identities are unknown to him, and he used these eloquently in films such as *Nobody's Business* and *The Sweetest Sound*. The archival imagery in Jay Rosenblatt's *Human Remains* was selected not to tell any chronological story, but because the men it captures on screen—men known to history for the atrocities they committed—are seen doing disturbingly ordinary things, such as eating or playing with dogs and children.

How you use the archival material is also important. THE CIVIL WAR, mentioned above, used archival imagery to illustrate and advance a powerful and thematically rich narrative. That series has also spawned a wealth of knock-offs. Take two parts archival material, the thinking seems to go, add one part emotional music, a dash of brand-name actors in voice-over, and you've got a film. The missing element, too often, is *story*. With archival films, that story is often driven by narration, with visuals playing a supporting role. In rare cases, however, where sufficient archival resources exist, the visuals can drive the storytelling.

This was the case with two public television series, VIETNAM: A TELEVISION HISTORY and EYES ON THE PRIZE. In developing EYES, executive producer Henry Hampton decided that rather than present a survey of the civil rights movement, roughly a 30-year period, he wanted to tell a selection of stories within that period and let them unfold, as dramas, on screen. To a large degree, this type of archival storytelling was made possible by a heyday of network news and documentary reporting, from the 1950s to the early 1970s, when stories were covered in depth and over a significant period of time. Editors on the documentary series had sufficient archival footage to craft scenes with beginnings, middles, and ends; there were cutaways and on-camera interviews that could then be augmented with modern-day interviews. Narration occurred only where it was needed to seam together other elements.

Both of these series established rigorous rules for the use of archival material. An image could not "stand in" for something else, and the rules of chronological order applied to footage just as it did to facts. This meant that if you were telling the story of rioting in Detroit in 1967, you couldn't use a great shot that you knew had been shot on a Thursday if your narrative was still discussing events on Tuesday. The intent was to create a series that would itself be authoritative.

On VIETNAM: A TELEVISION HISTORY, particular care was also taken with sound effects and the layering of sound onto otherwise silent film footage. "We sent all our silent archival footage to the Imperial War Museum in London," remembers archivist Kenn Rabin, "and they matched sound effects." If the footage showed a particular helicopter or a particular weapon firing, the sound effect would be of that model helicopter or that model weapon. "We were very careful not to add anything that would editorialize," Rabin adds. "For example, we never added a scream or a baby crying," he said, unless you could see that action on screen.

Many historical films and series do not have access to such a wealth of footage, and must rely on images from diverse sources such as original shooting, archival material, and artwork, to bolster a visual record that's sparse. The degree to which one historical image may stand in for another is a subject of some debate among filmmakers and historians. Producers of THE CIVIL WAR grappled with this issue in making their series. At a conference in 1993 ("Telling the Story: The Media, The Public, and American History," a project of the New England Foundation for the Humanities in association with the Massachusetts Cultural Council), Ken Burns presented a clip from THE CIVIL WAR and then said that, with two exceptions, none of the "illustrative pictures" actually depicted what the narrative implied. "There is a street scene taken in the 1850s of a small Connecticut town, which is used to illustrate Horace Greeley's 1864 lament about the bloodshed of the Civil War," Burns offered. "There are Southern quotes over pictures of Northern soldiers. None of the hospitals specifically mentioned are actually shown, particularly Chimborazo in Richmond. . . . The picture of Walt Whitman is, in fact, several years too old, as is the illustration for Dix." Burns added, "There's not one photograph of action or battle during the Civil War, and yet nearly 40% of the series takes place while guns are actually going off. What do you do? What are the kind of licenses that you take?"

His question is an interesting one and not yet sufficiently explored by filmmakers or the public. In the skilled hands of a filmmaker who has the resources and commitment to work with a stellar group of media and academic personnel, the storytelling may override the limited imagery. But too often, and increasingly, as archivist Kenn Rabin describes in Chapter 20, substitutions are made not for historical or storytelling reasons, but because schedules and budgets mandate shortcuts. Not every image needs to be specific to time and place, of course; Michael Moore's montage of bowling works for his film, and it doesn't matter when the images were originally created, or why. They're kitsch, and they work as such. But if you're using archival stills or motion picture footage to illustrate an historical story, be aware that the images you select will generally be taken at face value by your audience.

RECREATIONS AND DOCUDRAMA

Many filmmakers use what are known as "recreations" to suggest a historical past, either to augment a sparse visual record or because the recreations better serve their storytelling needs. There are many ways to film recreations; it's a good idea to watch a range of styles to decide which works best for your film—or determine an innovative new approach. You may choose to shoot partial reenactments—a hand here, legs marching, a wagon wheel. Human figures may be kept in the distance, silhouettes against a skyline, or people may be filmed close up and asked to convey emotions. Entire scenes might be played out, whether by professional recreators such as those who stage actual battles from the Civil War and the Revolutionary War, or by actors hired to recreate a crime scene or the investigation that followed. You also need to decide what role recreations play in your film; will they be part of your evocation of the past, as in Ric Burns's *The Donner Party*, or will they play a central role in the storytelling, as in *Murder at Harvard*, discussed below?

A film moves from recreation toward "docudrama" as elements are fictionalized, even when they closely adhere to known facts. This is especially true when actors speak dialogue that is based on something other than factual transcript; for example, when they improvise a murder scene based on evidence alone. In effect, they're choosing and recreating a single version of what happened, when other versions may be possible: Was the murderer really that angry? Did the victim actually see him coming?

Some filmmakers make the process of recreation and its inherent doubt a part of their storytelling. Errol Morris's *The Thin Blue Line* offers several versions, depending on testimony, of the shooting of a police officer. Laurie Kahn-Leavitt's *A Midwife's Tale* focuses on the efforts of historian Laurel Thatcher Ulrich to tease meaning and understanding from a diary kept by a Maine midwife between the years 1775 and 1812. Once the viewer understands how Ulrich knows what she knows from the historical record, the midwife's story comes increasingly to the fore, in detailed recreation. Another example of this is *Murder at Harvard*, produced by Eric Stange and Melissa Banta, which explores the 1849 murder of Dr. George Parkman and the subsequent trial of Harvard chemistry professor John Webster. The film includes actors performing scenes and speaking dialogue that have been imagined for these historical figures. But in this documentary, the imagining is attributed to historian Simon Schama, who wrote about the case in his 1991 book, *Dead Certainties (Unwarranted Speculations)*. In the documentary, he and other historians discuss the line between fact and informed speculation, and those elements of the past that can't be truly known, such as emotions and motivation. In working on the case, Schama had found that there were even variations in the trial testimony. "The testimony in the trial is from the record," notes Boyd Estus, the project's director of photography. "But there was no court stenographer in the sense that we know it today. What would happen was that several different people would compile their notes, and often the lawyers would get together and say, 'We think this is what happened.'" The film plays out several possible scenarios, and Schama explains why he finds one to be the most compelling.

Recreations that pretend to be something other than they are, such as footage that you shoot and then manipulate to appear to be archival (altering it to appear grainy, black and white or sepia-toned, scratched) are questionable, unless you make the artifice of what you're doing transparent to the viewer. In other words, you set the rules of your documentary storytelling. As long as you make those rules apparent, there is plenty of room for creativity.

SCIENCE FILMS

The approach to science filmmaking varies widely, with the tone being set by the long-running PBS series, Nova. Michael Ambrosino says that when he created the series in 1973, American broadcasters were skeptical. "People thought that a science series would be nice to have in the schedule," Ambrosino says. "It probably wouldn't get a big audience, but it was something that should be done." He was convinced that the show would not only succeed but that it would draw a larger audience than anything else on air at that time, he says, "and in its first season, Nova proved just that."

The reason? "We conceived Nova as a series that would explore and explain the way the world worked. We would use science as a tool, but we would primarily think of ourselves as journalists looking for the stories of science," Ambrosino says. "It's not possible to make a film about the crab nebula and have you be interested in it or understand it. It *is* possible to tell the story of the dozen or so men and women who are trying to find out what was the core of the crab nebula, and in telling their story of discovery, you had a story that was understandable."

There is opportunity across the broadcast spectrum for science programming—not programs that *teach* science, but programs in which science, like history or politics, is the setting for a compelling story. Unfortunately, the trend seems to be toward tabloid science, whether stories are about extreme behavior (animals that kill, insects that swarm), extreme weather, or the paranormal. These films often use documentary techniques, including interviews and narrated questions ("Was it possible that aliens had left these marks?") that lead viewers to conclusions that may have no factual basis. Fortunes are spent to bring dinosaurs to life through the magic of computer technology, but not enough resources are devoted to stories that advance beyond predator and prey scenarios. Why not present science with as much substance as possible, using storytelling to motivate viewers to want to know more? Rather than posit that *these* experts with *this* equipment can figure out the height and age of the victim, for example, why not allow viewers into the process so that they understand *how* the expert knows? Creative documentary filmmaking could make a difference, as those concerned with science literacy, including potential financiers, are aware.

Part II

DEVELOPMENT

Research

7

Good documentary storytelling, with few exceptions, depends on good research. You need to find a subject, understand your story, and be sure you're presenting a balanced and accurate point of view—at least, you do if you want to get the program to a general audience. Remember that balance and accuracy do not mean you can't, as the filmmaker, take a particular position or that your subjects can't take one. But if you expect the audience to take you seriously, you must allow them to weigh the evidence for themselves, which means that you need to research and present that evidence. This is true for what may seem like a surprising range of filmmaking styles.

- In an interview by Jason Silverman, filmmaker Alan Berliner describes working on his personal documentary, *The Sweetest Sound*. "I began where I always begin, with a tremendous amount of research, with a passion to understand the total landscape of whatever subject I'm entering."
- Susan Froemke and assistants at Maysles Films spent about six months researching poverty and looking for potential stories in several states, including Wisconsin, Maine, Iowa, and Missouri, before they settled on the stories and characters of *Lalee's Kin*, filmed in the Mississippi Delta.
- Filmmaker Jay Rosenblatt creates unusual documentary stories from bits of old films and "found footage." In press material submitted to the San Francisco Jewish Film Festival, Rosenblatt says that it took about eight months to do the research for *Human Remains*, a half-hour film about the banality of evil. In it, he presents black-and-white footage

of five of the 20th century's most notorious leaders—Hitler, Mussolini, Stalin, Franco, and Mao—over reminiscences voiced by actors but scripted from actual quotes and/or factual biographical information. "One of the challenges," Rosenblatt notes, "was to find images of the dictators that didn't include hats or uniforms, since they had to look . . . like the guy next door."

Do all documentaries require research? No. Liane Brandon's memorable and deceptively simple film, *Betty Tells Her Story*, while evoking powerful themes, began when the filmmaker heard something of interest in a colleague's story and asked her to tell it on camera. Not everything has to involve experts and advisors and location scouting. But many films, if not most, do involve research to some degree. With that in mind, here are a few suggestions.

Ask Questions, Dig Deeper

Whether you're looking for a story or finding the best way to tell it, a good film is one that surprises, challenges, and often, informs. This means that the information going into that film needs to be surprising. All too often, documentaries just repeat information that everybody knows. The easiest way out of that trap is to stop and challenge yourself. "Energy equals mass"—what does that *mean?* The Apollo 13 space mission—why was it named Apollo? "Everybody knows" that Rosa Parks was the tired seamstress who didn't feel like giving up her seat on that bus in Montgomery in 1955, right? It's a nice story, this downtrodden woman who has reached her breaking point. What if you found out that she was an active member of the Montgomery chapter of the NAACP, a group fighting for civil rights? Suddenly she's not so much a victim of oppression as an activist who sees an opportunity to fight it. You're telling better history and bringing fresh details to an old story that everybody *thought* they knew.

Good research is a sequence of questions, answers, and more questions. As mentioned previously, why start a project if you just want to prove a point? We've all seen films like this, where the filmmakers are out to prove that strip mining is bad or that a certain election was rigged. Have you ever seen a group of people telling each other what they already know and agreeing with each other since no one disagrees? That's how stimulating your film is going to be.

If you want to change someone's mind, or at least raise doubts, hopes, and ideas, you have to trust in that person's ability to make an informed decision. Give him or her *information* that will lead to that decision. That kind of information comes from a research process that is open-minded.

Do Your Own Research

One of the problems of faster and cheaper filmmaking is that original and up-to-date research is often beyond the scope of a project's resources and budget. It's much easier for producers to rely on a few authoritative articles or books rather than explore what's new in a field, who's doing innovative work, or what a more diverse group of storytellers might add to the audience's understanding of familiar topic. The same tired experts are approached time and again to speak about the same subjects, in part because the producers have already seen them on TV and know both what they look like and how well they speak on camera. But why tell the same story again, particularly if there's a newer or more complex angle you could explore? It may take more effort to gather and master up-to-date information and balance it with previous understanding of an issue—but as a documentary filmmaker, especially if your work has a life beyond broadcast (many documentaries end up being used by classroom teachers and community organizers, for example), this is exactly what you want to be doing.

Don't Be Afraid to Ask Basic Questions

Although you should gain a thorough grounding in your subject, you can't possibly, in a few days or weeks or even months, become an expert. Don't, in the interest of appearing "professional" to your advisors or experts, fake an understanding that you don't have; if you're confused, speak up. Your expertise is in knowing how to communicate a complex subject to a general audience; it's important that you understand the subject well, and that's why the experts are there. Most people who have spent their lifetimes mastering a subject are also passionate about it, whether it's professional football or nuclear physics, and enjoy sharing their knowledge with

Bayard Rustin, late 1940s, from *Brother Outsider: The Life of Bayard Rustin*. Photo courtesy of the estate of Bayard Rustin.

other, particularly when the person asking the questions is prepared and professional.

WHEN DO YOU RESEARCH?

The amount of research you do, and when you do it, varies from project to project and depends, to some degree, on your chosen topic, your approach, and your strategies for fundraising. Some public funding sources, such as the National Science Foundation or the National Endowment for the Humanities, as well as some private foundations, require that your grant application include evidence that your film project is built on a solid and current academic foundation. Projects that are funded "in house"—by public or commercial broadcasters directly—may be less rigorous in their up-front requirements, but producers will still need to do at least some research in order to effectively pitch their ideas and make their programs.

With many films, therefore, research begins with the development of the initial proposal(s), but begins again—and at greater depth—once financial support is available. (As discussed in Chapter 8, support may come in stages: development, scripting, production, post-production, etc.) Research generally is ongoing through the development of outlines and shooting treatments, and continues as needed until the film is complete. A flurry of fact checking often occurs in the last weeks of editing.

ADVISORS

The input of academic and non-academic advisors can be crucial to a project. These people offer their insight and experience behind the scenes; some of them may also be asked to appear on camera as experts, if that fits the program's style. On any film that's intended to be the least bit authoritative about a subject, advisors can help tremendously by getting you up to date quickly on current research in the field and directing you to people, places, and content to be explored. They can help you to see how such a film might contribute to the public's understanding of a subject and who, beyond a general audience, might be able to use the film (in classrooms, for example).

It's useful to seek out advisors and experts who represent a variety of viewpoints. If you're doing a film about the role of First Ladies over the years, for example, you might find biographers of specific First Ladies as well as scholars whose specialties cover presidential history, American history, women's studies, and political history. You might also look for non-academic experts, such as a former or current First Lady or someone who has worked closely with her. Advisors tend to be paid an honorarium for their services; the work might include a couple of meetings as well as reviews of outlines and/or treatments and other consultation on at least one, if not two, cuts of the film as editing is underway.

Good advisors—and they are often extraordinary—understand that they are advisors and you are a filmmaker and that their job is to push for content and inclusion and yours is to try to tell the strongest and most accurate story you can. What a film can do best is excite viewers about new and complex material; it's up to library and web resources to satisfy the hunger you may create for extensive detail. You won't and can't do everything the advisors want, but if you have truly considered their expertise and understood their concerns, chances are you've found a way to address them that also serves your purposes as a filmmaker.

When do you approach advisors? As Jon Else summarizes, "You read the ten most important and widely respected books about the subject, and then you read the two fringe books at either end of the subject. Then you do the basic primary research; you figure out who are the ten important living people and what are the ten important available documents or pieces of stock footage. And then you call the experts."

As mentioned, some of the people you'll be contacting as advisors may turn out to be people you want to interview. It's good to avoid confusing these roles initially because what you need at the moment is background help. If someone asks whether or not he or she will also be asked to appear on camera, you can honestly say that it's too soon to tell.

Advisors' Meetings

On some larger-budget documentaries and documentary series, funds are raised to enable at least one in-person gathering of filmmakers, advisors, and invited experts. These meetings might take place as the funding proposal is taking shape, and maybe again as production gets underway. With EYES ON THE PRIZE and other major series produced by Blackside, Inc., production also began with what was called "school." Production teams, researchers and others joined invited scholars and other experts in panel discussions that continued over a period of several days and were invaluable in setting out the work ahead.

If you can afford them, in-person meetings spark an exchange of information and ideas that isn't possible when the filmmaker speaks individually to this advisor, then that one. Valuable information can result from their interaction not only with you but with each other.

PROFESSIONAL CONFERENCES

Another way to conduct a lot of research quickly, as well as find potential advisors or candidates for on-screen appearances, is through attending professional conferences in the field and subject matter you're researching. For a film she's currently developing to help teachers and other education professionals understand and protect the civil rights of gay and lesbian students, filmmaker Liane Brandon and some colleagues attended an all-day conference that allowed them, as a group, to immerse themselves in nearly 40 sessions on the subject. Brandon took a similar approach when researching her documentary, *How to Prevent a Nuclear War.* "I spent a year just meeting with different grassroots groups to see what they were doing, what they thought was effective, who was doing it, how they did it," she says. The diversity of the groups she met also allowed her to select individuals who could represent a variety of perspectives on screen, in terms of age, occupation, and location.

TELEPHONE RESEARCH

Some of your research, whether searching for people, fact-checking, or just trying to get a handle on a subject, will inevitably be done by phone. Be as prepared as possible for these calls. Knowing as much as you can (within time limitations) about the person you're calling and his or her area of expertise will sharpen your questions and make the call more productive.

FACT CHECKING

Fact checking means being able to footnote your treatment and eventually, your script. Any fact stated, whether by you as the filmmaker or by someone on camera, needs to be verified through not one but two credible sources. Why do this? Because *everybody* makes mistakes. If you've ever read a read or watched a news story about something you know well, you'll have seen firsthand that there are often errors. Nonfiction books, too, contain inaccuracies, whether on the part of the author or in the underlying material.

Errors of interpretation are also common, if more slippery. Have you ever been at a rally that seemed packed, only to hear it described on the news as a "small number" of protesters? Or sat through an afternoon in which the majority of speeches were credible and coherent, and the radio coverage featured a couple of speakers who clearly had no grasp of the issues? The reports may be factual, but do they accurately represent the events? Another example is a writer profiling an anti-poverty activist might point out that the activist grew up in a town that, she notes, is "a wealthy suburb of New York." The fact may be true, but 50 years earlier, the town was still quite rural and had not yet become a bedroom community for the city. And even then, the activist was from a family living well below the means of other townspeople. Yet the reporter has used factual material to create the false impression, whether intentionally or not, that the activist grew up wealthy—an impression that has a direct bearing on any portrayal of the activist's current work.

Suppose you're making a film about this activist's life. Because you're using multiple sources, you should realize that the picture being painted by this reporter doesn't match others that you're seeing. You should also be doing your own reality checks. Is it really possible that the description of a town in 2003 also applies to the same town in 1953? Furthermore, even if the majority of townspeople *were* mega-wealthy back in 1953, can you really know, without checking, that the activist's family was also wealthy?

Suppose you've plowed ahead without considering this, however, and have become attached to the idea of using the man's childhood in a wealthy town as a motivating factor behind his work on behalf of the poor. Maybe you've even talked to experts (unfamiliar with the activist in question) who explain that growing up wealthy can plant seeds of guilt in the minds of certain children. So the information and motivation ends up in your narration, whether they are accurate or not.

This is a relatively minor example of a situation in which having advisors on your side can be invaluable. A biographer of the activist, if given a chance to read a treatment of your film or screen a rough cut, will respond to narration such as, "He grew up in the wealthy community of X," and cry foul. This doesn't mean that you have to remove the fact; it does mean that you will need to put it into more accurate context.

A note about fact checking: primary sources can be as biased or inaccurate as secondary sources. This is why you will want to double- or even triple-check the facts, especially those central to your story.

THE TELLING DETAIL

Facts are not just something to ensure accuracy; they can also be the lifeblood of the "telling detail" that will enrich and inform your storytelling (depending, of course, on the kind of film you're making). Facts can be a source of humor and irony; they can illuminate character, heighten tension, and underscore themes. So throw the line in the water, pull up what you can, organize it and file it, and then throw the line back in. Bess Myerson is known as the first Jewish Miss America. She was also the first to have a college degree. Which detail will you choose to use? Hold onto them both, for now. Famed Norwegian playwright Henrik Ibsen liked to read the comics. Russian author Fyodor Dostoevsky loved ice cream. Are these useful details? Maybe. They certainly add a human face to authors who've attained a certain stone-like presence in literary catalogues.

As you do your research, begin to keep track of the details and tidbits that strike your fancy, as well as the ones that answer questions essential to your storytelling. Find a way to keep track not only of the information but also its source. Make sure to note the source material as completely as possible, so that (a) you don't have to track it down again and (b) you could track it down again if necessary.

STATISTICS AND OTHER FORMS OF DATA

Statistics must be scrutinized and put into context. It's always a good idea, when you come upon a statistic you want to use, to trace it back to its source. Suppose you find an article in a magazine that says that a certain percentage of teenagers in the 1950s smoked. Somewhere in the article you may be able to find the source of that information, something such as, "according to the National Institutes of Health." You should always question someone else's interpretation of raw data, meaning that if you really want to use this statistic, you need to go back to the NIH data yourself. Maybe it was X% of all 17-year-olds who smoked, or maybe it was X% of 17- and 18-year-olds in Philadelphia. People often misinterpret statistical information, whether intentionally or not. The interpretation may satisfy your story, but don't trust it until you can get it corroborated by someone with sufficient expertise.

CHRONOLOGIES

Chronologies are one of my favorite tools for storytelling, especially in the early stages of a film. I begin by going through the material that directly relates to my story and charting in sequence what happens and when. This helps me to see the story more clearly, without the overlay of someone else's narrative. Second, I add other columns to my notes that indicate what's happening in the world beyond my immediate story. (There are various "Timetables of History" available in bookstores.) By putting these chronologies together, I can see new areas of research to be explored.

For example, the first Miss America pageant was held in 1921. Prior to that, according to scholars, beauty contests were held in the pages of America's newspapers. But this wasn't possible until the photographic half-tone was invented—in 1880—I find out when I look that up. What else was happening between then and 1921? A flood of immigration and migration was increasing the ethnic and racial diversity in America's growing cities, sparking differences of opinion about what constituted an American feminine "ideal." Add to all of this the emergence of mass media and a consumer culture, and the stage is set for the first official Miss America pageant in 1921. But note the date. A year earlier, in 1920, American women had finally won the right to vote. Is this relevant?

The truthful answer is, "Not necessarily." So while you can note the interesting dateline, you can't draw any conclusions about it. Cause and effect is a slippery slope; the fact that two things happen in succession does not mean there is a link. This is an excellent example of the kind of question you explore with your advisors, which is just what the production team of *Miss America: A Documentary Film* did.

The extent of the chronology depends entirely on the project. There were several chronologies done for the series I'LL MAKE ME A

WORLD: A CENTURY OF AFRICAN-AMERICAN ARTS. The initial chronology was a grid. There were ten columns, left to right, one for each decade of the century, and then six rows down, one each for literature, theater and dance, music, the visual arts, African-American political history, and American social and cultural events. As the series developed, separate chronologies were made for each story. The lives and vaudeville career of Bert Williams and George Walker, for example, was charted by month and year alongside events in American history.

This may not work for everyone, but I find that a chronology helps me to keep track of a story, look for a structure within it, and find some telling details that might enrich it and prevent mistakes. A song commonly believed to have been popular among soldiers during the First World War may, in fact, have been written in 1919—which a good chronology will show you is *after* the war's end.

In addition, by listing the major events in your story in chronological sequence, you can sometimes see possible points of attack—places to begin the story—and from there you can think about what moments you might drive toward and why, and which events can serve as backstory.

One final benefit of a chronology is that everyone can share it; the production team sees the timeline and is grounded in it just as you are. Note that chronologies should also be fact checked.

PRINT AND INTERNET RESEARCH

I love the Internet. It's a tool that puts unbelievable amounts of information into your hands almost too easily. But the Internet *augments* libraries; it doesn't replace them. Keyword and subject searches on the Internet are limited by your ability to come up with the right combination of magic words, spelled correctly (or the way they were *misspelled* by someone else) to find what you want, and if you don't come up with those words, you'll wind up empty-handed. Perhaps even more frustrating, web searches can land you at sites that are not sufficiently credible.

Libraries and bookstores are also great places to go when you're looking for ideas or you have a topic in mind but aren't sure how to approach it. By wandering among the shelves, you can cast a fairly wide net, finding books and connections you might not have considered and information that you wouldn't have known to search for on the web. Even better, you can find material such as magazines and newspapers that significantly predate the limits of most web databases. Furthermore, you can see this material in the context of everything else on the page and in the issue; you can see the price of shoes and mattresses at the time, read reviews of whatever entertainment form was being offered, and look at the way stories in general were covered. Not only do you get a better sense of the period (whether the 1970s or the 1870s), you also get ideas for visual storytelling and narrative context.

Be Organized

You'll need to keep track of the material you're citing. If you are taking notes on published text, make it clear that you are copying. Note the source, put it in quotes—do whatever it takes to make sure that six months from now, you don't go back to this material, think that you've written it yourself, and incorporate it into narration, only to find out that you've lifted entire sentences from Stephen Hawking or Alice Walker.

A few other tips:

- Note the source. An article that's not referenced is a waste of everyone's time. On the copy of the document itself, note the bibliographic data. It's also useful to note which library you found it in and even write down the call numbers. Otherwise, you may very well find yourself having to look it up again.
- Be sure you've got the whole article. If you're photocopying an article or printing one off a microfilm reader, check to be sure that the entire piece is actually readable. If it's not, try again or take out a pen and fill in the gaps. *If an article is footnoted, photocopy the footnotes.* It's very frustrating to the producer to find great material in the body of an article and not be able to use it without sending the researcher back to the library.
- Don't editorialize. Do not, as the researcher, take it upon yourself to annotate the photocopy (unless you're asked to do so). Pages and pages of underlined and highlighted material can be annoying. Steer the production team to relevant passages, but let them form their own impressions.

- Be organized. For example, do your best to keep bibliographies in alphabetical order. It will save you from looking up the same source more than once, by mistake, as you go down the list. Make use of file folders, so that you don't end up with a massive stack of paper that you will find yourself sorting through over and over.
- Neatness counts. Research is a lot of work, and everybody gets tired. But you must take the time to write legibly, or at least to copy any scribbled notes within a short period of time, before you can no longer decipher them. And if you're keeping a research notebook, keep it current.
- A plea on behalf of libraries—never mark up in a library-owned book or magazine. Never bend the pages down, and if you must spread the book face down to photocopy, do it gently.
- Go a step further. If you're doing research for someone else, get the material you've been asked to retrieve and then look through it. As mentioned, photocopy footnotes if they accompany an article. But then scan those footnotes to see if there's additional material you could pick up while you're at the library. Does a more current book by the same author come to your attention? If there's a reference to a primary source within a secondary source, can you dig up the original material? Come back with these unexpected treasures and you will make the producers very happy. Primary sources, especially, tend to be wonderful finds that take more than Internet digging.
- Again, be cautious about what you find on the Internet. It's an amazing tool. In a matter of minutes, it's possible to learn the population in Sioux City, Iowa, in 1910, or learn how many American presidents were married to a woman named Eleanor. But there is an awful lot of beautifully produced but less-than-useful information on the web, too. An impressive-looking history of the civil rights movement might turn out to have been produced by Mr. Crabtree's eighth-grade social studies class; a scientific-looking report on the "myths" of global warming might have been produced both by and for the oil industry. As you search the web, pay careful attention to the source of the material and read everything with a skeptical eye.

VISUAL ARCHIVES

Depending on the story you're telling, you may or may not need to explore what's available in terms of stills or motion picture footage in the archives, whether public (such as the National Archives) or private (such as Corbis). Extensive visual research is most commonly done once a film is at least partially funded; the visual research becomes part of the overall research and development leading to a shooting treatment, and often continues as needed (or begins again) as the story takes further shape in the editing room.

Knowledge of at least some of the material available can add a note of veracity to your fundraising material, whether you're submitting a treatment or script. For example, "Grainy black-and-white photos, a recent find in the collection of the McGooey Foundation, show the inventor as a child hammering together a contraption that he clearly meant as a flying machine."

As with the print material, organization of your visual research is everything. Many productions have a separate person (or people) responsible for keeping track of archival material, in part because the effort of acquiring rights to use footage (after it's been definitely selected for use in the film), as well as the logistics of ordering broadcast-quality reproductions, can be significant. In any event, you will have to find some way to keep track of visual images, such as a "stills" notebook that the production team can refer to when searching for images. However you choose to keep this visual record, it is critical that source information be recorded; it's very frustrating to realize that a particular image is perfect, only to find that the researcher doesn't remember the source or whether it was photocopied from a book or printed the web.

Archival stills and motion picture footage, no less than print materials, should be subject to scrutiny as to veracity and completeness. Sure, that footage undeniably shows teenagers looting a store, but you can't tell from the few kids crowding the frame how representative their behavior was of the event as a whole. Archival material, whether motion picture or stills, was created for a purpose. To the extent possible, you need to understand what the source of the material is and what else might be available to balance out that one particular viewpoint.

Doing Archival Research

Archival research is a specialty, although plenty of first-timers have made their way to the various film, video, and photographic archives to search through material. (Some searching can now be done online) As with print materials, it's important to do your own research as much as possible. Archivist Kenn Rabin, interviewed in Chapter 20, says that all too frequently these days, filmmakers research archival material mostly or even solely by screening other films that have used archival material on the topic. This creates problems for a number of reasons. In the first place, it will be very difficult to find out exactly where the shots came from; an edited sequence may have shots and stills from a variety of sources. You have to go to the original source, not the previous filmmaker, for rights. Secondly, you're trusting the journalism of the previous filmmaker, who may be trusting the journalism of a previous film-maker.

Suppose Producer A uses a shot labeled by the archive as "civil rights protester, Chicago, 1934" to stand in for a shot that doesn't exist (or he wasn't able to find) of Jonathan Miller, leader of a fledgling union of black workers in Detroit in 1937. Suppose Producer B then uses that shot, labels it "Jonathan Miller, labor leader," and uses it for a story that explores the extent to which charges of communism among labor organizers were or were not true. Producer C might take that same footage, drop the "Jonathan Miller," and label the guy "communist sympathizer, 1930s." It gets messy.

MOVING FORWARD

Research of every sort will be ongoing for most of the film's production, but there comes a point when the filmmaker has to decide that it's time to move to the next stage—production. But first, at least some of this information must be put down on paper, whether for your own use (a production treatment), for funding, or for the go-ahead (the "green light") from a supervising or commissioning executive.

Knowing when to stop researching, at least for now, can be tough. There's always more to learn, and the more you learn, the more you want everybody to know what you've found out. Just because something is fascinating or important doesn't mean it can or should make it into your final, edited film. As Alan Berliner said about working on *The Sweetest Sound* (in the same interview that started this chapter), "one of the hardest things I had to do was let go of everything I knew—to accept that the film could not possibly contain everything I had learned about names."

8

Pitching and Proposal Writing

Chances are, you'll be pitching your story until the day it's broad-cast or screened, if not after. Your pitch is the way to excite people about your project, which you need to do in order to get them to fund you, work with you, work for you, give you a broadcast slot, or distribute your film. Your pitch is your first and best ticket in; it's also, it turns out, a very good way to see if you really have a good film story. There are exceptions, but in general, if you can't pitch your story clearly and succinctly, it's likely that you don't yet have a handle on it.

PITCHING

A pitch very quickly lets the listener or reader "see" your film and understand why it needs to be made. An ineffective pitch intro-duces the topic but not the story, as in "This is a film about the ethics of genetic testing and about how some people face hard choices." An effective pitch does both. "This is a film about genetic testing in which we follow an actress making the tough decision about whether to be tested for a disease that claimed her mother's life." The pitch works because it compels the listener to ask follow-up questions. What will she do if the test is positive? Will she let you follow her through the process? What if she doesn't take the test?

Here's an example of a weak pitch. "Four years ago, Vietnam veteran Martin Robinson decided he would scale the heights of Mount Whatsit at the age of 53—with one leg. He succeeded, and in the years since has inspired veterans' groups across America." There's just one hitch. Where's the story here? There *was* a story (his efforts four years ago), but unless you have some plan for telling it now, what's holding the film together? A 57-year-old man standing before various groups of veterans.

A better version of this pitch, assuming you can find a more dynamic angle, would go something like this. "Four years ago, Vietnam veteran Mark Smith became the first amputee to scale the heights of Mount Whatsit. Now, he's going back—and bringing two Gulf War veterans, amputees who thought their best athletic days were behind them—along with him." Not a bad pitch, especially if you can follow it up with good access to these people and some information about your own skills as both a filmmaker and a mountaineer (to show you'll be capable of following them up the mountain). In many cases, the pitch will be even stronger if you show a tape that introduces your main characters, allowing people to see that they're appealing and will work on camera.

Tailoring the Pitch

If you're pitching to a specific program or foundation, you'll want to emphasize those aspects of the story and your treatment of it that meet the needs of that group. If you were pitching the film about genetic testing to a foundation concerned with issues of medicine and the public's ability to make informed choices, that would be your emphasis. The exact same film, pitched to a television executive, might play up the emotional aspect of a young woman facing tough life choices.

Tailoring the pitch doesn't mean changing the film to suit the financier; it means highlighting those elements of your project that are likely to be of greatest interest and helping the reader or reviewer see the relevance of your material to his or her goals or mandate.

This means, of course, that you need to know as much as you can about the individuals or groups to whom you're pitching. Don't throw ideas at just anybody. If you're pitching to a network or the producers of an existing series, watch their programs, go to their web sites, and find out everything you can about the programming they've done and if they're moving in any new directions. Are they interested in character-driven stories? Would they want an historical survey film? Do they tend to use on-screen presenters? Can you submit a magazine-length story, or do they only want broadcast hours? If they commission work, do they tend to work with the same handful of known producers? In panel after panel, commissioning editors complain that people approach them without knowing enough about who they are, how they work, or the kind of programming they do. So do your homework, and be prepared before you pitch.

This is no less true if you are approaching government or private agencies, whether it's the National Endowment for the Humanities, the MacArthur Foundation, or the Pew Charitable Trusts. Not all foundations support media projects, and those that do have a mandate for the work they support. Go to their web sites, which generally offer detailed information about the kinds of programming they support. Often, foundations also have program officers who are willing to answer questions. It can take time to find your way around the various funding agencies, but the good news is that, while some potential financiers require detailed and lengthy proposals, others only require an initial query letter.

With the caveat that fundraising is an area of expertise beyond the scope of this book, what follows are some tips for presenting your story as effectively as possible, as part of your overall fundraising strategy. No matter how serious the mission of the foundation, the bottom line of your approach is as writer to reader, filmmaker to audience.

When to Pitch

There is no single way to raise money or support for a project. Some filmmakers pitch an idea verbally or in an introductory letter. Others walk into a meeting with a handful of ideas, none of which has, as yet, been significantly researched and developed. It can be very difficult for independents to get financial support for development, but the odds of doing so increase as you establish a solid track record in production. In addition, you may find yourself pitching as a staff person, or you may be pitching to an independent company that regularly provides programming to a network and therefore has some funds for development. Every scenario is different. But for many documentarians, it all gets a bit jumbled together—pitching, development, and proposal writing—in a cycle that's generally underfunded. The process is bearable for the following two reasons: the passion you feel for the story, and the conviction that the film will eventually get the support it needs.

Pitching on Screen

At times, you'll run across programmers who would rather see footage than paperwork, and many times people want to see both. What this means varies, depending on the scale of the project. Sometimes, you only have to provide footage of other films or tapes you've made, as evidence of your skill as a filmmaker. But it's not uncommon for people to want to see even raw footage of your story as a way of seeing your characters in action. In any case, a good, short promo reel can be an effective way to excite people about your project and make it clear that you know what you're doing.

Pitching to Hone Storytelling

Outsiders aren't the only ones to whom you might be pitching. On some projects, producers pitch their stories at development meetings, not once but several times as the films or series take shape. The following is adapted from an in-house pitch that I helped to construct for the opening hour of I'LL MAKE ME A WORLD. The six-hour series told two to three stories in each hour, and the hours themselves were arranged sequentially, in an order that was both chronological and thematic.

> *The pitch:* Hour One: Lift Every Voice (1900–1924)
>
> *This film begins at the turn of the 20th century, a time when the United States is emerging as a modern, industrialized nation and the culture that will come to be known as 'American' is still being formed. The first generation of African Americans to be born in freedom is also coming of age. This hour is about their efforts to add their voices, ideas, and visions during this time of possibility and hope. This hour includes three stories:*
>
> Nobody *follows Bert Williams as he teams up with George Walker and they head for the Broadway stage, where they face an audience whose expectations of black entertainment have been shaped by sixty years of minstrel traditions. Can they reject these stereotypes and still attract a mainstream audience? This story continues through the death of George Walker; we end with Bert Williams performing with the Ziegfeld Follies alongside stars including W.C. Fields, Will Rogers, and Fannie Brice—and yet, as actor Ben Vereen portrays him, still facing racial discrimination.*

> *Our second story,* The Good Mad Music, *follows a talented young trombone player, Edward "Kid" Ory, as he arrives in New Orleans in 1908 and sets about creating his "Creole Jazz Band," drawing together such future notables as Sidney Bechet and King Oliver. Together, they help to create the controversial new sounds that many call America's first original music: jazz.*
>
> *Our last story,* Within These Gates, *explores the promise of the brand-new motion picture industry and the efforts of filmmaker Oscar Michaux to create films that present the complexity of African-American life at a time of growing racial division, embodied in 1915 by D.W. Griffith's acclaimed epic,* The Birth of a Nation, *a dramatic portrayal of the rise of the Ku Klux Klan. We follow Michaux to his artistic triumph of 1924,* Body and Soul, *starring activist and actor Paul Robeson.*
>
> *By the end of the first hour, white resistance to African-American advancement has closed doors to opportunity in jobs, education, housing, and voting rights. African-American leaders seize upon one of the few avenues open to opportunity: the arts. They launch a movement that—as we see in the series' next hour—comes to be known as the Harlem Renaissance.*

The story titles listed above were never used on screen; they were simply a way to summarize the stories within each hour and differentiate them from the other stories. (In the editing room, these stories were woven together, meaning that one story would start, continue partway, and then be put on hold while a second story got underway.)

Pitching helps you to streamline how you think about a story, its themes, and its important action. Eventually, if the story is to be told using a three-act structure, you'll want to be able to pitch it as such. In other words, "Our first act begins here . . . We drive to the moment when . . . As the second act begins, such-and-such is happening. The second act drives to the point where . . . "etc. If you're pitching out loud, it's a good idea to practice beforehand so that you don't get bogged down in unnecessary details and sidebar information that will lose your listener. ("Oh, and you'll find out along the way that he's gotten married to so-and-so and I should have mentioned that they toured in Europe . . . ") You want to tell a clean and exciting story, which means that as your pitch changes over time—as your familiarity with the story and how you want to tell it evolves—you'll need to practice and deliver your pitch again.

PROPOSAL WRITING

Many filmmakers complain that they spend more time writing proposals than they do making films. Proposals are the documents you submit in order to request funding from grant making agencies, whether public or private. In general, the following are stages at which financial support might be available prior to the completion of your film: planning, scripting, production, post-production, and finishing. The first two fall under the category of "development" and can be very difficult funds to raise. The easiest, arguably, are finishing funds, which are awarded at or after the rough cut stage. The financier can see your film, there are few surprises, and there is a higher likelihood that you'll be able to complete the project.

While each proposal must be tailored to the guidelines and mandates of the particular agency, there are a few basic things that they'll usually want to know, whether in a letter of introduction or a 25-page narrative. They include the following:

Nature of the Request

Who you are, what your project is ("a 90-minute program to be shot on digital video on the history of the can opener and its impact on American cuisine"), how much you're requesting at this time from this grant maker ("$X,000 for scripting" or "$XX,000 for production of one hour of this four-part series"), what activities are to be supported for the amount requested, and what the end result of the grant will be (for example, if you ask for a scripting grant, you should end up with a script or, in some cases, a production-ready treatment).

Introduction to the Subject

This section offers the proposal reviewer a general grounding in the subject matter to be treated on film. In other words, this is not your film treatment and does not have to include detail about how you will treat the subject on screen. It's an overview of the subject, presented clearly and concisely, and written in a way that will hopefully bring the reader to share your conviction that the subject is interesting, relevant, and worth a commitment of resources.

Rationale

A more focused opportunity to convey the significance of the project and, in particular, its relevance to the financier. Another way to look at it is, "Why this project now? How will it advance public understanding and awareness of the topic? Why is it useful for this topic to be presented on film? In what way will audiences be served by this project?"

Goals and Objectives

What your project is designed to accomplish. There will be a handful of these; for example, *Goal: To explore the historical context in which Title IX legislation was originally passed and the inequalities it sought to address, and to evaluate the law's impact, intended and unintended, in the context of current efforts to repeal it. Objective: Viewers will better understand the complexity of Title IX legislation beyond the issue of school sports, and appreciate the social and political processes by which legal change is brought about.*

Related Projects

What other films have been done on the same or related subjects, how does their success (or lack of success) inform your approach to your story, and how does your story build on or differ from these projects? As mentioned previously, the fact that a topic has been covered is not necessarily a deterrent, given all the different ways a topic can be treated and the different venues available. But you should demonstrate that you know what's out there.

Ancillary Projects

These are sometimes *also* called "related projects," which makes for confusion. An ancillary project is something that you're developing to bolster your film's shelf life and reach. These might include web-based materials, radio broadcasts, material for educational outreach, and/or material for community engagement, which uses media as the catalyst for action and discussion within and between community groups. At a time when the television landscape is cluttered with choices, including documentary choices, it's becoming increasingly important to financiers, especially those who support public television programming, that you demonstrate ways that you will extend the impact of a broadcast.

History of the Project

Some information on how the project got underway and on the financial or institutional support you've received to date.

Audience and Broadcast Prospects

Information on your target audience(s) and how you intend to reach them.

Organization History

Information about the organizations involved in submitting the proposal, including the production company and possibly the fiscal sponsor. As elsewhere, you may want to highlight those areas of your expertise that mesh with the interests of the potential financiers.

Project Staff

Information on the media team and academic advisors (where appropriate). If you or your media team aren't experienced in the kind of production you're proposing, consider taking on other team members who will add to your credibility. If it's your idea but your first film, figure out what you need to get out of it, personally and professionally, and then determine what you might be able to give up in the interest of getting it made. It's difficult to get anything funded these days, so you need to do what you can to be competitive. (Alternatively, you might work to get farther into the production before requesting funds, so that you have a film-in-progress that demonstrates your ability.)

Another note: Be diverse. Seek a good balance of people on both sides of the personnel fence, in terms of expertise and points of view as well as ethnicity and gender. This will not only add to the complexity of your storytelling, it more accurately reflects the diversity in American professional and academic circles.

Plan of Work

A detailed description of the work that will be done, and by whom, with the funding requested. Be sure that this plan of work doesn't exceed the scope or length of the grant period; if you're asking for scripting money, your plan of work shouldn't continue through production and editing.

Appendices

Resumes, letters of commitment, research bibliography, lists of films on this or related subjects, description of materials to be used, if appropriate. (For example, for a film that will rely on archival footage, a list—even a preliminary one—of archival materials pertinent to the subject will need to be included.)

Treatment

Many financiers want to see some form of written treatment in order to consider a request for scripting or production funds. A treatment is a prose description of the film as you envision it; in other words, it is not a research document but a description of how you will treat that research on screen. Depending on where you are in your research and development, this treatment may be fairly preliminary. Even so, it should be well-written and make the strongest case possible for your film. Treatment writing is discussed further in Chapter 9.

Budget

Financiers often want to see a breakdown of how you'll spend the money you're asking them to provide. They're also likely to want to see your entire production budget, to get a sense of how funds will be allocated overall.

A Few Extra Pointers

Much of the advice for proposal writing can be applied to the entire production, including the editing. For example:

- Accuracy is important. It's standard practice for funders to ship proposals out for review by people who know the subjects well. If you spell names incorrectly, get titles and dates wrong, or misrepresent factual information, it will (and should) be held against you. The proposal and the quality of work that goes into it are indicative of the film to come. Besides, the fact checking you do now, if filed carefully, will be useful later.

- The storytelling matters. The people reviewing your proposal, whether they're scientists, historians, mathematicians, or teachers, are as aware as you are that audiences don't watch a film because the topic is important; they watch because they're interested in your story. So while they'll be on guard to see that you don't cut academic corners, you also need to show that you know how to attract and hold an audience's interest.

- Good writing goes a long way. Beyond the basics of spelling and facts, the proposal should present a coherent argument that flows from paragraph to paragraph. Your readers are likely to be plowing through several proposals, and you don't want to trip them up with writing that's unclear or ungrammatical.

- Be your own first audience. Ask yourself if you'd be interested in the film you're pitching, and if the answer is no, work on it some more.

- Anticipate resistance. If you are going to propose a history of the American soap opera as a way to look at important themes in American cultural and social history and women's history, be prepared for the reviewer whose first instinct is to laugh. Get some experts on your side and, with them, make your case. Answer the nay sayers with solid research. Producers have gotten funding for films on all sorts of subjects that might not, at first glance, have seemed "suitable."

- Arm people with what they need to know to understand the proposal. A producer can sometimes get so close to a topic that he or she forgets that other people aren't immersed in the subject and may need either to be reminded or introduced to key characters and events. Assume that your audience is smart but seed information throughout your proposal in a way that brings readers along with you.

- Passion is important. It comes across in the presentation of a proposal in subtle ways, but mostly it shows in the quality

of the work—how thorough the groundwork, how cre-
atively the ideas have been transformed into a story, and
how well that story is presented on paper.

- Avoid overproduction. Teachers are known to get wary
  when they receive papers with fancy, multicolored covers
  that clearly took hours to design and execute because
  they know that the effort spent on the cover hardly ever
  went into the paper. The same is true of proposals. Put the
  effort into the contents (and where appropriate, a sample
  reel); include a few pictures if they help evoke the subject
  and charts and chronologies where they're helpful, but
  otherwise, don't worry about fancy graphics.
- Avoid unfounded hyperbole. "This is the most amazing
  story that the XYZ foundation will ever help to produce,
  and nothing that XYZ has done to date will have the kind of
  impact this film will have."
- Avoid paranoia. "While we are pleased to share this proposal with you, we ask that you keep it in strictest confidence as we are certain that others would grab this idea the
  minute they got wind of it." Foundations keep proposals in
  confidence unless or until they are funded and produced.

PROTECTING YOUR IDEAS

When you become passionate about an idea, you're convinced that
it's so great, everyone will want it right away. The truth is, ideas are
cheap, and it's the whole package—your experience, your treatment of the idea, your ability to make the film happen—that will
sell it, not the idea alone.

With that said, there are ways to protect your work. The first is
through copyright, which is a form of intellectual property law.
You cannot copyright an idea, but you can copyright your treatment of an idea, whether as an outline, treatment, script, or finished
film. For more information, go to the Library of Congress web site
(www.loc.gov).

Another way to protect your work is through the Writer's
Guild of America (www.wga.org), which represents writers in the
motion picture, broadcast, cable, and new technologies industries.
The WGA offers a registration service to nonmembers as well as
members. For a fee (currently $22 for nonmembers), you can regis-

ter anything from an idea to a scenario, synopsis, outline, treatment, or script. By writing down your pitch—the basic story and your unique approach to telling it—and then registering it, you'll have a record of the idea's origination, should it become necessary to prove that you came up with it first. It's best to register at least an outline or treatment (e.g., enough detail to indicate how you'll be approaching the story and what story you'll tell). For example, "a look at skydiving" is far too vague. "A film about skydiving that follows the stars of the NBC sitcom *Friends* as they learn together how to do it and then take their first skydive together" is better; a two-page, ten-page, even twenty-five page treatment is even better.

Know, however, that ideas are in the air. A story that caught your attention on the local news probably caught someone else's attention as well, and it was probably picked up and carried in newspapers all across the country. Books, other films, and current events all trigger film ideas. Anyone who's reviewed proposals, whether for a station or a financier, will tell you that they often come in waves—surprisingly comparable proposals from disparate sources.

At the same time, it's not a perfect world. Keep track of where your material's been, who's seen it, and when. In other words, don't be paranoid, but do be organized.

9

Outlines, Treatments, and Scripts

The role of outlines, treatments, and even scripts in documentary storytelling varies from project to project, but their basic purpose is the same: to help you and others see, on paper, the film as you imagine it. There is no one style for any of these: their level of detail depends, to a large degree, on your schedule, budget, and reasons for writing them. For some filmmakers, it's necessary to write out the story (usually in treatment or preliminary script form) because a potential financier requires it. For others, such as those shooting a film designated for a specific series or broadcaster, a treatment or script may be necessary in order to get the "go ahead" to film. But even for filmmakers working more independently, creating written material at various stages can focus the storytelling.

OUTLINES

An outline is a sketch of your film, written to expose its proposed structure and necessary elements. In most cases, the outline is a working document for you and your team; the prose doesn't need to be polished, and you can use shorthand if your meaning is sufficiently clear. For an hour-long film, the outline might be four to five pages long, double-spaced. It would include a synopsis (one or two paragraphs) of the overall film story, and then a program outline broken down by acts (if applicable) and sequences, with detailed information on elements such as archival footage or specialized photography and interviews.

The outline is a chance to begin imagining your film as it will play on screen. Be careful to focus it as you intend (for now) to focus the final film. Is it about the expedition leader or the group of retirees on the expedition? The parents waging a legal battle against commercialism in the public schools or the budget-starved principal actively courting soft-drink contracts?

If the film is about events in the past or events you have control over (a series of demonstrations set up for the purpose of an essay, for example), it's easier to begin outlining the film and finding an appropriate structure. For films of events that will unfold as you shoot, it's still possible to draft an outline (and treatment) based on what you anticipate happening. If you intend to follow an eighth grader through a summer at basketball camp, you could certainly do research to find out what the experience is typically like, and what scenes or sequences offer possibilities for meaningful interaction. Do the students board at the camp or go home at night? Do they tend to form close friendships? Are there one-on-one sessions with coaches? Is there much pressure from parents? Knowing these things can help you begin to think about what a sequence will *do*, as opposed to the specifics of what it is. If you know, for example, that you want a sequence that you're tentatively calling "The end of innocence"—a sequence that looks at the commercial pressure on young phenoms—then you arrive on location knowing what you're hoping to find.

The same is true when considering the people you'll want to film. As you're doing the outline, you'll begin sketching in the names of people you need, from those you "have to have" to those you'd ideally like. Sometimes you won't know *who* you want specifically, but you know approximately who you're looking for—"We need someone who was at the dance with her," or "We want to talk to janitors and others who keep the physical plant operating." An outline can help you see if your story or argument is building, if you have enough variety of sequences, and if there is redundancy.

Over the course of filming, decisions about story and structure are bound to change, but for now you're taking the first steps in organizing your story into a workable film.

TREATMENTS

There are many reasons to write a treatment, and they differ in length and style because of this. If the treatment is your detailed "pitch" to a financier or executive, it should reflect the interests of that audience. A treatment for the National Endowment for the Humanities, for example, will fold significant humanities scholarship into its storytelling; a treatment for a commercial broadcaster is more likely to be shorter and catchier. A treatment written for use in-house may be less polished in terms of prose, but might include more details about specific shots needed, especially those requiring special gear, as a means of beginning the process of planning for the shoot. The bottom line, though, is this: The treatment is your way of working out *a* film story—not necessarily the *final* film story—on paper, so that even if nothing wonderful and unexpected happens on location to make your film a thousand times better, you'll at least end up with a film that works.

Treatments for an hour-long film may be 5 pages or 25, depending on what you need. (For some examples, see the end of this chapter.) They should be double-spaced, for ease of reading, and written in the present tense—a film story moving forward in time, even if the story is set in the past. Unlike the outline, the treatment may hide the structural underpinnings of the film, especially if it's for public dissemination. As written, the treatment should mirror the experience a viewer of your film will have the following: where and how the film opens, what moments it's driving toward, where it ends. People and places should be introduced in screen order, including a description of how information will be presented. For example, if you plan a sequence about the New York City marathon, it should be clear in the treatment when and how it occurs in your film. Does it start the film, or do you drive to it? If you're going to explore the history of the race, will you do so with archival material, interviews, or something else?

In general, in a detailed proposal, you want to avoid too much shorthand, for example, "Washington crosses the Delaware; military historians explain; Smith reviews the mythology." A better treatment might read, "Over Emanuel Gottlieb Leutze's famous painting, 'George Washington Crossing the Delaware,' we learn through narration of Washington's triumphant crossing of the Delaware River on the stormy night of December 25, 1776. As our historians make clear, all had seemed lost for the Americans. Now, Washington and his army of 3,000 surprise Britain's mercenary forces at Trenton and capture one-third of the men. They also gain a foothold in New Jersey that puts a halt to the British offensive. It's a decisive moment in the war for independence. We return to the painting, as art historian Jane Smith compares the history to the mythology. The painting was completed in 1851, 75 years after the event . . . ''

Note that the treatment hasn't said what images you'll be weaving into and out of between historians; hopefully by this point in the treatment it's clear how you're handling the war history. Nor does it list all of the specific historians talking about this particular event, because by now the reader probably has a sense of which historians you've involved. You can't describe every image and every voice-over and every anticipated sync bite, or you might as well write the script. What you're doing is making the story and progression of events clear, and including the most important details, in this case, the use of the painting and the art historian.

Explanatory Materials

If you are submitting a treatment for outside review, one way of adding information other than what's in the film—because at best, the treatment can't possibly capture everything the film will deliver—is to include a preface, often called "an approach." For example, the filmmaker can state his or her objectives for the program and raise questions to be explored. "Was Father Divine an inspired religious leader who helped to reinvent the rules of social ministry? Or was he a potentially dangerous man deluded by power? This story will examine . . . " The approach can offer explicit information about the themes and ideas that will be explored in the storytelling; it can also make the filmmaker's position on an issue clear. "We are committed to exploring the overwhelming evidence that manufacturers of XYZ knowingly withheld information about its dangers . . . " Note, however, that there must still be questions to be explored; in this case, they might be, "Were regulatory agencies aware of these dangers, and if so, why did they not take action sooner?"

Be Complete

Especially if your treatment is to be read by project outsiders, don't leave your reader in the dark. Rather than drop names like "Copland" or "Bismarck," weave enough information into the treatment to remind readers the significance of these names. A quick sketch is usually enough, (e.g., "the German battleship the Bismarck, whose sinking in the Atlantic Ocean in May 1941 marked a turning point in the Second World War.'').

Quoting People

Suppose you know who you want to interview, but you haven't spoken with them yet, either in a pre-interview or a filmed interview. You should never make up quotes based on what you hope someone will say, even if you have a good idea of what it might be, if only because the world is small and if Professor X finds out that you attributed a statement to him he hasn't made or wouldn't make, the chances that he'll cooperate with you in the future are slim.

Instead, there are a few options for sprinkling in quotes from sources you haven't directly spoken with. First, you can simply describe what someone will be asked about, for example, ''Dr. Hunter offers an introduction to photosynthesis . . . '' Second, you can quote from the individual's published writing. Third, you can quote from interviews that others have conducted with the person. *But*—if you do any of these, you need to be clear that you have not yet contacted the person directly, and that he or she has not yet agreed to participate in the film. You might say, ''Except as noted, quotes are taken from print material published elsewhere.'' *Suggestion: If you decide to do this, write a version of your treatment with footnotes, so that you can go back to this source if necessary. Remove those footnotes in copies for outside review; they're distracting and unnecessary for readers—they are ''seeing'' your film on paper, not reading a research report.* Another possibility would be, ''We have gained the cooperation of Dr. X and Rev. Y, but have not yet spoken with Mr. Z and Dr. P, who are also quoted here.''

In any case, quotes should be used sparingly. This is your treatment, not your script.

Unknown Information

Even the most polished treatments are written before all of the pieces are in place; you don't know what you'll discover on the film shoot or what terrific visuals you'll find in somebody's attic. Most importantly, it's very often the case that you're writing the treatment to raise money to do necessary research; you're doing the best you can with the resources you have, but you know that there is a lot more you'll need to learn before you can go out to shoot. One solution is to acknowledge these gaps in your writing, by describing, in general terms, types or scenes that you believe you'll need. For example, "A trainer describes what it's like to work with thoroughbred horses and takes us through the paces of an early-morning work-out." Or "We are searching for an expert in queuing theory who can apply his or her theoretical work to the design of amusement parks, and we will find parents who know from experience that there is a limit to how long their children—and they themselves—are willing to wait in line."

Writing Treatments for a Series

Writing treatments for a multi-part series is not much different than for individual films, except that the approach (and the films themselves) may need to serve a series story as well as individual film stories. What is the overall series story? Where does each film begin and end? How does that film set the stage for the next film in the series? The build doesn't always need to be chronological; the evolution of a mathematical concept, for example, could form the spine of a series. Sometimes a series has no overall story. Each film simply explores a different aspect of a subject.

Reflect the Work You've Done

Surprisingly, one of the most common problems I encounter when reviewing treatments is that they seem to be based on an afternoon's worth of research, when in fact the filmmakers have spent weeks or even months on the project and in some cases, have shot a significant portion of the footage. Your treatment should sell your project and play to its strengths. Add the details that will make your efforts show. For example, "In an interview filmed last May on the steps of her brownstone in Brooklyn, author Celia Jones offered her perspective on the housing crisis." Or "Our crew follows Mr. Smith down spiral stairs leading to a dusty basement filled with old newspapers, magazines, and a rare collection of photographs that he offers to show us." Provide enough detail to make it clear that you know your subject inside and out, even if you also know that there is a lot more you need to learn.

Tell a Good Story

An important trick of writing treatments is to convey your passion early on. You think you've found an excellent subject for a film—convince the reader. A good story, well researched and well told, goes a long way. As someone who's reviewed proposals, I can say from experience that many submitted treatments are little more than research documents, or, even worse, ideas that haven't progressed much beyond a basic topic. Treatments that attract attention are those that set up and deliver a compelling story, one that's informed by research and enlivened by something different—an unusual perspective, a new angle, unique access to people or places.

Tell a good story as best you can. Then run your treatment past someone who knows nothing about your movie and preferably is not related to you, so that you get impartial feedback before you send your material to the people you're likely to need most at this stage—financiers.

THE SHOOTING TREATMENT

A "shooting treatment" is the most polished form of film treatment; on some projects, it's the only form. It may be the same as the treatment you submit for development or production funding, but it's more likely to be a treatment you write once significant funding is in place. The shooting treatment represents all of your research and development prior to shooting; it's the document in which you work out, in detail, how you anticipate telling your story on film.

For many filmmakers, this treatment serves as a blueprint for production. It is a baseline guide to the elements you need to tell the story that you *anticipate* telling. At the same time, the understanding that you've gained from creating this document often prepares you to recognize and take advantage of even better storytelling opportunities in the field.

Depending on the project, a treatment for an hour-long film can be anywhere from 15 to 30 pages, double-spaced. It is written in the present tense, and does not include information that cannot be conveyed on screen. (For example, instead of writing, "As a young man, Henry was a talented aviator," you let us know how we'll know this. "In a montage of stills from Henry's barnstorming days, we see . . . ") The film's structure should be implied in the treatment. If you are using a three-act structure, for example, your film's first act should *roughly* be a quarter of the length of your treatment.

The most important thing to know about treatment writing is that your emphasis should be on the story, not the shots. Filmmakers often get distracted imagining the powerful images they're going to capture or the technical requirements needed to get certain shots and fail to head out on the road with a real understanding of the particular story they're telling and why. They come back to the editing room with a great beginning that goes nowhere or without the storytellers they need to paint a detailed picture—but they've got that great sunset or the aerial view.

Get the story in order by writing a treatment that you're satisfied with, and then go through that document with your production crew, including the cinematographer. Together, you'll be able to effectively determine the best way to capture your *story* on film.

SCRIPTS

Documentary scripts tend to evolve over the course of production. In the case of programs that are significantly driven by narration, the script might begin to take shape during pre-production, only to be significantly revised and rewritten during editing. (Rarely, a film will be entirely scripted prior to shooting. Unless the filmmaker is extremely skilled, however, this can lead to a program that is little more than an illustrated lecture.)

On programs in which narration augments visual storytelling, scripts are not usually written until editing or shooting is complete (or nearly complete). At that point, filmmakers will assemble a paper script. This script builds on the original treatment but takes into account changes to the story as filmed, and it incorporates interview, sync, and archival material in proposed screen order as a blueprint for the editor to follow (for more details, see Chapter 12). As editing progresses, this script is revised and rewritten, until no more changes are to be made (script lock and picture lock). Note that not all films are edited in this way, and some editors rely solely on an outline that is revised over the course of editing.

Fundraising Scripts

There are funding agencies that require a script as a condition of granting production money. If you are already editing, you will be able to submit a draft of your script in progress. If you are still seeking funding for production, however, what you submit is more akin to a very developed treatment or a document that is part treatment, part script. You do the best you can, adhering to the guidelines for a treatment but generally presenting the material in a more script-like format.

Script Format

Don't go out and buy a commercial screenwriting software program; these are designed specifically for dramatic feature films and serve that function well, but they're of little use for documentaries. Most documentary filmmakers seem to use Word or WordPerfect (files cross these platforms without much difficulty), using them to create scripts that are formatted in either one or two columns.

If two columns are used, one is for visuals, the other for audio. With a single-column format, visuals, if mentioned, are put in parentheses. In either case, narration and interview bites should stand out from each other; for example, the narration might be in bold, or the interview bites indented. On films with significant interview material, whether or not there will also be narration, it can be helpful to create a separate block (whether you're working with one column or two) for each interview bite that's pulled, so they can be quickly moved around. Some filmmakers also use the outlining function to keep sequences intact, again, so they can be quickly rearranged.

Narration Script

When it comes time to record narration, your narration pieces are generally numbered and then isolated into a script of their own—a "narration script"—which is often single-column, double-spaced, with very wide margins to the left and right for ease of reading. Don't put the narration in all capitals, as this makes it more difficult to read.

Sample page, outline, *Ain't Gonna Shuffle No More*

PROGRAM TITLE: *Ain't Gonna Shuffle No More* (1964–1972)

Synopsis: This hour looks at rising Black consciousness through the transformations of Cassius Clay, who becomes Muhammad Ali and takes a stand against the war in Vietnam; students at Howard University, who fight for a curriculum that recognizes their Black heritage; and elected officials who join Black nationalists at a National Black Political Convention in Gary, Indiana.

Program outline:

Sequence 1: Tease: Black is Beautiful

A montage of archival images and sync material that introduce the Black Arts and Black consciousness movements of the 1960s.

PEOPLE: Interview with Sonia Sanchez, poet

FOOTAGE: Archival of Amiri Baraka (at the Congress of African Peoples, 1970) and the Last Poets

Sequence 2: "I Shook Up The World"

We begin the first act of our first story: Olympic champion Cassius Clay challenges World Heavyweight Champion Sonny Liston. Rumors are spread that Clay is spending time with Malcolm X, spokesperson for the Nation of Islam. Fight promoters want Clay to deny the rumors; he refuses, and after he defeats Liston, he publicly announces his new Muslim identity: Muhammad Ali.

PEOPLE: Edwin Pope, sportswriter; Kareem-Abdul Jabbar, student; Angelo Dundee, trainer; Herbert Muhammad, son of Elijah Muhammad

FOOTAGE: Archival of Muhammad Ali, Ali with Malcolm X, the Liston fight

Sequence 3: A Heavy Price

As associates and the press react to Muhammad Ali's new identity, he embarks on a tour of Ghana. Nigeria, and Africa, where he is welcomed as a hero. Returning to

Episode five of the second season of EYES ON THE PRIZE. This page was written as demonstration only. The initial outline for *Ain't Gonna Shuffle No More* was for a program called *New Definitions*.

Sample page, preliminary treatment, *You Could Grow Aluminum Out There*

Not fact checked/interview subjects not confirmed   4

ACT I, THE CENTRAL VALLEY PROJECT
FIRST CAUSES

In California we name things for what they destroyed.

Real estate signs whiz by the windshield. . . . "Quail Meadows," "The Grasslands," "Indian Creek," "Riverbank Estates," "Elk Grove Townhouses," "Miwok Village."

Before the Spaniards came, 300 tribes shared the Central Valley of California. . . . . Maidu, Miwok, Patwin. A few weeks of flooding each winter fed the great marshes and seasonal lakes, but for most of the year—the seven month dry season when Indians moved to the cooler surrounding foothills—the Great Central Valley got, and still gets, less rain than North Africa. It was the American Serengeti

Spanish maps.

Richard Rodriguez, or perhaps Maxine Hong Kingston or Jesse De La Cruz pick up the story.

The wet winters and dry summers unique to California had gone on for a hundred thousand years before Europeans came. A rich, complex ecosystem had evolved with such intelligence that the great condors, elk, delta smelt, cougars and bunch grass could survive in the natural cycles of drought and flood. Each carried genetic information for the next generation to thrive in arid land, and the next and the next. Bidwell saw 40 grizzlies in a single day, and Central Valley salmon ran in the millions. Muir, standing on a hill south of San Francisco looked 100 miles east toward the Sierra and saw ". . . . a carpet of wildflowers, a continuous sheet of bloom bounded only by mountains."[2]

Program produced, directed, and written by Jon Else; page 4 of 40; episode three of CADILLAC DESSERT; broadcast as *The Mercy of Nature.* © 1995 Jon Else, reprinted with permission.

Sample pages, NEH treatment, *Getting Over*

HOUR THREE: *Getting Over* (1910–1939)

> Tell me how we got over, Lord;
> Had a mighty hard time, comin' on over.
> You know, my soul looks back in wonder,
> How did we make it over?
>
> Tell me how we got over, Lord;
> I've been falling and rising all these years.
> But you know, my soul looks back in wonder,
> How did I make it over?
>
> "How I Got Over" (gospel song)

THE PRESENT

"Where is hope? Hope is closer than we know!" declares the Reverend Cecil Williams, pastor of the Glide Memorial United Methodist Church in San Francisco.

> I want you to know this morning that this is Bethlehem! The rejected are here. The wretched of the earth are here. Poor folks, rich folks, middle-class folks. You can be yourself here. You don't have to run from yourself here. You don't have to put yourself down here. You can embrace love here. Where is hope? Hope is here! Amen!

Glide Memorial Church in the Tenderloin district of San Francisco, an area of tenements, crack houses, and shooting galleries, lies at what Rev. Williams calls "the intersection of despair and hope." Williams took over the church in 1966, when the congregation included about 35 people, nearly all of them middle-class whites. Today, it has 6,400 members and a reputation, as *Psychology Today* reported in 1995, as "an urban refuge for the spiritually disenfranchised . . . a faith steeped more in heart and soul than in scripture."

Powerful and influential visitors like Oprah Winfrey and President Bill Clinton speak of Glide as a model religious institution. Poet Maya Angelou, a parishioner for nearly 30 years, calls it "a church for the 21st century." Glide is San Francisco's largest provider of social services, offering recovery centers for substance abusers, domestic-violence workshops for batterers and victims, anger management classes for youth, job skills and computer training for the unemployed or those wishing to further their education. Its tradition of outreach is a hallmark of African-American religion, especially as it developed in the decades following the Great Migration.

On a Sunday morning, we watch as Rev. Williams evokes the past in his demands for the future:

> Faith and resistance are the fuels that power the train of freedom and transformation. . . . The train of freedom and recovery chugs on daily. Claim your place on this train. The freedom train is passing you by. Catch it. Then listen. Listen carefully. Those on the train are singing. Can you hear the voices of a New Generation? They are singing and shouting with unchained abandon. Lift your voice, raise your fist. You sing, too.

We will return to Glide throughout this program, as its ministry informs the historical events in this hour. For now, we cut to:

THE PAST:

A train rushes by, seen in grainy black-and-white footage reminiscent of the early years of this century. A woman can be heard singing softly, unaccompanied, as if comforting a sleeping child on board: *Plenty of good room, plenty of good room in my Father's kingdom.* A few cars back, we catch a glimpse of a window, the curtain drawn. Inside, a man's hand sets words to paper:

> I am writing on board a Jim Crow car . . . a horrible night ride. . . . Why does the negro leave the South? . . . You feel a large part of that answer on this train . . . and share for one night the longing of the people to reach the line . . . which separates Dixie from the rest of creation.

Everyone Is Welcome

The third hour of THIS FAR BY FAITH begins with the onset of the greatest internal population shift to have yet occurred in the United States. In 1910, more than 90% of African Americans live in the South. Between the turn of the century and 1930, nearly two million will make their way north in a mass exodus. They are "led as if by some mysterious unseen hand which was compelling them on," reports Charles S. Johnson, an African-American sociologist in Chicago at the time. A group of nearly 150 Southerners, crossing the Ohio River, a divide "between Dixie and the rest of creation," kneels together and prays.

3-4

Treatment written by Sheila Curran Bernard and Lulie Haddad, episode three of THIS FAR BY FAITH, broadcast as *Guide My Feet*. © 1998 Blackside, Inc., reprinted with permission.

Sample treatment, *The Milltail Pack*

The Milltail Pack

At the edge of a dirt roadway which runs along a thick wooded area, three red wolves appear as dusk begins to fall. The leader of the pack is an old male in his twilight years with a thick auburn coat and a long nose. Though he's not as fast as he used to be, his gait remains quick, his eyes and ears alert. Close behind are two noticeably smaller wolves. They are siblings, a male and a female just turned three years old. The pack is heading to a corn field just at the end of the road. In the brown dry stalks of last month's corn live mice, rabbits and voles - tasty appetizers for the Milltail Pack.

At nine years old, the aging male is raising, in all probability, his last offspring. He's seen a lot of change over the years, and he's survived to tell the story of how a species on the brink of extinction came to be saved by a handful of dedicated humans and a branch of government. Known to biologists at the Alligator River National Wildlife Refuge in North Carolina as #331, this old male is living proof that predators and people can live together and flourish. The only remaining red wolf that was born in captivity and reintroduced into the wild, his life parallels the timeline of a unique government initiative.

In 1980 the red wolf was declared biologically extinct - in the wild. In answer to this, the US Fish and Wildlife Service implemented the Red Wolf Recovery Plan - an all-out effort to save the species using captive wolves. This was the first re-introductory program of its kind for any carnivore in the world! Against overwhelming odds and after countless setbacks, the program has managed success.

In 1987, a red wolf breeding pair was reintroduced into the Alligator River Wildlife Refuge, and by the next year their first litter of pups was born in the wild. Since then wolves have been introduced on three island sites, three wildlife refuges, a national park, and a number of privately-owned properties in North Carolina, Tennessee, and South Carolina. But it wasn't easy. The recovery plan had to insure genetic diversity, hope the wolves tolerant of people in a captive setting would shy away from them once wild, and enlist public support for reintroduction of a predator in their neighborhoods. And the ultimate goal of the plan, not yet realized, is to have a total population of 220 wild red wolves.

Today there are about 70 wolves living in northeastern North Carolina, and all but one were born in the wild. Number 331 and his brother, 332, were released when they were just under one year old. Running together they sought out a home range that was occupied by a resident male. They killed the wolf and began consorting with his mate, 205. Together the young males shared the area with 331 mating with 205 and 332 taking up with 205's daughter. But 332 was killed by a car leaving 331 the leader of the Milltail Pack. Like gray wolves, red wolves mate for life, but 331 lost his first mate several years ago. He then mated with his step daughter, 394, who was mother to the siblings he takes hunting today. Last year, she died leaving him without a mate and the youngsters without a mother.

The Milltail Pack ranges through farmlands, wooded areas, public roadways and along the banks of Milltail Creek in search of food. They mainly eat white-tailed deer, but their diet also consists of raccoons and small mammals like rabbits and mice. Similar to gray wolves, they tend to shy away from people and stay close to woodlands or farm edges that provide cover. In their home in North Carolina the habitat ranges from farmland to wooded areas including marshy wetlands, and even a military bombing range!

Before becoming extinct in the wild, red wolves populated the southeastern United States, but as man began clear-cutting areas for wood, drainage and farms, wolves and men came into closer contact. Fear and misunderstanding led to indiscriminate killings and bounties. In addition, as coyotes adapted stretching their habitat from western states into the southeast, they interbred with red wolves, threatening the wolves' genetic purity.

The Milltail Pack has lived through the successes and failures of the Red Wolf Recovery Plan and now stands on the threshold of a new debate. Can man use this program as a model for other species and can we learn from our mistakes? Despite the success of such re-introductory programs, there will always be opponents of predators. In 1995, gray wolves were reintroduced into Yellowstone National Park and today their fate is questionable because opponents to the reintroduction have waged a court struggle to have them removed. In North Carolina opponents to the Red Wolf Recovery Plan still threaten to shut down the program with lengthy court battles. Last year 11 Mexican wolves were released in Arizona after 16 years of planning, and today they are all dead - most were shot by angry ranchers. For conservationists and biologists these programs represent a chance for society to learn from our mistakes. Without the existence of top predators, prey animals go unchecked and often overpopulate areas. And not only is it important to save wolves because of their role as predators, but they are a leading symbol of wild nature.

Because red wolves were virtually extinct until 1987, little was known about their behavior. But biologists are learning that their social structure, feeding and breeding habits are similar to gray wolves. Ten years after reintroducing the first red wolves into the wild, their numbers are growing -evidence of their adaptability, strength and stamina. The leader of the Milltail Pack has survived to sire 4 litters and he and his offspring have a unique story to tell.

Wolves have been in the news for the past few years and are a hot topic. But little has been said about the red wolf or this recovery project. Most of the national press has focused on the gray wolves and their reintroduction to Yellowstone. While there has been regional press about the Red Wolf Recovery Plan, this film is the first documentary to offer an in-depth look at these beautiful animals and the circumstances that have brought them back into the wild.

Film Approach

This film offers an opportunity for a rare glimpse into the lives of a fascinating species, and the film's goal is to tell a success story. Using the Milltail Pack we'll chronicle the program from the early days of life in captivity, move to life today in the wild, and finally speculate about the future of the recovery program and these amazing animals. We have access to footage of wolves in captivity, footage of animals being released, and filming in the wild today. {In order for the biologists to monitor the health and movements of released wolves, most of the animals are radio collared which makes it easy for us to locate packs and differentiate between them.}

This film will take the viewer on an odyssey of survival through the eyes of an aging red wolf. Filming will include captive animals at the Alligator River National Wildlife Refuge, wolf capture and tagging, wolf release, and behavior of family groups in the wild. In addition, interviews with biologists who have been working in the program for 11 years as well as area farmers and townspeople will help illustrate how these wolves came to be accepted on both private and refuge land and how they've managed to survive. While the focus of the film is the red wolf, we'll round out the piece with a look at what's happening to the Mexican wolf and the grays in Yellowstone.

Treatment written by Holly Stadtler, film broadcast on Explorer Wild as *America's Last Red Wolves*. © 2000 Dream Catcher Films, reprinted with permission.

Sample editing outline, *Lalee's Kin*

AUGUST

A NEW SCHOOL YEAR BEGINS

LLW AND KIDS ON PORCH
    Intro kids
    Main flunked first grade

BOYS BATH – before school

LOST CLOTHES (night before school)

TELEPHONE GAME

FIRST DAY OF SCHOOL – LW brushes Redman's hair

PARKING LOT ADVICE – LLW and Redman

REGISTRATION – LLW and Redman

SAN'S HOUSE
    Supplies

DON'T NOBODY KNOW

SUNSET
    Praise Jesus

GRANNY CRIES ON PORCH
    No pencils

KIDS GET ON SCHOOL BUS/ ARRIVE AT SCHOOL

REGGIE – If kids don't come to school first day we're not going to solve anything
    We have a test Oct. 1 and instruction begins now
    Someone has to be Level 1, but we don't want to be it

GRANNY IN SCHOOL

SADIE DILLS

COTTON FIELD

LALEE AND REGGIE RE COTTON PICKING AND PLANTATION MENTALITY
    R- Closed schools

© 2002 Maysles Films, Inc., reprinted with permission.

Sample page, script (single column), *The Donner Party*

VOICE 001: It is odd to watch with what feverish ardor Americans pursue prosperity – ever tormented by the shadowy suspicion that they may not have chosen the shortest route to get it. They cleave to the things of this world as if assured that they will never die – and yet rush to snatch any that comes within their reach, as if they expected to stop living before they had relished them. Death steps in in the end and stops them, before they have grown tired of this futile pursuit of that complete felicity which always escapes them.

Alexis de Toqueville

TITLE: THE DONNER PARTY

NARRATOR: It began in the 1840s, spurred on by financial panic in the East, by outbreaks of cholera and malaria, and by the ceaseless American hankering to move West. When the pioneer movement began, fewer than 20,000 white Americans lived west of the Mississippi River. [Ten years later the emigration had swelled to a flood, and] Before it was over, more than half a million men, women and children had stepped off into the wilderness at places like Independence, Missouri, and headed out over the long road to Oregon and California.

In places their wagon wheels carved ruts shoulder-deep in the rocky road.

The settlers themselves knew they were making history. "It will be received," one emigrant wrote, "as a legend on the borderland of myth." But of all the stories to come out of the West, none has cut more deeply into the imagination of the American people than the tale of the Donner Party high in the Sierra Nevada in the winter of 1846.

INTERVIEW HS24: Human endeavor and failure. Blunders, mistakes, ambition, greed – all of the elements. And if you call the rescue of the surviving parties a happy ending, it's a happy ending. But what about those that didn't make it. Terrible, terrible.

Harold Schindler

INTERVIEW JK1: We're curious about people who've experienced hardship, who have gone through terrible ordeals. And certainly the Donner Party, you know, 87 people went through a crisis the like of which few human beings have ever faced. And we're curious about that.

1

Written by Ric Burns. © 1992 Steeplechase Films, Inc., reprinted with permission.

Sample page, script (double column), *Lift Every Voice*

SERIES TITLE	*I'LL MAKE ME A WORLD: A CENTURY OF AFRICAN-AMERICAN ARTS*
NAME OF SHOW	*EPISODE 1: LIFT EVERY VOICE*
Lower third: **Melvin Van** **Peebles Filmmaker**	**Van Peebles**: People always talk about the—the down side of racism. There's an up side, too. The up side is that nobody thinks you're smart. They don't even know why they don't think you're smart. Don't woke 'em, let em slept. Just go ahead and do the deal you have to do. Racism offers great business opportunities if you keep your mouth shut.
clips of Bert Williams – *Nobody*	(hearing a few bars of *Nobody*) *When life seems full of clouds and rain* *And I am full of nothing and pain* *Who soothes my thumping, bumping brain?* *NOBODY.*
lower third: **Lloyd Brown** **Writer**	**LLOYD BROWN**: Bert Williams combined the grace of a Charlie Chaplin, imagery and all, and at the same time with a very rich voice too. And so he—he was . . . wonderful comedy.
lower third: **James Hatch** **Theater Historian**	**HATCH**: He has a . . . (laughing) song where he's obviously explaining to his wife who the woman was that he was seen with. And the refrain chorus line is "She was a cousin of mine." He has that line, I would say, six or seven times in the song: "She was just a cousin of mine." Every time it's different. Every time it's a new interpretation. (v/o) The man was a genius.
Stills of Bert Williams	**NARRATION 1: In the earliest years of the 20th century, Bert Williams was the most successful black performer on the American stage. But each night, he performed behind a mask he hated: blackface.**
Lower third: **Ben Vereen** **Performer**	**VEREEN** (v/o): Bert Williams didn't want to black up. But socially during that time, he had to. And he realized that. He was a very intelligent man. . . . We have to hide our identity by putting on this mask, in order to get things said and done. (o/c) But we did it. We did it. And today we don't have to do it. But we cannot forget it.

Written by Sheila Curran Bernard; episode one of I'LL MAKE ME A WORLD. © 1998 Blackside, Inc., reprinted with permission.

10

Casting

Not all documentary filmmakers would call it "casting," yet all would agree that the people you see on screen—whether they're interacting with each other, talking to an off-screen interviewer, or acting as narrator or host—need to be researched, contacted, and brought onto the project with care. Decisions about who will be filmed, how they will be chosen, and what they're expected to contribute to the storytelling are important. Even the people who appear through archival means, whether in archival footage or through a reading of their letters, diaries, and other artifacts of the past, are important to the overall casting of a story. In fact, how you cast your documentary is so important that some executives want to see footage of your main characters before they'll approve or commission a project.

WHEN TO CAST

In general, you begin thinking about casting even as you're considering a topic and story to film; it's part of the conception of a film's style and approach. If there are specific people whose involvement is critical, you'll need to cast them (or at least know that they would be available and amenable) prior to your inclusion of them in any pitch. After that, casting takes shape as the outline and treatment do, and you begin to know who or what type of people you're looking for and why.

WHO TO CAST

For a film that requires experts, it's wise to cast a range of viewpoints. This means that instead of just shooting "five experts" on a subject, you know how each of the five differs from the others in expertise and outlook, offering a means of adding complexity and balance to the overall film. There are only so many people an audience can follow in a half-hour or an hour, and you don't want all of those people talking about the same issues from the same perspective.

One way to think about casting is to regard each individual who appears on screen, whether as a character you're following or as someone you interview (or both), as having a job to do in the overall film. Sometimes they stand in for a particular aspect of an argument; sometimes they represent an element that you could not otherwise film. For example, you could get three people to talk in general about Title IX legislation, but it might be stronger to find a lawyer who'd fought for its enforcement, a female athlete who got a college scholarship because of it, and an athletic director who opposed it out of fear that it would limit resources for his school's football program. They may each know a little bit or even a lot about each other's areas of expertise, but it muddies the storytelling if they don't stick to the part of the story that they best serve.

Along the same lines, if you're creating a historical film, you might want a biographer to stand in for Martha Washington, for example. He or she would be asked to comment specifically and only on your story as it relates to Martha. Without attention being called to it, the audience will learn this cue. When they see that expert, they'll know that—in a way—Martha is now on screen, or at least her proxy.

Do Your Homework

A significant part of casting effectively is doing some research before you start indiscriminately calling around looking for experts or "types." The less generic the casting is, the stronger the film will be.

Casting Non-Experts

Sometimes, you're not looking for experts but for real people willing to give you access to lives and situations that embody themes and ideas you've set out to explore.

- For their film *Troublesome Creek*, Jeanne Jordan and Steven Ascher decided against casting or interviewing any experts, and instead focused on Jordan's family members especially her parents. "We absolutely did not want any expert testimony about anything having to do with farming or economics that would make it seem like this was a subject being studied as opposed to a subject that was being lived," Ascher says.

- The producers of *Hoop Dreams* were fortunate in their discovery of the two young basketball players featured in their film, Arthur Agee and William Gates. According to their press material, filmmakers Steve James, Frederick Marx, and Peter Gilbert initially planned to make a half-hour documentary on street basketball in Chicago. In 1986, they approached producer Gordon Quinn of Kartemquin Films, and Quinn, in turn, approached KTCA, the PBS station in St. Paul. By this time, the filmmakers had found Agee and Williams, both freshmen in high school. The plan now shifted, and they followed the players over a period of years to see where their basketball dreams would take them. Each player, on his own, would have been interesting, but their two stories interwoven provide a far more insightful look at the various ways in which opportunity, family, skill, and luck can impact an athletic career.

Casting Opposing Voices

How do you get people to participate in a film when it's likely that the viewpoint they hold is contrary to yours or the audience's? A primary way is by making it clear that you are open to what they have to say, intend to treat them fairly on screen, and believe that their point of view, while you might disagree with it, is important to the subject at hand and the public's understanding of it.

Don't misrepresent yourself or your project just to gain someone's cooperation. If you want to explore the notion that the 1969 moonwalk was faked, don't imply that your film is a look at manned space flight. Does this mean that you can't approach credible experts on subjects that strain credibility? No. It means that you need to bring them with you, not trick them into cooperating. Give them the option of adding their credibility to

Ken "Spike" Kirkland, in *Sing Faster: The Stagehands' Ring Cycle*. Photo courtesy of Jon Else.

the project, and then use their credibility responsibly. (If you *are* an expert and are approached for a documentary, do some homework before saying yes. A quick web search should tell you a bit about the producer and/or the series that will be airing the interview.)

Casting for Balance

Balancing the point of view of a film does not mean simply presenting opposing sides. In fact, it almost never means that. Two opposing sides talking past each other do not advance anyone's understanding of an issue. When the opposing sides are actually very uneven, as when a majority of credible experts takes one position and a small (and often fringe or invested) minority disagrees, then giving these two views equal time and weight creates a false impression that the issues are more uncertain than they actually are. This is not balanced, it's inaccurate. Instead, you look for people who can offer shades of gray, complexity, within an issue.

Note that casting for balance also means letting the appropriate people present their own points of view. This doesn't mean that individuals can't speak to experiences outside their own; a

French historian whose expertise is Native-American education at the turn of the century, for example, might be well qualified to discuss life on a particular Oklahoma reservation in 1910. It's more of a stretch to ask a biology major who happens to be protesting foreign sweatshops to tell you what goes on in an overseas sneaker factory, unless you limit your questioning to a frame of reference relevant to that person. "Why am I here? I'm here because I read an article that said . . . " If your film storytelling requires that you convey conditions in the factory, you'd be better off trying to find someone who has witnessed those conditions firsthand (as a worker or owner, for example, or as someone who toured the facilities on a fact-finding tour) and/or a labor expert who has studied those specific conditions.

When you hear someone on camera talking about "them"— for example, "The people living in government housing thought we were being unfair to them"—it's likely you need to find individuals from within that community or qualified experts to speak instead.

Expanding the Perspective

It's very easy, when casting (and especially when casting quickly), to go after the people at the top, the leaders and figureheads. Often, they are known to be charismatic and articulate. But they rarely represent the whole story or, often, the most interesting part of it. Dig deeper, and ask yourself who else might add perspective to a story. If you're talking to policy experts for a film on education, you might want to explore what a second-grade teacher would add. If you're doing a film about corporate scandals, an interesting perspective might come from a realtor trying to sell the homes of some former executives who are now in prison.

Part of looking further involves making an effort to seek out diversity. Look further than the list of people interviewed for the last documentary or the most recent news report on a particular subject. Times have changed, the experts have changed with it, and if you can't find female and minority astrophysicists, structural engineers, construction workers, social historians, and pretty much everything else, chances are you're not looking very hard. This isn't about political correctness; it's about accuracy and a commitment to updating the subtle and not so subtle messages that films send to viewers.

HOSTS AND NARRATORS

There is a wide range in how and why people use on-camera hosts for documentary films. The PBS series THE AMERICAN EXPERIENCE uses historian David McCullough to set the stage for each program and then to serve as the program's off-screen narrator. Lifetime has used celebrity hosts to front documentary programs, as when Camryn Manheim hosted and narrated the documentary special, *100 Years of Women*. Meryl Streep hosted and narrated SCHOOL: THE STORY OF PUBLIC EDUCATION, which aired on PBS. A host can bring publicity to a film and, depending on the individual, may bring credibility and a commitment to issues raised.

Other programs involve the host in the filmed storyline, as when WILD NATURE brought celebrities on journeys around the world, including Goldie Hawn and Julia Roberts. These hosts help to bring a narrative structure to the filmmaking, as discussed in Chapter 3. It's also possible to have one person introduce a show and another narrate it. And it's possible—in fact, quite common— that a celebrity or non-celebrity narrates the show without ever being seen on camera. In any case, you want the narration to be recorded by someone who can enunciate and whose voice will carry even when placed against music or sync sound.

The narrator's voice sets a tone for the film. Will it be male or female, or have an identifiable ethnicity or regional accent? How old do you want your narrator to sound? How do you want this person to come across to the audience? As an expert or a friend? Sounding humorous, somber, remote, or warm? Your narrator has a distinct presence in the film, and is part of the overall balance of voices that are heard.

PAYING YOUR SUBJECTS

Some filmmakers pay their subjects (whether interviewees or those filmed vérité) indirectly, whether through buying them groceries or making a contribution to a charity. The general rule in journalism is that if you start paying for stories, people will come up with stories for which they want to be paid. There is a big difference between paying an actor to portray Thomas Jefferson and paying a scholar or expert to discuss him. One is a craftsman in an art frequently supported through freelance employment such as this.

The other is usually a career scholar and/or author who benefits by advancing his or her expertise and, in many cases, published work, for whom you are providing a significant audience. Scholars and experts are not traditionally paid, although this is a current issue of debate and there are some new precedents being set.

Don't be confused by the difference between experts who appear on camera and those who work off camera as advisors—and don't assume that they are the same people. As discussed previously, advisors work behind the scenes, often for the duration of the project. They are usually paid an honorarium for their time and given a credit that flies by all too quickly at the end of the film.

What about those people who agree to appear on camera but have nothing to gain, no book to build an audience for or business that benefits from publicity? People participate in films for a number of reasons. They believe in their work or struggle and hope that their stories may raise awareness or help others; they've suffered an injustice or a personal loss and hope that publicity may gain them support or bring perpetrators to the attention of law enforcement people; they are asked to cooperate by their employers or sponsors. There are a number of good reasons to participate in a documentary. Being paid shouldn't be the most significant one.

Part III

PRODUCTION AND POST-PRODUCTION

11

Shooting

Telling a story in the field means working closely with the sound recordist and cinematographer to ensure that you get what you need and, even more, that you find material you couldn't have anticipated but soon won't be able to imagine making your film without. Done well, the visuals (and audio) can play a critical and distinct role in your storytelling. Is your film dependent on interviews and narration, or can scenes and sequences be played without sound and still convey story? Ideally, language alone is not driving the film, but instead images and ideas together advance the overall narrative. In addition to live action photography, the visual elements might include time-lapse photography, archival images (including innovative or unusual material, such as home movies or clips from old feature films), still photography, computer animation, recreations, and demonstrations. They're all part of the palette for telling a story.

SHOOTING WITH THE STORY IN MIND

With live-action filming, the best way to ensure visual storytelling is by *not* hiring a cinematographer the day before production starts. You want a crew that knows the story and has the expertise to help you tell it well. Boyd Estus, a director of photography whose credits include the Academy Award-winning *The Flight of the Gossamer Condor*, has shot both documentary and drama for venues including the BBC, PBS, Discovery Channel, and National Geographic. When a documentary producer calls him about shooting, Estus always asks to see an outline or treatment, something that gives him an idea of the big picture—not only what's being filmed, but why. In cases where a crew is filming an *event*, the sound recordist, too, should be in on the story, in part because he or she is often better able to anticipate, through listening to the conversations of key players who've been miked, where the action is going next. "They often will hear things that nobody else hears," Estus says, adding that when he shoots vérité, he also wears a headset so that he can hear the radio mikes directly.

An example of how this pays off comes from SURVIVOR, M.D., a PBS series that followed seven Harvard Medical School students over a period of several years as they became doctors. Estus had been filming a student who was assisting in a heart operation. The patient, an elderly man she'd grown close to, died in surgery, and Estus watched as the student walked off by herself, to the back of the operating room. "By then, I knew her well enough to know she would have trouble [with the loss]," Estus says, and because he was wearing a sound monitor, he could hear that she was crying. He stayed in the distance but continued filming as the senior surgeon approached the student and consoled her, but also reminded her that as a physician, she had to balance her own feelings with the family's need for her professional guidance. She nodded, and together the doctors went to speak with the patient's family.

Since the story was about the making of a doctor; the emotion shown by the tears was important, but not as important as the lesson—another step on the road to becoming a physician. The moment feels intimate, despite the fact that Estus stayed several feet away (he shot the scene hand-held until a tripod was slipped underneath the camera as it was rolling). "Normally I'm right on top of people, especially for that kind of shooting," he says. "But I didn't want to break the spell. And also, I felt the perspective was appropriate, the two of them meeting." Estus says that he encounters both situations while he's filming: times like this, when he's afraid to move a muscle for fear of interrupting the moment, and times when he can be very proactive in ensuring that he gets the coverage he wants.

What you shoot and how you shoot it, involves more than simply documenting an event. It's a way of contributing to the story. "Think about what the scene is supposed to say, as much as you can, both before it and during it," says Steven Ascher, who shot *Troublesome Creek* in addition to numerous other films. He adds that the same applies "on the broader structure, in terms of how you go about deciding what to film, how much of it to film, and who to film."

In many cases, you may be filming a scene or sequence without knowing exactly how it will come out or how the overall story will ultimately be structured. "But you should be asking yourself, what seems important, who's compelling, how might the story be structured?" Ascher says. He notes that first-time filmmakers often have trouble projecting ahead like this. "They haven't done it enough to think about, what is a narrative spine, what is structure, how will scenes get distilled? They tend to overshoot and at the same time not shoot in a focused way that makes themes emerge."

SHOOTING WITH THE EDITING IN MIND

It's important that footage be shot in a way that it can be edited. In other words, there needs to be sufficient coverage to give the editor options. You want to establish the time, place, and people, looking for ways to do so that might let you cut back on verbal introductions. Look for the telling details that reveal character, whether it's the cigarette burning untended or the pile of liquor bottles in the recycling bin. Look for shots that show how people behave in relationship with each other and how skillfully they handle the tools of their work. You might want to look for humor. And you need to be sure that you have a sufficient range of angles, shots, and cutaways that your editor can condense hours of material into a final film that tells a coherent and visually satisfying story.

Cinematographers try to "cover scenes to leave as many storytelling options as possible open," Jon Else says. "I have kind of written on the inside of my eyelids a list of basic storytelling shots that I have to have coming away from a scene, about a half dozen shots." These include the widest possible angle of a landscape or cityscape, a proscenium shot in which all the figures involved in the action are in the frame and large enough that their faces and actions can be seen, several angles on any process being filmed and close-ups "on every single face of every person, both talking and not talking."

If there's a sign saying, "Joe's Orchard" or "The Henry Ford Motor Company," Else says, you want to get a "nice picture of the sign, preferably one picture with something happening in the foreground or background and one picture without anything happening." If there are time markers such as clocks, you want to get a shot of them. "A lot of it's cliché stuff, and 90% of the time you don't use it," he says, "but that one time you need to show that time has passed, the clock is invaluable." And finally, he notes that you want to be sure to shoot simple indicators of direction. "If you're next to a river," for example, "you want to make sure that you get a shot that's close enough that you can see which way the current's going."

For those who shoot in film, the cost of stock and processing seems to mandate careful shot selection. "I used to joke that there should be a dollar counter in the viewfinder instead of a footage counter," says Ascher. "In film you're really thinking ahead about each camera move, how can it cut with the others, what will it mean. 'I'm now doing a close shot, I'm now doing a move from character A to character B.' People who learn to shoot with video often shoot more continuously, and it's a real problem. They don't stop the camera, they're not thinking about where shots begin and end, and sometimes that results in uncuttable footage."

CREATING VISUALS

Not all film ideas are inherently visual, especially those that concern complex or technical issues. If you haven't found a visual story through which to explore these issues or if your stories alone don't sufficiently cover the subject, it's likely that you'll try to find general visuals that will at least put some images on screen as your experts and/or narrator speak. For a story on educational policy, for example, you might spend an afternoon filming at a local elementary school; for a story on aging, you might attend a physical therapy session at a local hospital. This material is often described as "wallpaper" because the visuals themselves are generic, in that they're not linked to any particular character or story. With that said, they're often necessary to a film project, and the more creative you can be with them, the better.

In developing a film on the controversial diagnosis of multiple personality disorder, for example, filmmaker Holly Stadtler and her co-producer came up with a variety of visuals. To demonstrate the concept of dissociation, they filmed a child in her bedroom, on the bed, playing near the bed, standing, sitting, and then combined these images in the editing room. The result is a portrait of the child surrounded by "alternate" versions of herself engaged in a range of behaviors. Stadtler also mounted Styrofoam heads (wig forms) on turntables and had them lit dramatically. "I wanted to have some footage I could cut to that wasn't specific and wasn't someone just sitting in a park or something," she says. To further explore dissociation and compare it to the common phenomenon of "highway hypnosis"—losing track of where you've been while you're driving—they combined point-of-view shooting from within a car (including a car going through a tunnel) to a more dizzying "drive" through corrugated steel pipe, shot with a lipstick camera.

Demonstrations may also be devised specifically to advance your overall story. Michael Moore set up a sequence in which he opened a bank account in order to receive a free gun in *Bowling for Columbine*; while the offer was open to the general public, Moore himself would not likely have opened the account except that the filmed scene advanced his overall narrative. For the series THE RING OF TRUTH, we arranged a number of demonstrations of scientific concepts, from a technician weighing the dot of an "i" to a surveyor making a rough map of Monticello, Thomas Jefferson's homestead in Charlottesville, VA. These events would not have occurred had we not set them up; we needed these sequences (which each told an individual story) to illustrate non-visual concepts.

Visual Storytelling in the Wild

Creating visual stories out of nature and wildlife footage can be very expensive and time-consuming. Filmmaker Holly Stadtler produced a documentary about the making of *The Leopard Son*, a Discovery Channel feature produced in 1996 by noted naturalist Hugo Van Lawick. *The Leopard Son* started out being called *Big Cats*, she says, "a story about lions, cheetahs, and leopards in the Serengeti." It was filmed on 35 mm over a period of a year, and the story evolved on location and in the editing room as the leopard footage stood out. The final film is a real-life drama about a young leopard coming of age.

Stadtler spent several weeks on the Serengeti with the production crew and saw how Van Lawick captured natural behavior by "getting the animals used to his presence, staying with it and persevering, and not manipulating things in the environment. And so I became this purist," she says. " 'This is the way to do it.' '' With the growth of cable and the decrease in the amount of money available for production, however, filmmakers must often find ways to make quality wildlife films that don't require the time needed to fully habituate animals to a film crew's presence.

This can be a tricky business due to ethical issues involved in wildlife shooting. Concern has long been raised over such practices as tying carcasses down so that animals will come to feed at predictable spots, for example. Stadtler also notes that some people object to filmmakers using vehicle lights at night because it can affect the outcome of a kill. Stadtler recently produced *America's Last Red Wolves*, a half-hour film for the series NATIONAL GEOGRAPHIC EXPLORER. ''What I try to do is find a happy medium,'' she says. ''For instance, there's no way you can get 25 feet from wolves feeding in the wild—they're going to take the carcass and go—or that you could get that close to a den site. We had a lot of discussion about setting up remote cameras that could be tripped by censors, which I had done on *Troubled Waters* (a one-hour film for TBS), but you get a shot or two and the animal leaves.''

Red wolves were once extinct in the wild; they were bred in captivity by the U.S. Fish and Wildlife Service and then reintroduced into the wild at the Alligator River National Wildlife Refuge in North Carolina, beginning in the mid-1980s. Some wolves remain in captivity, however, and Stadtler took advantage of this to get the close shots she needed. She and the crew masked the fencing behind the wolves; the cameraman stood about 25 feet away from the wolves on the other side, poking his lens through the fence and filming as a deer carcass was put out for the animals. ''That's how we got some beautiful images, close up, of wolves,'' Stadtler says. ''The only other way we could have done that is if we had, in essence, habituated the wolves in the wild to our presence, which would have required months of being there—and even then, I'm not sure how close they would have allowed our camera people.''

TONE AND STYLE

Visual storytelling goes well beyond *what* you shoot; how you shoot, how you light, and how you treat the material in post-production are also critical. Tone (does the light convey something harsh and cold or warm and familiar?), point of view (from whose point of view is a scene shot? Is it from a first-person point of view, or is it omniscient? Is the camera shooting up at the subject, or looking down?), and context (does the subject fill the frame, or does he or she appear small and overwhelmed by the surroundings?) are all important considerations. Knowing the answers in advance can help you plan your production needs, including lights, lenses, filters, and whether or not to use special equipment such as dollies and cranes.

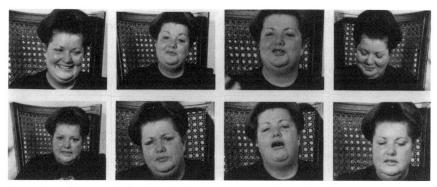

Betty, from *Betty Tells Her Story*. Photo courtesy of Liane Brandon.

INTERVIEWS

Before shooting, look at films that contain interviews and decide what you like or don't like about an approach and what you want to do in your own film. Do you plan to appear on camera along with your interviewees, as Judith Helfand did in *Blue Vinyl*? Do you want your interviewees to appear to be addressing the audience directly? Do you want to take a less formal approach to interviewing, asking your subjects questions as they go about their lives or filming them as they discuss specific subjects with each other?

Your answers to these questions will affect how you conduct and shoot your interviews. If you're not going to appear on camera, and your questions won't be heard as voice-over, you'll need to frame the question in a way that elicits a full answer, not just "Yes. Sure. Oh, yes, I agree with that." You might want to ask the person being interviewed to incorporate part of your question in his or her answer, as in "When did you know there was trouble?" Answer: "I knew there was trouble when . . . " In any case, you'll need to listen carefully as the interview is underway to make sure that you're getting something that will work as the beginning of a sentence, thought, or paragraph. If necessary, ask the question again, maybe in a different way.

Go into the interview knowing the handful of specific story points the interview needs to cover, and then include other material that would be nice to have or questions that are essentially fishing—you're not sure what you're going to get, but the answers could be interesting. Note that if you've cast the person you're interviewing in advance, you probably already know what ground the interviewee can best cover. It's rarely productive to ask everyone in a film the same twenty questions.

Conducting Interviews

Everyone approaches interviewing differently. Some people work to put the subjects at ease, starting with more "comfortable" questions before easing into material that's more touchy. As mentioned, filmmakers whose style is more confrontational may show up with the cameras rolling. Sometimes you're asking someone to relate an event he or she has told many times, and the story's taken on a polished quality that you want it to lose; it may take getting the person riled up, or challenging something about the story, to accomplish that.

Another strategy for interviewing, notes Estus, "is for the person asking the questions not to look at the interviewee as a source of information but to get them involved in a conversation, which often involves playing Devil's advocate. 'I really don't understand why this is better than that. Can you explain that to me?' So the person's engaged, as opposed to spouting a pat answer."

The Interview Setup

Only rarely is an interviewee asked to speak directly into the camera; few "regular" people can do it well. Filmmaker Errol Morris achieves this effect through an elaborate setup in which the person is actually speaking into a monitor, not the camera. More likely, the interviewer is seated close to both the camera operator and the person (or people) being interviewed. Although some people work further away, Estus likes to position the camera fairly close to the interview subject, within five feet or so. "It does two things," Estus says. "If the person moves, they change size in the frame, which makes it more three-dimensional, whereas if you're on a long lens they're plastered against the background. But . . . more importantly is that the person they're talking to is right on top of them." This kind of intimacy may also be enhanced by conducting the interview over a table. If both parties lean forward, they're very close, and their hand gestures will be in the frame. Estus notes that wooden chairs with arms (often found in academic institutions) can be especially good, because the arms tend to be higher than normal. "The gesture's in front of your face, and if you're leaning forward you look more energetic." You don't want the chair's frame or headrest to show behind the person, and as a rule, try to avoid chairs that swivel or rock.

Another decision to make is whether the interviewee should be looking slightly to the left or to the right of the camera. If, for example, you know that you want two people to be "answering" each other on film, you might want them to be facing different directions. This isn't always possible to do, but if it's a style you like, you'll need to plan for it in advance.

You and your crew also need to think about the other visual content in the frame. "Part of the job is to sell the person so that the audience really wants to hear what they say," says Estus. "My approach is to try to make an environmental portrait, so that the setting the person is in and the way they look tells you something about them and the subject matter. In wide screen (16:9) television that's much more important because no matter how tight you are on the head, there's half the screen hanging there empty, and a wall of books doesn't tell you anything."

Additional decisions, stemming from the style of film and approach to storytelling, include how you light the interviews and whether you strive for some kind of consistency in look throughout the film (or series). How do you want the interviewee to come across? There are ways to light that will flatter someone's face and minimize the distractions that could leave viewers focusing on the appearance of an interviewee, rather than his or her words. What are your subjects wearing? For more formal interview setups, some producers ask subjects to bring a few clothing options. (For some films, a stylistic decision might be made to ask interviewees to dress one way or another; Estus did a series with gothic themes in which the interviewees were asked to wear black.)

The visual context of an interview and the visual cues contained within it can be very important to the storytelling. How tightly do you frame the interview? Some cinematographers will stay wider for expositional information and move in closer as the interview gets more intimate and/or emotional. What do the interview setting and subject's clothing convey? In *The Thin Blue Line*, Randall Adams and David Harris are interviewed in a setting that suggests confinement, and in fact both turn out to be in prison. Law enforcement people are all filmed indoors, in suits and ties. David Harris's friends are all filmed outdoors, in casual clothing. Since Morris uses no lower thirds (on screen titles) to identify speakers by name, these visual cues serve as a form of identification.

If you've filmed someone involved in his or her work or at home, you probably have footage that advances our understanding of the character (we can see that she is confident as she works very complex machinery, or that he is devoted to his children) even as we hear who the person is. But it's still common to see typical and uninformative introductory shots of the interviewee—Walking into the Building or Entering the Office or Working at the Computer. Even some films that are otherwise excellent resort to these shots. In hindsight, there are almost always better alternatives.

Interview Styles

Interviews need to have an energy and immediacy about them, as well as a credibility. They also need to serve the story being told. Watch a range of interviews and you'll see that they can be very different. Is the interviewee talking *about* a subject from a distance, or is he or she speaking as if the event is ongoing? It's not only experts who talk *about* subjects; people often shape stories after the fact, especially if they've told them before, and it creates a kind of distance between the storyteller and the story, which is sometimes desired, but not always.

Filmmaker Liane Brandon discovered this when she made *Betty Tells Her Story* (1972). Brandon had met Betty when both were consulting for the Massachusetts Department of Education, and during a coffee break, Betty told her a story about buying a dress and then losing it before she had a chance to wear it. The story stuck with Brandon; the women's movement was in its infancy, "and we were just beginning to think about women and clothing and culture in addition to the larger equal rights issues," she says. At first, Brandon thought of turning the story into a short drama, but soon realized that what intrigued her was as much the story-teller as the story.

On a teacher's salary, Brandon could only afford three ten-minute magazines of black and white film (at a time when color film was more expensive). "I borrowed Ricky Leacock's camera, and John Terry, who worked with Ricky at M.I.T., volunteered to do sound," she says. At Betty's house, Brandon set up the camera and lights and then asked Betty to simply tell her story. "The first version that you see in the film is the first take that we did. I never told her how long a magazine was, but somehow she ended the story just before we ran out of film." It was basically the story as Betty had first told it to Brandon; a witty anecdote about a dress she'd found that was just perfect—and then she never got to wear it.

To be sure she had what she needed, Brandon asked Betty to tell the story again, which she did. It was essentially the same as the first take, "but in the middle of it a truck stopped in front of her house," Brandon says, "and the horn went off, and it wiped out a couple of minutes of audio. I was really upset, but I knew I had one more magazine left."

They all took a break. Brandon worried that she was imposing on Betty, who'd never been on camera before, "but was being a really good sport." Out of curiosity, the filmmaker asked Betty how she *felt* when the events were taking place. "Betty's eyes opened wide and she said something like, 'I don't think I ever thought about what I was feeling; I mostly think about how I remember the story.' You know how people change and shape stories to make them good stories? Especially good storytellers."

With the cameras rolling again, Brandon asked Betty to try telling the story as she felt about it while it was happening, rather than as she remembered it. "Everything changed: body language, eye contact," Brandon says. "The minute she started telling this story, I got chills up and down my back. I was very surprised by the feelings that she talked about; I don't think she'd ever told or even thought about the story that way." Told from within rather than without, the story is no longer a humorous anecdote; it's the painful memory of a plain, overweight woman who found a dress that made her feel beautiful, then lost it before she ever had a chance to wear it.

This was before people routinely exposed themselves on national television, Brandon notes. As a filmmaker, she didn't know what to do with two very different versions, filmed in three takes. "I thought one of those takes would have to be the story, because I'd never heard of a film where you show more than one take," she says. She showed the first version to some college students, who thought it was "cute." She showed the third version to another group, who said, essentially, "Bummer. Get a life, lady."

Neither story worked alone. "I tried split screening them, I tried intercutting them, I tried everything and nothing worked, and so I just let them sit. For a film that has almost no cuts, it took longer to edit than lots of films that have lots of cuts," she says. She finally got rid of the middle version and ran the first and third consecutively, with some black leader in between that reads, "Later that day, the filmmaker asked Betty to tell her story again." The contrast between the two takes is what gives the film its power, revealing information about the stories we tell ourselves, the selves we present to the world, and the different ways there are to tell a story. For filmmakers (and others), it's a fascinating look at the way in which a shift in interview style can lead to a very different response.

12

Editing

Many of the storytelling issues covered elsewhere in the book come into play again in the editing room. On the majority of films, story and structure do not truly come together until the editor begins to assemble and pare down filmed material. Several versions of the film may be cut before the best point of attack is identified; you may be cutting toward one ending for weeks before you realize that in fact, the film ends on an even earlier, and stronger, note.

While every project is different, the basic editing process is that you screen everything and make a long assembly of your footage, which is then honed into a rough cut, a fine cut, a picture lock, and finally a script lock. The assembly includes the material you've shot to date, as well as archival material, if any. (Often, you're working not with original archival footage but with "slop" dubs, such as preview reels or stills you might have shot quickly in the editing room. Later, when you know what images will stay in the film, you negotiate for rights to use this material, order broadcast-quality duplications, or arrange for broadcast-quality filming of still material and artifacts.)

As the editing progresses, you work toward a rough cut. This is a draft of your film that is significantly longer than the final show will be. But your general story and structure are in place, and you have some, if not all, of your elements on hand. The rough cut stage often the best time to reassess major issues of story and structure and experiment with alternatives; this becomes more difficult as the film is fine tuned. By the fine cut, the film is almost to time. (For example, a film that will end up being 57 minutes long might be 63 minutes at fine cut.) Major problems, hopefully, have been worked out. If there is narration, this is the time to begin polishing it. And for the movie as a whole, this is the time to make sure the facts are accurate. "Picture lock" means that all of the images are in place and to time. "Script lock" means that any outstanding issues of narration or voice-over are resolved and that the material can be recorded and laid in without further changes.

GETTING TO ROUGH CUT

The interaction between producer, director, writer, and editor (or some combination of these) differs with each project. Some teams watch the rushes (the raw footage) all together, and discuss which interview bites work, which scenes are strong, and how material might be assembled. Some editors screen the footage alone because they want to evaluate the material without being influenced by the producer's ideas of what worked or didn't work on location. "I really like to just look," says Jeanne Jordan, an accomplished editor. "I don't want people to even tell me, 'This was a difficult interview,' or 'I didn't get what I wanted.' "

As you screen the footage, you're watching for moments that affect you in some way, whether emotionally or intellectually. Look for scenes and sequences that can play on their own, interview bites that seem strong and clear, material that has the potential to reveal themes and issues you want to raise, and the special moments that you hope audiences will discuss with each other at work the next day.

"I'm looking for emotion, that's always my first thing," says Sam Pollard, who works frequently as an editor. "Then I'm looking for some tension and opposition, because that's going to always make those sequences work the best. And if I feel none of those elements are in there, then I figure I've got to convey another type of feeling. Maybe this is a moment where you just sit back and listen to some music; maybe it's a moment to be somewhat reflective. You've got to know what the material says." Each person will come away from a first screening with his or her own favorite moments; this memory of what was strong in the raw footage will be useful as you shape and trim the material into a coherent story, all the while working to retain the energy it held in its raw state.

Some editors work off a written outline of scenes and sequences, especially if the film consists primarily of live action, such as cinéma vérité. If there is a significant amount of interview material, however, whether or not there is to be narration, the producer may take transcripts of the interviews and cut and paste selected bites into a "paper edit." If the project was shot to a script or a script-in-progress, that working script will be adjusted to reflect the actual material on hand. In either case, rough narration can be written to seam together disparate elements, make a transition clear, or hold a place for a sequence that's still to be shot. In many editing rooms, "scratch" narration is recorded and cut in against the picture, to better evaluate its effectiveness.

As previously discussed, what works on paper won't necessarily work on film. The juxtaposition of two interview bites and two filmed sequences might read very well, but there may be something about the way a phrase is spoken or the scene plays out that makes it less than powerful on screen. This doesn't mean that you shouldn't do paper cuts; they can be a faster and easier way to "see" an edit before realizing the changes physically. But since a good portion of the paper editing won't work on film, it's also useful to know *why* you're suggesting a particular change, in addition to what it will be. Perhaps you pulled a bite because it conveyed two specific points; if your choice doesn't work, the editor might be able to satisfy those points in a different way, either through a different bite, a combination of bites, or perhaps through a scene that he or she's just edited that makes the interview bite unnecessary.

The editor, meanwhile, may be assembling scenes, whether from live action or archival footage, shaping them individually, and putting together the strongest beginning, middle, and end possible before sequencing them into the overall film. The editing process tends to be very collaborative. A producer or director coming into the editing room to watch a cut in progress can often see links and transitions that the editor may not have seen, or he or she may see something in what the editor has assembled that will spark a realization that additional material—a piece of artwork, a fragment of music, a different interview excerpt—will enhance a scene. It's a give and take process, with everyone in the editing room putting him or herself in the role of viewer as well as storyteller. Ultimately, there has to be a single person who makes decisions, usually either the producer or the director. But the give and take, especially when the discussion is not only about a specific scene or shot but on what it *does* in the overall storytelling, can be very productive.

Transcripts

If you've conducted interviews, you should get them transcribed, accurately and thoroughly. Not a summary ("Dr. Fisher talking about gravitational forces . . . "), but an exact transcription of what is said, including the "um, um, he said, he said, um, well, let me back up by saying that what gravity is not, is . . . " This will save you a lot of time later, because you're likely to go back to these transcripts repeatedly during the editing process in search of story solutions, and an inaccurate or incomplete transcript can mean that you assemble a scene based on what you *think* someone said, only to find out that it's close but not what you need or that it's great but the answer took forever. Some filmmakers will also transcribe scenes that have a lot of dialogue, such as a meeting that was filmed, a press conference, even a conversation.

In the case of foreign language interviews, filmmakers in the field often rely on quick translations to get a sense of what's being spoken. In the editing room, particularly if no one on the team is fluent in the interview language, it's good to get an accurate and detailed translation as soon as you can, but no later than rough cut. You don't want to fine tune a film to interview material that doesn't say what you think it says.

When viewing the interviews, make notes on the transcripts to help you remember what someone's energy level is like, if there are problems such as flies or a microphone in the frame, or whether someone sneezes. Some portions of the interview may be useable but only as voice-over; others may be useful as information only. Better to write it down once than to go back to the same bite three times in the course of the editing session because you forgot that there was a reason you didn't use it in the first place.

Another reason to transcribe interviews is that it's unfortunately very easy to cut someone's words up, assemble them with other interviews, and eventually lose track of what the person's original answer was. I always try to make a point of re-reading the transcripts as the editing nears completion, for three reasons: to make sure the interviewee is not being misrepresented; to make sure that there isn't terrific material that was overlooked earlier when the story was somewhat different; and to look for color and details that might be helpful to narration.

Editing Interviews

Chapter 5 discussed the issue of cutting interview material down for time. When these cuts are made, the editor often covers each of them with a cutaway. For example, an interview with a scientist about cloning might use cutaways of the scientist at work, or archival footage of Dolly, the cloned sheep, or cutaways to graphics illustrating the scientist's point.

It has become somewhat more accepted to simply cut the footage and allow the viewer to see the image jump—one minute the speaker is looking to the left, the next he is looking down, but still talking; this is known as a "jump cut." Sometimes an editor will soften this cut with a slight dissolve, or a fade in and out of black, but the cut is still apparent. Another style of jump cutting is to include a few quick images that inform the interview but do not imply a seamless whole. In interviews with former Alabama governor George Wallace for the documentary *4 Little Girls*, editor and co-producer Sam Pollard makes a series of evocative jump cuts to shots of Wallace with a cigar: lighting it, inhaling, blowing out smoke, looking away. Pollard says he was inspired by Oliver Stone's use of jump cuts in *JFK*. "Stone conveyed so much information through the way he cut it that I wanted to try to emulate that," he says.

Juxtaposition

The juxtaposition of two shots, or two sequences, adds meaning that is not necessarily contained in either of the elements alone. This works to your advantage, but it's also something to guard against if the juxtaposition creates a false impression. If you cut from someone saying, "Well, who was responsible for it?" to a shot of Mr. Smith, you are creating the impression that Mr. Smith was responsible, whether you meant to or not.

Entering Late, Exiting Early

As you edit, try to enter a scene at the last possible moment, and leave at the earliest possible moment. This doesn't mean chopping the heart out of a scene or losing its context, but it does mean figuring out what is the most meaningful part of that scene, and what is just treading water on screen. Suppose you've filmed a sequence in which a mother goes to the grocery store, chats with a neighbor or two, fusses with the butcher over a choice cut of meat, waits in line at the checkout counter, drives home, prepares a meal, calls her college-age daughter to the table, and then watches with dismay as her daughter storms off, angry that her mother has not respected the fact that she is a vegetarian—a fact that the mother says she didn't know.

Where you enter and exit this scene depends on what the scene is *about*. Is it about the mother going to tremendous lengths to make her daughter feel welcome at home, perhaps because of a recent divorce or the daughter's expulsion from school? Or is it about a chasm between mother and daughter and their inability to communicate even basic information? If it's the former, the scenes in the grocery store help to establish the mother's efforts to please; if the latter, the grocery store scenes aren't really relevant. You could convey their lack of communication with the following shots: the mother puts the steak on the table; the daughter refuses to eat it and storms away; the mother is left looking at the steak.

Where do you end the scene? Again, it depends on where your story is going. If the story is about the fuss the woman made to please her daughter, you might end it with the reversal: the daughter rejects the food and storms away from the table. But if it's about the communication between mother and daughter, you might want to go a bit further and see what happens next. Will the mother try to find some other way to reach the daughter, perhaps by cooking a vegetarian meal?

Again, you don't want to cut scenes to their tightest in terms of the action; you want to focus them so that their meaning and their emphasis in your film's narrative are clear.

Anticipate Confusion

In general, audiences are willing to do quite a bit of work to figure out what the story is and where you're going with it—that's part of what makes viewing a good documentary an active rather than passive experience—but eventually, if they become too lost, they'll give up. A good storyteller anticipates the audience's confusion and meets it in subtle and creative ways, skillfully weaving information in where and when it's needed and not before. It may take some effort to bring a general audience up to speed on what those gadgets actually do or how certain laws of physics work. But armed with that information and an understanding of how it furthers or frustrates the efforts of the protagonist to reach a goal, solve a mystery, unlock a secret, or prove a theorem, the audience can be one step ahead of the story. Those moments when the audience "gets it" just before you, as the storyteller, give it to them, are enormously satisfying.

Just as you want to present information at the moment it's most needed, you also want to be careful not to clutter a story with too much detail. Many film stories get diluted by details that the filmmakers are convinced are "important," although they are not directly relevant to the story at hand. If you're telling the story about a candidate's political campaign, for example, you might not want to spend a lot of time looking at his business career. If there's something about his career that he's promoting on the campaign trail—he wants to bring his cost-cutting strategies to the job of managing a state budget, for example—then it might be relevant. Otherwise, it's taking up space that you need for your story.

Be careful, though, that you don't "cherry pick" your information, selectively using only those details that support your argument or "take" on a story and ignoring those that contradict you. It's possible to be factually accurate and still create an overall story that is fundamentally dishonest. Choosing some details from a person's life as a means of focusing a story is not the same thing as selectively leaving out information you don't want the audience to know. Ultimately you'll be found out, and it weakens your film and credibility.

ROUGH CUT TO FINE CUT

As the film moves toward completion, footage is dropped and hard decisions must be made. Is the story working as filmed, or is new material needed? Does the story that was set up at the film's beginning pay off at the end? Is it being told for maximum audience involvement? Is this the kind of film that people will talk about? Will it keep an audience watching? If the filmmaker hopes to convey important but difficult concepts, are those concepts being communicated accurately and well? To get the film to a broadcast length, would it be better to delete an entire scene or subplot, or should time be shaved off a number of scenes?

One way to begin answering these questions is by showing the film to an impartial audience. Often this is done at rough cut and, schedules and budgets permitting, again at fine cut. You want to invite people who don't know the story and aren't necessarily interested in it, as well as people who know the story better than you do. If, in previewing your film, you discover that the message you *think* you're sending is not the message being received, there's a problem. As simple as this seems, it's not uncommon for film-makers to simply decide there must be something wrong with the audience. "I've said it clearly; I don't know why they're not getting it." Or they fear that if they "pander" to an audience, they will be toning down their "message." It doesn't work that way. If one person doesn't get your film, maybe it's just not that person's cup of tea. If two people don't get it, fine. But if a significant portion of an audience has missed your point, your point isn't being made.

Screening Tips

You want to invite a manageable number of filmmaker colleagues, scholars, and a general audience of "others" to these screenings. If you have a very small screening room, it may be necessary to show the film more than once to get an adequate cross-section of reactions.

Before the screening starts, make sure everyone has paper and pencils for note taking. You or an appointed moderator should explain what stage your film is at, mentioning, for example, that it's running several minutes long, that narration is provisional, and the footage has numbers and other information printed on it that will be gone by broadcast. In other words, it's a work-in-progress, and their input and help are extremely valuable to you. Make it clear that you will be asking for their reactions, both positive and negative. Ask them to please stay in the room for a few minutes immediately after the film ends. Then dim the lights, but not so low that people can't see to scribble occasionally in the dark. As the film plays, notice the audience's reactions. When do they seem intent on the story? When is there a lot of shuffling and coughing? Is there laughter? Are there tears?

After the film ends, ask people to jot down their first impressions, anonymously if they'd prefer. Then start the discussion, with you or the moderator asking for broad impressions—what worked, what didn't, what was surprising or confusing or fascinating. After a while, move on to specific questions agreed upon by the production team, such as, "Were you confused by the transition to France?" "If you had to cut eight minutes out of this film, what would you cut?" "Did you understand that Dan was more concerned about Marcie's health than about his job?" Concrete responses can be very helpful.

Two important points. First, during a feedback session, the members of the filmmaking team should be quiet. Don't answer questions, offer explanations, or defend any aspect of the filmmaking. You are there to receive information, period. It will waste the opportunity afforded by this valuable audience if you take fifteen minutes to explain why it was important to keep the sequence with the demolition derby in, or to explain the backstory that left this audience mystified. Even if it kills you to sit there and listen to people debate subjects that you know the answer to, restrain yourself. You're not there to educate this audience on the topic or show them that you do know more than was up on the screen; you're there to get a good sense of what actually *was* on screen and where it needs work.

Second, take any and all suggestions, say thanks, and keep going. You know, and your entire production team knows, that you can't possibly afford to shoot another four interviews, as the guy in the hat suggests, or that cutting out the trial sequence would make your entire film irrelevant. After this audience goes home, however, consider *why* these suggestions were made. Non-filmmakers don't always know how to articulate a problem, and they can't be expected to know how to fix it. You can and do. If your audience thinks that you're missing significant interviews, is there information that those interviews would add that you could convey in some other way? If you believe the trial sequence is critical and they think it's disposable, what's wrong with it? Is it edited badly? Is it in the wrong place? Is the narration not effectively setting it up so the audience can see its relevance?

You don't have to take anything that anyone says as marching orders. But you do need to pay attention to which elements of your film are working and which will send your audience racing for the remote, or the door.

With that said, it is your film. Know when to trust your gut. Understand that there will be a degree of criticism that is not about your filmmaking but about your ideology. Someone doesn't understand why you would even give the skinheads a chance to speak. Someone else thinks it's invasive to stay focused on the woman sobbing because her son has blown his mind on inhalants.

This is useful information to have, as it anticipates some of the criticism the final film might receive. But if the issue is not one of fact, or clarity, but of style, the choice is yours to make. Hear that people don't like it, but decide for yourself what makes you and your team comfortable.

The same is true of scholarship. Tell an accurate story, but don't feel compelled to tell everything. It's sometimes difficult for scholars who care deeply about their subjects to see that the entire section on primate behavior is only six minutes long or that you decided not to include that powerful letter that John Adams wrote. Accept the criticism and really consider whether or not it would enrich the story you have chosen to tell on film. If not, file this information away for use later in the companion book, if there is to be one, or for the teachers' guides and other educational and community engagement components of the project. Your film is successful if it appeals to a wide audience with a strong story and motivates part of that audience to go to the library or the web for more information.

FINE CUT TO PICTURE LOCK

The process as you get down to the wire is more of the same, looking backward as well as forward. It's often very helpful at this stage to go back and re-read initial outlines and treatments to see if you've lost a story thread along the way that might prove useful. You might also re-read transcripts to see if the changes that you've made to the structure are better served by interview bites you didn't pull because you were looking at a very different film back then. It's even useful to look back into research files, to make sure there aren't details and other tidbits that might speak volumes. And of course, you are by now immersed in the task of making sure that everything that will end up on screen has been fact checked, not once but twice.

Fact Checking

Fact checking means going through your script line by line, finding the information that needs to be verified through at least two credible sources. If you can't confirm a fact—and it happens— find a way to write around it. Maybe you don't need to say that

25,000 bikers rode into town. If your sources all agree that it was "over 20, 000," then say that instead.

What needs to be checked? Pretty much everything:

- "Brilliant and fearless, Admiral Marks now seized command of the troops." *Brilliant* and *fearless* both need corroboration, as does *seized command*. You don't want to find out after broadcast that Marks was widely considered a coward, or that command was thrust upon him when the admiral before him came down with food poisoning.
- "The congresswoman was exhausted and frustrated, convinced now that the bill she'd authored would not be passed." *Exhausted* and *frustrated* need to be confirmed, and you should have solid evidence that at this point, she truly was *convinced* of the bill's failure, and that she had *authored* it and not simply supported it. *(Confirming an emotional state depends on reliable reports from reliable eyewitnesses, recorded as close to the event as possible.)*

You need to fact check interview and sync material as well as narration. For example, an auto manufacturer says, "Forty percent of the tires we got in had the problem. They all had to go back." He's the expert, but you find out that in fact, 25% of the tires were sent back because of the problem. You can't hide behind the argument that "he said it, I didn't." As the filmmaker, you are incorporating the statement into your film and therefore, it will be your statement as well. In this case, the line has to go. Of course, if the falsehood is deliberate, and that's part of your story, or if it's clearly a lie and therefore reveals character, you don't need to cut it. But when it is presented as significant evidence to support the argument you're making, then it must be accurate. However, there is also some room to maneuver. For example, if you've confirmed that 38% of registered voters in Millville voted for a rise in property tax, and the mayor says, "I don't know, about a third of the voters wanted it," that's probably close enough to use.

PROBLEM SOLVING

Every film has its own problems, but the following ones seem fairly common.

No Story

You have scenes and sequences that are interesting but aren't adding up to a coherent whole. One reason for this may be that there really wasn't a clear story to begin with. What you can do at this point is take a step back and return to the earlier stages of the process; knowing what you know now, try to write up an outline that identifies what the story is about, whose story it is, what the key moments are that you're driving toward, how the story is resolved, and what you're hoping the audience will take away from the film. Then look at your material with this structure in mind, and see if you have what you need. You may need pick-up material to fill in the gaps, but you also may be surprised to find that your gut did lead you in the right direction.

Be prepared for the fact that you may have to drop favorite scenes because they don't serve the story that you now realize you're telling. If a shot or a scene or even a sequence is a distraction rather than an addition, it's got to go, no matter how expensive it was to shoot or how difficult it was to get. You can spend some time trying to fiddle with it, see if you can possibly make it work, but if ultimately the material is beside the point, it goes. The same standard should be applied to interview material. If you didn't plan ahead but instead simply shot a few available experts, it's very possible that there will be redundancy and somebody's interview will be dropped. (If you end up cutting people out of a show, do them the courtesy of letting them know before the program is aired.)

You Start One Story and End Another

A related problem is that the film starts one story and then drifts onto a different track. As discussed in earlier chapters, outlining the film story can help, along with an openness to changing your initial concept of the film, given the natural direction it has ended up taking. Otherwise, you need to accept that the film you now wish you'd shot just isn't covered in the footage and either go back out to get what you need for the story you want to tell or make a different story out of what you have.

Be careful, however, when bending material to tell a story other than the one for which it was originally shot. Be especially careful in situations in which the editing team is separate from the production team, and the link between subject and original story-teller has been lost. It's possible to tell a great story that fundamentally misrepresents the material that was filmed. It's also possible to tell a different but still highly accurate story, especially if you take the time to explore your material with the new story in mind and can conduct additional interviews or shoot pick-up footage as necessary. It's a *lot* of work. Getting useable and accurate material out of footage that was shot for a different reason is time-consuming and often frustrating.

Additional note—what you don't want to do is use footage of one thing and pretend it's something else. Footage of Sally's graduation party should not be substituted for the engagement party you didn't film. Find a way to use the party footage to make a more generic point, if need be.

Too Many Characters or Story Threads

You didn't want to give up the incredible research you did or the wonderful people you found, so now you find yourself telling the stories of eight people, all with different goals but perhaps a common thread—maybe they're all recent college graduates looking for work in the United States. But your film is only an hour long and everybody is getting short shrift, or audiences can't keep track of which person was having trouble with his neighbors and which was being investigated by the Immigration and Naturalization Service and which one was going to move her business to Seattle. You may need to make choices as to which people best embody the themes you are trying to convey or the policy issues or areas of discrimination you want the audience to know about.

You can also get distracted by too many details within an overall story. No matter what style film you're making, you need to keep track of the one primary story you're telling, folding in additional threads (or subplots, backstory, etc.) as they serve that one story.

Too Many Beginnings and/or Endings

The film opens with a look at the farming industry and the cultivation of wheat. The narration offers some information as to what's being presented, and the audience thinks, "Oh, it's a documentary about farming." Then it seems to start again with a look at the processing of wheat into bread. "Oh, it's a film about food as big business." But then it starts again, and gradually it becomes clear that your film is really a look at the health issue of wheat intolerance or sensitivity. An unfocused opening is a fairly common problem, so it's good to watch out for it, asking yourself as the story unfolds, "What do I *think* this story is about at this point?" The primary story you're going to tell should start soon after your film begins, and it should be possible, from the way that story is launched, to anticipate—not to know, but to *anticipate* and be curious about—how it will end. In this case, the remaining details of wheat farming and the baking industry can be folded in to that overall story.

Where you end your film is also very important. Appearing to end it, and then ending it again, and then ending it again can dilute a film's overall power; furthermore, there's generally just one ending that will truly bring a satisfactory resolution to the story you set out to tell. Resolution does not mean things are *resolved*; it means that you've reached a conclusion that satisfies the questions and issues initially raised in your film's opening moments.

Not Enough Breathing Room

In the rush to cut a film down to time, to get everything tight, and to make every point, it's possible to trim interviews or scenes into oblivion. The production team doesn't necessarily notice; they've been looking at this guy day after day and week after week, so they know what he's going to say, they've heard it before, and the joke is no longer funny. Or they realize that they can say in two lines of narration what that scene takes nearly two minutes to convey. It's important to resist this—you need the energy that real people bring to a film and the enthusiasm they bring to their storytelling. While radio and television news reports may cut interviews or scenes into fragments, you generally want to let material play for a reasonable period of time.

It's often better to offer a little less information or a smaller number of scenes than to include everything and give all of it short shrift. Filmmaker Jon Else discusses this in terms of "the parable of the peach pits," which the producers came up with on the first season of Eyes on the Prize. "There are various versions of it, but it boils down to the idea that there's a wise king who has no heirs, and he says that he'll give his kingdom to whoever among his subjects can fit the most satisfying collection of peaches into a box that is a given size, say, 57 minutes on a side," Else says.

"It's a long shaggy dog story, but people start trying to put peaches in the box. They kind of squish them, to fit one more in, and then some fellow gets the bright idea that without letting the king see, he'll shave a little bit off the back of one of the peaches. So he shaves a little bit off and manages to get 13 peaches in instead of 12, and then he sees that if he shaves a little bit off another one he can get 14 peaches in, and he's shaving away at these peaches and cutting little chunks off them and before long, what he has is a box full of peach pits."

The moral, says Else, is that in making films, "we often try to cram so many different episodes and so many different pieces of incident and character and policy in, that in the process we wreck them all." At the end of the parable of the peach pits, the winner is the person who finds "a few perfectly ripe, naturally soft peaches that perfectly fit into this box without violating any individual peach." Less can be more.

Insufficient Casting

You may discover, in editing, that an important voice is missing, or that someone you've interviewed is filling a storytelling role that would be better filled by someone else. If possible, you might shoot an additional interview, trying to match its tone and look to your film's style. Otherwise, you need to find another way to bring this point of view forward, such as through archival voices or the way a scene is edited. It's also possible, as your story becomes more focused, that you've neglected to ask someone important story-related questions. Depending on how significant the problem is (and the size of your budget), you can either do another interview with that person, intending to either replace one with the other or somehow use both (although cutting directly between them may prove difficult), or you can work to match the audio enough so that you can use the pick-up material as voice-over.

Occasionally, an entirely new sentence *can* be crafted from someone's existing interview, a sentence the person never uttered but one that you think he or she would agree with. If you really want to do this, and it's your only option, *you must run this new sentence past the person and secure permission to use it.*

GETTING UNSTUCK

Even the best creative minds get tired. You try six ways of cutting something and it doesn't work, or the editor thinks it works one way, the director hates it, and the producer is thinking that now might be a good time to get that law degree. Assuming that you have at least something strung together in sequence, take a step back and try throwing all of the pieces up in the air.

This is easier done at rough cut than fine cut, but it's a useful exercise in any case. You've got a story and structure that maybe aren't great, but they're fine. Open the door, for a short period, and let everyone throw out the craziest ideas they can think of, without anybody becoming scornful or arguing about why it won't work and that it's already been tried. "What if we started where the film now ends? What if we held off on the fireman's story until after his wife is in the accident? What if we told the story from the child's point of view, and not his parents'?"

Just throw it all out there and then try a few things. Maybe none of them will work. But in the difference between what was boring and safe and what is outrageous and stupid, you might see things you weren't looking for. In other words, two wrong answers may lead you toward one that's right. You can't do this indefinitely, and at some point whoever's in charge has to make the final call. But what you end up with might be really interesting.

BE YOUR FIRST AUDIENCE

A mark of a good storyteller is the ability to look with fresh eyes— with the audience's eyes—at material each time a new cut is available and honestly assess its weaknesses. If you see problems, don't ignore them because audiences are uncanny in their ability to see that one flaw you thought you could gloss over or the transition whose absence you thought you'd masked with some fancy music and images.

At the same time, you can't cut a film or tell a story with a critic on your shoulder. Don't second-guess yourself; that's not what this process is about. Instead, ask yourself every step of the way, "Is this interesting? Would I keep watching? What do I care about here? Who am I worried for? Am I confused? Where do I need more information?"

Chances are, if it works for you—the editor, producer, director—it will work for the audience.

13

Narration

Narration is not the worst thing to happen to a documentary, but *bad* narration might be, which might explain why so many filmmakers want to avoid it at all costs. We've all spent way too much time watching films that were talky, preachy, hyperventilated, and dull. But there's also narration that makes films funny, sarcastic, spare, poetic, and elegant. *Bowling for Columbine, The Donner Party, A Brief History of Time*, and *Recording* The Producers: *A Musical Romp with Mel Brooks* all have an effective off-camera narrative voice. *Bowling* is narrated in the first person by filmmaker Michael Moore, *The Donner Party* is narrated in the third person by historian David McCullough, and the last is "narrated" through material culled from a filmed interview with Mel Brooks.

Narration done well can be one of the best and most efficient ways to move your story along, not because it *tells* the story but because it draws the audience into it. Who narrates your film, and why, is up to you. It can be someone young or old, famous or not, someone personally connected to the story or an expert commenting upon it. You can even use more than one narrator and weave the voices together.

"When documentary makers dive into fairly complicated historical policy or legal and legislative issues," notes Jon Else, "narration is your friend. It may mean that you have only two or three lines of narration in a film, but something that might take ten minutes of tortured interview or tortured cinéma vérité footage can be often disposed of better in 15 seconds of a well-written line of narration." Nor does narration need to be spoken. I helped to write a few lines of text that were presented on screen in *Lalee's Kin*, for example, and worked to bridge gaps in the narrative. An example of this is the card that read, *Two months later, Granny sent a message to her grandfather and Auntie Michelle. "Please come get me. I want to live with you."*

NARRATOR'S POINT OF VIEW

If you have an unseen, voice-over narrator, you'll need to decide on a point of view both from which to tell the story and from which to narrate it.

- First-person narration is when the narrator speaks of him or herself. "I needed to find out." The point of view is limited to what the narrator knows at a given point in the story.
- Second-person narration is rarely used, even in fiction. It has the narrator addressing the audience as "you," as in, "He asks if you want a soda, and you say yes."
- Third-person omniscient is the most commonly used form of narration; it is written using "he" or "she," and the narrator can slip in and out of anyone's thoughts or actions. "The mayor was well aware of Smith's plans. And from his campaign headquarters, Smith knew that the mayor's response, when it came, would be fierce." Most often, this narration is also "objective," meaning that it is limited to factual information that can be observed or verified. However, it still has a point of view; as discussed in the first chapter, any reporting of any kind, no matter how strong the intent to be neutral, contains—to some degree—the point of view of the reporter.
- Third-person subjective, used by some fiction writers, uses the "he" or "she" form but is limited in narrative to that individual's point of view.

Omniscient narration does not give you free reign to jump back and forth between points of view. To keep your audience with you, you need to be careful how and when you switch. For example, if you begin to narrate a battle from the point of view of the advancing British, you don't want to suddenly switch to the American side without signaling to the audience that you've done so. In other words, the following (imagined) scene is confusing: *British forces prepared their charge as the Americans assembled near Boone Hill.*

General Washington ordered his men, a ragtag group of 300, to stand firm. The soldiers advanced, a force of nearly 2,000 in territory that offered little resistance.

Told from the American point of view, the scene might go like this: *The Americans were assembled near Boone Hill when they got word that British forces were advancing. General Washington ordered his men, a ragtag group of 300, to stand firm, as nearly 2,000 British soldiers advanced toward them.*

From the British point of view, it might go this way: *British forces prepared to charge on the Americans who were assembled near Boone Hill. A force of nearly 2,000 men, they had little difficulty with the terrain as they approached Boone Hill, where General Washington was waiting with a rag-tag force of about 300.*

Obviously, your writing should fit the visuals. But it's very easy in a case like this to quickly lose track of who's fighting whom, who's advancing where. One way to help, as the filmmaker, is to maintain a consistent point of view.

"Voice of God"

People refer to omniscient narration, occasionally with derision, as "voice of God" narration. Presumably this is because it seems to know all and come from thin air, and historically it's carried with it the stentorian tones of an anchor such as Walter Cronkite. But lose the "voice of God" aspect and omniscient narration can be an important part of your storytelling. A neutral third-party voice can bring a distinct tone and trustworthiness to your account. Imagine EYES ON THE PRIZE without the calm voice of narrator Julian Bond, a civil rights activist, politician, and broadcaster, or FRONTLINE without the voice of narrator Will Lyman, a professional actor. Note that it's not simply the quality of their voices that makes the narration of these series distinctive; it's the way that program producers write with their particular tone in mind.

In some cases, the narrator isn't hired until a series is completed. If the narrator's identity becomes an additional factor in the storytelling—if, for example, you've gotten baseball star Cal Ripken or writer Toni Morrison to agree to narrate your program —you'll fine tune the narration (and probably the show) to suit their unique voices. Note also that the content of the show makes a difference. Cal Ripken's narration for a tribute to a recently deceased athlete will be different than his narration of a light-hearted look at spring training.

You can also surprise people with narration. Suppose John Glenn agreed to record third-person narration for a documentary about the American manned space flight program. At the point when he appears in archival footage, he might adopt a first-person approach, "And that's me, about to do something most Americans only dream of."

WHEN IS NARRATION WRITTEN?

When you write narration varies from project to project. A film adapted from a book might begin with the text. Sometimes a narrative device doesn't suggest itself until well into the editing, as happened when the producers decided to use voice-over excerpts of an old diary as the narrative spine in *Yosemite: The Fate of Heaven*.

In general, if you are creating a "traditional" third-person narration track, meaning that you're writing narration to seam together visual images, interviews, and perhaps archival material, the final narration won't come together until you're editing. You may assemble other elements first, such as filmed footage, archival material, or interview bites, and then rough out narration as needed to help move the story along. Sometimes you need to write "into" a talking head, which means that your words are needed to make the meaning of the upcoming interview selection clear. Sometimes you need narration to set the stage for a scene that can then play out, uninterrupted, on camera or to make a transition from one sequence or story to the next.

WHO WRITES THE NARRATION?

Film writing is a different skill than magazine or book writing. While some prose writers make the transition successfully, not all do. Writing to picture—writing words that will be heard rather than read—and structuring a film story within the confines of thirty minutes or eight hours, are specialized skills, and just as a great poet might be a terrible screenwriter, a great print journalist might not write a good movie.

On many documentary projects, the film's producer is also the writer. But there are no hard and fast rules. Some projects involve a writer from the beginning; others bring a writer on board at the assembly or rough cut stage. Some directors write. Some editors write or at least draft out scratch narration that is then polished by or with the help of a writer.

If you are going to bring in an "outside" writer (as opposed to involving the producer or director in that role), it's best to do so as early in the production process as possible. This might mean, for example, that the writer consults on and off until editing is underway, at which point he or she works on a more regular basis. An experienced film writer can point out potential structural weaknesses in an outline or treatment and help develop a "must have" list for production. At the assembly stage, a writer can help develop an editing script, focusing not just on narration but on the structure of the storytelling itself. A writer, ideally, knows all of the storytelling elements well and plays a significant role in using them to tell the strongest story possible.

To bring a writer on simply to polish narration works if the film is in good shape, but it can be frustrating for everyone if improving the narration doesn't solve a problem that might better have been addressed through different story or structure choices earlier on. By the time you're polishing narration, most of your editing resources are gone, and it can be very hard on everyone to have to pull things apart and look at the film with fresh eyes.

WRITING TO PICTURE

The camera pans across a sepia-toned still photograph of a wagon train on a dusty road. To the side, an old farmer stands, watching as the wagons pass. The shot ends on a hand-painted sign tacked to the back of one of the last wagons: CALIFNA OR BUST. As you watch this shot on screen, which line of narration would be more useful to you?

- *The wagons set out along the dusty road.*
- *On August 4th they set out; four men, five women, and eight children determined to find gold.*

Which narration breathes life into the photograph? And which just states the obvious? Narration should add information to picture, not simply describe it. Above all, narration should advance the story that you are telling.

Here's a second example, from a film that follows a group of college friends as they face their first year in the job market. In a live-action scene set in a private home, a group of young women sits down to a fancy dinner. One of them, dressed in an expensive-looking suit, sets a roasted turkey on the table. Which narration is useful?

- *Donna is the most vivacious of the group, and the most fashion-conscious.*
- *Donna, who graduated with high honors from Harvard Law School, hopes to pursue a career in advertising.*

Obviously, what you say depends on what the audience needs to learn. But we can tell from watching the scene that Donna is vivacious and well-dressed. We *can't* tell from looking at her that she went to Harvard Law School. That narration adds to picture.

There is another approach that people sometimes use, designed to create a sense of tension. Here's an example.

- *Donna, the organizer of this gathering, would soon learn that her life would change in ways she couldn't imagine.*

What exactly does this add? Are you on the edge of your seat wondering how Donna's life will change? No. This sounds like it's intended to build tension, but it's just words. Tension comes from the story, not a narrator's hints.

Just as you should write to picture, you should never write *against* picture. A common mistake people make is to write in a way that sets the film up to go in one direction, when in fact the images are going somewhere else. Here's an example. We see a group of executives sitting around a table, talking. Narration: *The board decided to hire a consultant, Jane Johnson.* Cut to a woman talking. Wouldn't you assume it's Jane Johnson? If it's not, it's going to take a moment to readjust your thinking, to figure out, well, if it's *not* Johnson, who is it? By then, you'll have missed at least part of what this woman has said.

Suppose the woman that we cut to is on the board of directors, and she's explaining why they're hiring Jane Johnson. The edit makes sense. But the narration gets in the way. Try again. We see a group of executives sitting around a table, talking. Narration: *The board decided that a consultant was needed.* Cut to the woman from the board, who explains, "We were spinning our wheels. And so . . . " It's a minor difference but an important one.

Words and picture should work together, each adding to the buildup of your story. Words should also accurately identify the picture. Suppose that you are telling the story of a man and woman who met at a USO dance the night before he was shipped off to fight in the Second World War. This meeting took place in Ohio. But other than family photos (taken five years later, after he's returned from the war and they've married and had a child), there are no visuals. There is no footage anywhere of that particular USO dance or even of the club in which it was held. Can you use footage of another USO dance, from another state and another year?

Of course you can, but your narration should avoid creating the false impression that the audience is seeing the real thing. For example, suppose the editor cuts in footage of a USO dance held two years later in a different state. The narration says, *On February 2, 1942, at a USO dance in Columbus, Ohio, Tim finally met the girl of his dreams.* The audience may think, "Gee, isn't that amazing, there was a film crew there to capture it." I think it stretches credibility, and if the audience assumes that this couldn't possibly be *the* USO dance on *the* night in *the* city, they will see your footage for what it is—wallpaper. From that point on, the archival value of the footage is diminished, and the rest of your material becomes a bit suspect, deservedly or not.

There is an alternative, using the same scene, same footage. Open the narration wider, as in this example, *USO dances were held in gymnasiums and hospitals, canteens and clubs throughout the U.S., and it was at a dance like this that Tim met the girl of his dreams.* You're not writing as closely to that one particular image; at the same time, you're offering a valuable reminder that your characters are just two people caught up in a time and a situation that's bigger than both of them. The footage is no longer generic wallpaper, but illustrative of an era.

Writing to picture also means that the words you choose work in tandem with the visuals. Here's an example. You are making a film about a team of cyclists competing in the Tour de France. You need to introduce Ralph Martinez, riding for the Americans. In the scene you're narrating, it's early morning and the cyclists are gathered in a village square, drinking coffee or juice, eating pastries, and psyching themselves up for a day on the Tour. The specific shot starts close on a croissant. A hand wearing a bicycling glove reaches in and picks up the pastry; the shot widens and pulls back as we follow the pastry up to a rider's mouth, and see that it is a young man (Ralph) perched on his bike, sipping coffee as he laughs and talks with teammates. Some narration options:

- *Pastry and coffee start the day for Ralph Martinez and his American teammates.* Too on the nose—we can see the pastry and coffee for ourselves.
- *Ralph Martinez, getting ready for his third tour, is riding with the American team.* This won't work, because the words "Ralph Martinez" will fall too soon, probably when we're still looking at a big glob of jam on a croissant. You want your narration to roughly mirror the picture and to arrive at Ralph when the visuals do.
- *Riding with the Americans is Ralph Martinez, in his third Tour de France.* This might work—it's hard to tell until you see and hear it against picture! Note that you don't need to say "team" because it can be assumed. Chances are that by this point in the film you also won't need to say "de France." You want to be as economical in word use as possible. Better to have a moment for natural sound than to keep yammering away at the viewers.

Writing to picture can be difficult, especially for those who resist rewriting. While a film is being edited, nearly everything is subject to change. A scene needs to be cut down to give another scene more time. An archival shot needs to be changed because the rights to it aren't available. A sequence is moved from the last half of the film to the first half and therefore needs to be set up differently. From the assembly through to script lock, narration is a moving target. You must be willing to make changes. When enough changes pile up, the editor or someone else on the production team will record a new scratch narration track and lay it against picture. As you'll discover, at least some of these revisions will need further revising. Eventually, though, the script will be locked, the picture will be locked, and the narration will be finished.

WRITING NARRATION TO BE SPOKEN

Narration scripts are, by design, written to be spoken out loud. Every word counts. Important words have to stand out in a sentence or paragraph. Sentences should be short and written in an active voice. Phrases should be reviewed to ensure that they don't create a confusing impression, such as, "Mark left Philip. Underneath the house, a skunk was waiting." Reading it, the meaning is clear; hearing it, you wonder if Mark left Philip underneath the house, or if the skunk is going to catch Mark unaware. "The remains were sent to the local anthropology lab. There, they believed Dr. Smith could provide vital information." The *remains* believe something about Dr. Smith?

You also need to avoid tongue twisters and quotation marks—audiences can't hear the irony when a narrator says, "Eleanor was 'sorry,' but no one believed her." On paper, a reader could reasonably figure that Eleanor had made an apology but it was taken as false. To the listener, it sounds like the narrator has determined that Eleanor is, in fact, sorry, but no one believes her. There's a small but important distinction. (For the same reason, you need to be wary of words that sound alike but have different meanings, and of conjunctions, such as "shouldn't," which may be misheard as "should.")

The solution is very simple. Read your narration out loud, even as you're writing it. You will find it far easier to hear the rhythm, feel where the strong words are falling, and get a sense of what's hard to say or where words are superfluous. Then read it aloud again (and again, and again) against picture. There are a few ways of doing this, and you'll use them all. You can read to picture on the fly, although it's tough to look at the screen and your script simultaneously. You can have someone read aloud as you watch. Time permitting, the most effective way to check narration against picture is to have someone on the production crew record a temporary ("scratch") narration track, which is edited into the film.

SOME GENERAL GUIDELINES FOR NARRATION

Reapply the Rules of Grammar

As with proposal writing, narration writing must be grammatical. Common problems include the following:

- Dangling and misplaced modifiers. *Three sheets to the wind, the police officers stared up at Rodney as he stood on the window ledge.* It's Rodney who's drunk, not the police officers. The line should read, *Three sheets to the wind, Rodney stood on the window ledge as police officers stared up at him.* But what if you're writing to picture? What if you see the police officers first, and then Rodney? You reveal the information as you see it. *The officers stared up at Rodney, teetering on a ledge, three sheets to the wind.*

- Dangling participles. This is when you start a sentence with a verb and go to another verb without inserting a subject. *Having been recently fired, getting a job was a priority for him.* Instead, try: *Having been recently fired, he made getting a job a priority.* Or, *He'd recently been fired, so getting a job was a priority.*

- Confusing use of pronouns. *When she was just six, her beloved horse, Yum Yum, died.* Was the horse six, or was it the "she" that we're talking about? A simple solution is something like, *Jennifer was just six when her beloved horse, Yum Yum, died.*

- Lack of parallel form. Avoid statements such as *Four men in Texas, three in Ohio, and one in San Francisco.* That's two states and a city. Either three cities or three states should be used to make the construction parallel. In this case, since there's the possibility of having to list eight cities in total, I'd say, *Four men in Texas, three in Ohio, and one in California.* Here's another example. *He liked running, fishing, and to build model airplanes.* Try this instead. *He liked running, fishing, and building model airplanes.*

- Incorrect use of "fewer" and "less." Fewer is for things that can be counted, like students. *There were fewer students this year than last.* Less is for quantities and measures that can't be counted. *There's less support for the new tax law.*

- Other incorrect word usage. Here are some words to be careful of. *Since*—It can be a measure of time (*since the 1980s*) or it can indicate cause (*Since no one bothered to show up, the meeting is cancelled.*) *As* and *like*—In general, *as* refers to a similarity. *She dances as if moved by the wind.* *Like* refers to similarities between nouns. *He hopes to pass regulations here like those already being enforced in Cleveland.* And finally, *and* and *but*—While both are used as conjunctions, *and* is for clauses with similar weight or similar meaning. *The students staged a local sit-in on Saturday, and on Monday they attended a city-wide rally. But* is used when you want to imply a difference in emphasis or a contrast. *The students staged a local sit-in on Saturday, but on Monday they attended a city-wide rally.* The implication is that the rally has greater weight in your story.

- Non sequiturs. These are statements or phrases that follow each other but don't have any logical connection. *Investigators call on a team of forensic scientists to establish the victim's time of death and bring his killer to justice.* There's no indication here of a link between knowing the cause of death and bringing the killer to justice.

The list of common mistakes goes on. Some excellent style books are available, including *The Elements of Style*, a classic by William Strunk, Jr. and E.B. White; *The Associated Press Stylebook and Libel Manual*, edited by Norm Goldstein and *The New York Times Manual of Style and Usage*, by Allan M. Siegal and William G. Connolly. In addition, there are likely to be people on your staff who are good at grammar, know all the rules by heart, and actually enjoy diagramming sentences. Ask one of them to review your narration before you lock it.

Use Anticipation

Narration needs to follow the arc of the story, not lead it. In the film's opening minutes, you want to set up the questions that will drive your story forward. You then want to anticipate the audience's needs and almost intuitively seed information in, just as—or just after—the question or confusion begins to flicker in the viewer's mind. Pay attention as you watch a well-made film, and you'll notice this happening. You turn to a friend and say, "I don't understand; I thought she couldn't run for governor." and seconds later, the narration answers your question. "A loophole in electoral law had worked to her advantage."

Avoid Stereotyping

Use the most gender-neutral terms available (e.g., firefighter rather than fireman, police officer rather than policeman, business people rather than businessmen). This is important for two reasons. It more accurately represents the world in which we live, and it's a step toward acknowledging (and involving) an audience of diverse backgrounds.

Avoiding stereotyping also means being careful of "code" words (saying "suburban" when you mean white or middle class, for example) and watching out for an overlay of judgment based on stereotypes, such as, "She was pushing 40, but still attractive." Whose point of view does a statement like this reflect? "Pushing 40" implies that this is an unbelievably ancient age, and the "but" is a dead giveaway that nobody on the production team could imagine anyone over 25 being worth a second glance. Stereotypes—dumb jock, dumb blonde, little old lady, "not your grandmother's store"—have no place in documentary narration. Mothers-in-law run corporations and countries; "geezers" set foreign policy or rob banks.

Watch Out for Anachronisms

If you are telling narration from a point of view within a story, stay within the boundaries of that point of view. This means respecting the limitations of your character's frame of reference, including time and place. An example of narration that fails to do this comes from *When Dinosaurs Roamed America*, an animated series from the Discovery Channel. Narrator John Goodman is speaking from the point of view of a dinosaur, trying to size up a new beast he's encountered. "The raptor's never seen a dinosaur like this before," Goodman says. "Is it a predator, or is it prey? No other creature in the world looks like a half-plucked turkey and walks like a pot-bellied bear. Still, an oddball can be dangerous." This narration has the dinosaur comparing what he sees to animals he has no knowledge of, since they won't exist for several million years. For the audience, the comparison may be valuable, but its use here pulls us out of the story. To use the comparison, the producers should have acknowledged the leap in time by moving—even briefly—outside the raptor's point of view. For example, *The raptor's never seen a dinosaur like this before. Scientists today say it probably looked like a cross between a plucked turkey and a pot-bellied bear. To the raptor, it just looks odd—and oddballs can be dangerous.*

You also want to be careful, when speaking of the past, not to impose your 21st-century values, assumptions, and knowledge. In an interesting way, renowned historian Simon Schama does this (albeit successfully) in his A HISTORY OF BRITAIN. Here is his somewhat breathless description of the pairing of Henry of Anjou (soon to become King Henry II)—"the most hyperactive king in British history"—and his "Guinevere," Eleanor of Aquitaine. "But the match was a gamble. He was 19; she was pushing 30. He was relatively inexperienced; Eleanor had seen as much of the ways of the world as it could possibly offer. Henry found himself at the altar in 1152 beside an older woman, described as a graceful, dark-eyed beauty, disconcertingly articulate, strong-minded, and jocular, hardly the frail damsel in the tower. One likes to think that for her part, Eleanor saw not just the usual feudal spur-clanking bonehead, but beyond the stocky frame and barrel chest, someone who was an intriguing peculiarity."

Look at the point of view in the paragraph above:

- There are two references to Eleanor's age, in terms that imply that this carried the same weight 850 years ago that it does today. It would need to be fact checked and presumably was.
- "Disconcertingly articulate"—disconcerting to whom? What is the cultural or political value that this runs counter to? We have to take Schama on faith that there was a problem with a woman of significant power having a brain in her head and the ability to speak her mind; there is no context for it given here.
- "Hardly the frail damsel in the tower" implies the groom's point of view, when in fact it's the narrator's. Schama noted earlier in the film that "this was the age of chivalry, when the myth of Arthur and Camelot was at its most popular," adding that Henry's parents were grooming him to become "a new King Arthur—and to do this of course, he would need a Guinevere." It may or may not have occurred to Henry to size up his bride with Guinevere in mind; the evidence in the film, however, makes this solely Schama's point of view.
- "One likes to think that . . . " furthers the impression that the point of view here is the narrator's and that in fact it is Schama who likes to think that Eleanor saw more than "the usual feudal, spur-clanking bonehead." Would this have been Eleanor's presumption of a man deemed suitable for her to wed? It's possible; it's just difficult to tell here.

This narration *does* move the story forward at a fast clip and brings characters to life. But Schama can get away with this, in my view, because of his considerable expertise; he carries a certain weight when he makes sweeping and very modern-sounding statements. It's one of those "don't try this at home" situations—or if you must try it, do so with professional (scholarly) guidance. Otherwise, it's very easy to slip up and inaccurately impose 21st-century assumptions on the past—about life, work, gender roles, class, race, all sorts of things.

Limit the Number of Ideas in Each Block of Narration

Your narration should convey only the story points needed to get to the next sync material; if you go too far or include too many points, your audience will lose track of the information and will be distracted or confused by what follows. For example, here's a piece of narration from *Not a Rhyme Time*, a program from I'LL MAKE ME A WORLD. "In the spring of 1967, Amiri Baraka was scheduled to address the Black Writers' Conference at Fisk University in Nashville, Tennessee. Gwendolyn Brooks was also on the program."

The tension comes from the fact that (as we already know from the program) Baraka represents the new school, the Black Arts Movement, and Brooks—a Pulitzer Prize-winning author who publishes with a large, mainstream publisher—represents the "establishment." The interaction of the two will help to spark Brooks's transformation, which is the focus of the story.

Look at what happens if we go too far and turn the corner with this narration. *In the spring of 1967, Amiri Baraka was scheduled to address the Black Writers' Conference at Fisk University in Nashville, Tennessee. Gwendolyn Brooks was also on the program. She had prepared to read her poem, 'The Life of Lincoln West.'* The paragraph now sets us up to learn more about this one poem and away from the anticipated meeting of Brooks and Baraka.

Foreshadow Important Information

The American troops battling the British in the Revolutionary War were promised in July of 1776, when the fighting broke out, that they would all be discharged by December 31. Don't wait to tell the audience this until it's December 31 in your film's chronology. Tell them in July, when they won't think it matters; remind them in September, when the war is dragging on. That way, when winter sets in, it will be on their minds—just as it must have been on General Washington's mind—when the troops are tired and demoralized, and there's no way that Washington can keep his word.

Understand the Different Roles Played by Narration and Sync Material

It's all too common for filmmakers to use talking heads to do work that is better done by narration, and vice versa. Sometimes, this happens because the casting is weak; everybody talks about everything, nothing is differentiated, and they all might as well be narrating.

Ideally, your interviewees should be advancing the story through the lens of their own expertise, experience, and point of view. This is information that is more valuable, in some ways, than narration, and it's certainly more personable. Using these characters to convey basic narrative points that narration could convey just as well is something of a waste. Conversely, if you replace too many of your talking heads or too much of what they say with narration, you risk pulling the heart and soul out of your film. Even people who are resistant to talking heads would prefer a good visit with an enjoyable character to narration.

Narration is also not generally the best way to contradict an interviewee, except in films that are driven by the filmmaker as narrator (Judith Helfand's *Blue Vinyl* and Michael Moore's *Bowling for Columbine*). Using the narrator to argue with or undermine an interview bite may not be the strongest way to make your case. The subject says, "No one knew about those documents," and a disembodied voice interrupts, "No one knew? It seemed unlikely."

So how do you contradict people on screen? You find another interviewee to offer a rebuttal, or you film scenes that contain evidence contradicting the interviewee's statement. Let the individuals, facts, and story speak for themselves, and trust that audience members can decide the truth for themselves.

Use Words Sparingly and Specifically

Screen time is a precious commodity, and you want your narration to be as spare as possible. Don't waste good airtime on words that are little more than filler, such as, "Salinas. A town of working people, it hardly seems the place for a murder. But on January 14, 1998, the owners of a house discovered something that would change that impression forever." A quick check shows that Salinas is a city of around 123,000 people, and that in the 20 years before the homeowners discovered a body buried beneath their house, a total of 218 people had been killed in Salinas, including 18 in 1997. The narration pumped emotion into the story, but it's not useful or even accurate.

The perceived need for hype often seems to lead to imprecise writing. "In rural Michigan, a search for a missing man ends in cold-blooded murder." Well, actually, it doesn't. If the *search* ended in cold-blooded murder, then someone involved in the search would have ended up dead. What happened is that a missing person case is revealed to be a murder case—the search for the missing man leads to a corpse. Why not say that?

Using words sparingly also means choosing the best word to describe what you mean, being careful of nuances. Does a teenager walk across the room or saunter? Does a CEO say that he doesn't have numbers for the fourth quarter, or does he "admit" that fact? Has the world leader made an impassioned speech or launched into a tirade? Was a nation's capital liberated, or did it "fall?" Was it a conflagration—a term that has specific meaning among firefighters—or simply a bad fire? Choose your words carefully, and be sure the meaning you want is not only the most exciting, but also the most accurate.

Along these lines, try to avoid the slogans of others, whether you agree with them or not. For example, rather than adopt the phrases "pro-life" or "pro-choice," state that someone is either for or against abortion rights.

Use Telling Details

A good detail, well-placed, can convey a tremendous amount of story information. If there were any doubts about the need for a campaign to register voters in Selma, Alabama, they were dispelled in EYES ON THE PRIZE by this fact. "More than half of Dallas County citizens were black, but less than 1% ware registered [to vote]". Details can set a stage where visuals are insufficient, as in THE CIVIL WAR. "Sherman began his march. Sixty-two thousand men in blue were on the move in two great columns. Their supply train stretched 25 miles. A slave watching the army stream past wondered aloud if anybody was left up north." And details can convey tone and wit, as in *Troublesome Creek: A Midwestern*. "Like a lot of families facing a real crisis, we immediately stopped talking about it."

Put Information into Context

Your narration needs to move the story along, which means it should not only impart facts but also make it clear how they are relevant to the story you're telling. "The 390 people in the club now fought their way to an exit," is interesting, but I have no way of knowing if that's a lot or a little. If the club is Madison Square Garden, it's a very small crowd. "390 people—nearly twice as many as the club could legally hold—fought their way to an exit," tells you that laws were broken even before disaster occurred.

The same is true for motivation. "The mayor called a late night meeting," may not advance your story as well as, "Hoping to avoid the press, the mayor called a late night meeting." *Motivation must be fact checked*, however. Never guess at what someone was thinking or feeling, unless your narration makes clear that it's speculation, as in, "She might have been concerned not to hear from him; perhaps that's why she got into her car that night."

If quantity is important to convey, offer it in terms that are comparative, rather than giving specific numbers. "From head to tail, the dinosaur would have been half as long as a football field." Comparisons and context are also useful when discussing quantities from the past. It's common for filmmakers to imply that someone making "only making $5 day" in 1905 was being exploited, without finding out what this amount meant at the time, what it might buy, and how it compared to other incomes at the time.

As you add this context, keep in mind that you're building toward story events. You need to remind the audience occasionally (not constantly) about what's at stake, what information we know, where we're going. "The board will stop hearing testimony at 9:30. At that point, their vote will decide the future of this regional school system." Offer gentle clues about the outcome as we move forward.

"He had gambled everything, and he had lost. As Ransom's troops trudged wearily north . . . "

Get Off the Dime

Like the story itself, narration needs to keep moving forward. It's surprising how often narration repeats the same information over and over, especially to remind viewers that they're seeing something for the first time, or that it's very dangerous, or that no one knows what's around the next corner. If you've told us once that a particular military unit is untrained and untested, don't tell us again; build on that information as you move the story forward.

Don't Drop Names

If people are worth mentioning, they're worth identifying. The first time someone's name comes up in narration, let us know who the person is, even if you think that we'd have to be living under a rock *not* to know. "Noted composer Leonard Bernstein once said . . . " "He was filmed in performance by cinematographer Gordon Parks, who said he saw in the young musician . . . "

Try to anticipate words that your audience may be unfamiliar with, whether they're spoken by the narrator (and can't be substituted) or spoken by an interviewee or someone on camera. If the word's meaning is not clear in the context, you may need to set it up. If, for example, you are cutting to a historic artifact, a bill of sale for a *frigate*, you might set it up as, "That day, the general placed an order for a new sailing ship, one outfitted for war."

Put Lists in an Order That Builds

This is fairly straightforward. You want your paragraphs to pack a punch. Look at the following line of narration from the series Liberty! The American Revolution, describing the British invasion of New York in 1776: "30,000 troops. 10,000 sailors. 300 supply ships. 30 battleships with 1200 cannons. It is the largest sea borne attack ever attempted by England until the 20th century." What's great about this is that the build is not by number but by power; in fact, the numbers decrease from 30,000 (troops) to 1 (attack). But the power goes from men to supply ships to battleships, and news of the force that's about to hit the newly-independent states is delivered with a sentence that jumps the chronology and lands us, very briefly, in the present (the series aired in 1997). It's very effective drama.

Use an Active Voice

You want your narration to be as active as possible. For example, "A decision was made to allow Coca Cola to advertise on school property." Who made the decision, and how? A more active way to say this is, "By a vote of 4-1, the school board decided to allow Coca Cola to advertise on school property." (Obviously, if we're watching a scene where we know it's the school board, and can actually see four hands up and one down, you won't say this. But if we're seeing a shot of the hallway with soda vending machines all lined up, you want narration that helps that shot along.)

Help to Differentiate Among Similar Things

Narration can play an important role in getting a viewer through a succession of battles, or medical interventions, or political gatherings. Since you've been careful to film a series of events that build on each other, and not just three or four examples of the same thing, your narration may be needed to simply make that build a little more clear or fill in the details. "The operation on Bill's knee had only improved mobility. Now Dr. Fishman needed to add cartilage . . . "

Do the Math for Them

If you write narration that says, "Born in 1934, she was 18 when she met Mark," there are viewers who will be so distracted trying to figure out the year she met Mark (1952) that they'll momentarily lose track of your story. Whether it's calculating profits or age or elapsed time, it's best to write it in a way that doesn't make the viewer do the work. This is not an issue of involving the audience in the story, it's a matter of not wanting to distract them from it.

Avoid Hype

If a story is truly astonishing or an event is truly chilling or a person is really sinister, it should come through the story or character or event and the way you present it. The cheapest and worst way to try to pump emotion into a piece is through adjectives and hyperbole. Frankly, audiences become skeptical when narrators begin to sound like over-caffeinated salespeople. If your story is really good, it'll sell itself.

Know When to Stop Narrating

Prepare the moment, and then let it play. If you're building toward the battle of Waterloo or a lifesaving operation or a statewide volleyball tournament, get us there and then let it play for a bit. Audiences need a respite from the talking; they need time to feel those moments of humor or pathos or fear. Anticipate those moments and build them in, whether it means a moment of silence or a moment with music or just action and sync sound. This is also true when the information is very complex and needs to be processed; or when it's very funny, and the audience needs time to laugh.

14

Storytelling: A Checklist

Here's a list of questions[1] to be asked at each stage of production, and especially as you near the end of the editing process:

- Given a choice between your film and the latest version of *Who Wants To Marry This Guy*, which would you choose? Are you telling a compelling and dramatic story and giving the viewer a reason to watch?
- Are there interesting questions being asked and answered throughout? Does your film offer mystery, intrigue, suspense?
- Are you offering new information or an unusual perspective or just rehashing tired, unchallenging material?
- Are you in the driver's seat of your film, steering toward emotional and intellectual highlights?
- Have you created moments of discovery for the audience, allowing them to reach their own conclusions that are then confirmed or denied in the film?
- If there is backstory in your film, have you motivated the viewer to care about going there?
- Have you grounded viewers in your story so that they can anticipate where you're going and will be surprised when you take unexpected turns?
- Have you cast the film carefully with a manageable group of characters who fairly represent the complexity of an issue and not just its extremes?

[1]Credit and thanks are due to Steve Fayer and Jon Else, who created earlier versions of this list for the producers at Blackside, Inc., in Boston.

- When you introduce new information, do you do it in a way that brings audience members along, or will they feel that you're speaking to an exclusive club and change the channel?
- Does the film seem like "just another documentary," or is it something that people might want to tell each other about the next day?
- Does the story that was set up at the film's beginning pay off at the end?

Part IV

CONVERSATIONS ABOUT STORY

Many documentary filmmakers, including those interviewed for this book, work in a range of job capacities and film styles, so identifying any one of them with any one type of storytelling is difficult. With that said, there are some organizing principles behind the following conversations:

Ric Burns (New York) was asked about his experiences as filmmaker who specializes in historical documentaries.

Jon Else (California) has created a diverse body of documentary work; he is also a renowned cinematographer. Our conversation ranged from visual storytelling to the pitfalls and possibilities of digital video technology.

Susan Froemke (New York) and I spoke about her distinguished work in direct cinema.

Jeanne Jordan and **Steven Ascher** (Massachusetts) have worked independently and together on a number of films; my conversations with them are focused on their personal documentary, *Troublesome Creek: A Midwestern.*

Sam Pollard (New York) has also served in a variety of roles as a filmmaker, but we spoke at greatest length about his experiences as an editor.

Kenn Rabin (California) is a filmmaker and writer, although I spoke with him here primarily as a nationally-recognized expert on the use of archival material.

Susanne Simpson (Massachusetts) spoke with me about her experience in giant screen (e.g., IMAX) filmmaking.

15

Ric Burns

Ric Burns won two Emmys for THE CIVIL WAR, which he produced with his brother Ken. Through his own company, Steeplechase Films, he produced *Coney Island, The Donner Party,* the six-hour series THE WAY WEST, and two Emmy Award winners, *Ansel Adams* and the seven-episode series NEW YORK, completed before the September 11, 2001 attack. At the time of the interview he was completing a sequel, *The Center of the World: New York,* about the World Trade Center.

Of the ideas that cross your desk, how do you decide which to make into films?

For me, in the bundle of words, "historical documentary film-maker," there's no question that the word "film" is the most important. And that's because of how powerful and dreamlike film can be. Certainly the experience of film that I value most is an experience of being taken to some very deep place by the flow of light and shadow and sound and words and music, which are the elements of film. It's always about contrasts. Visually, thematically, emotionally. Think about the Donner Party. Read a one-paragraph account of the Donner Party, and if it's accurate, you'll feel that interplay of bright-ness and darkness. In one of the biggest years of the American dream, 87 people go west thinking they're going to find Paradise and end up in a terrible nightmare. Say the words "New York" and try not to have in your mind, very swiftly, the New York skyline. Its most powerful moment is at twilight, where it's both tremendously, luminously shiny and also powerfully black and dark.

    In choosing a story, the pilot light goes on when you sense that this is material that will allow you to exploit that dream power of film. Use that basic feeling to ask yourself, well, what's the story here? What's the structure of a film that will penetrate and elaborate the story? And in the case of NEW YORK, I think the most gratifying thing about working on that project—which sprawled to 14.5 hours and now we're working on another two-hour film about the World Trade Center—is that, at the very center of it, a very simple, provisional explanation revealed itself as to, why did New York become such a shining and dark place? And that was that at the very beginning it was founded as a relentlessly commercial colony, unlike the religious colonies that were its rivals at the time.

From there, how do you focus a historical topic that's broad and complex?

Every step along the way you ask, "What's absolutely crucial to telling the story? What advances the story?" You've got to start with the Dutch [settlers], you understand that. Then there are the English; you don't spend that much time with the English—they did some things that were different, but many things that were the same. So you apply the basic narrative yardstick, which is: try not to tell any story more than once. So there's only one riot. There's only one fire. There's only one burst of skyscrapers. There's only one war. In other words, always find that moment where the nature of the particular story you're telling is caught at its highest arc. Tell the story of the draft riots of 1863, the most catalytic and, to this day, the worst instance of civil unrest in American history.

You try to be as severe as possible as you go through the chronology of your subject matter. Ask, "What are the central themes that structure the material? Which are the moments that elaborate those themes most powerfully?" And you use those central themes as a kind of divining rod to show you—amongst the literally infinite amount of material, in the case of something like New York—where the gold lies. Where's the stuff that's most powerful? Where is the stuff that most embodies the themes, elaborates them, and drives them forward?

How do you define theme, and how do you handle themes in your work?

Theme is the most basic lifeblood of a film. *This* is what this thing is about. The story is the vehicle and the theme is the tone and emotion; theme tells you the tenor of your story.

Theme makes you see and feel the correspondences between different elements of your story. How do Harlem in the 1920s, the explosion of mass media, Al Smith, the stock market rise, and the skyscraper wars all correspond with each other? Theme is, in a sense, vibrating through all of them. At its worst, the theme becomes a kind of cookie cutter which causes everything to look the same. At its best, it makes you understand the metaphoric relationships between things which are, on the surface, more or less dissimilar, more or less alike. Al Smith's pursuit of the presidency, F. Scott Fitzgerald's pursuit of Zelda and the great American novel, a modest investor's pursuit of wealth, and somebody else's pursuit of the highest building in the world, all stand in a corresponding metaphoric relationship to each other, which doesn't mean that they all *mean* the same thing. You understand them as resonating within the same ambiance, and that can't help but make each of them more powerful.

Not all historical documentaries explore themes; some present a story or situation without that added complexity

What I know from my own work is that if you do it quickly, you can't possibly get the themes. It's one thing to understand the theme and write it out on the back of a matchbook. But then to actually cause the theme to flow through the film, that's really difficult. First, you find the right theme. That can take a while. You articulate it correctly, in relationship to the actual material, the research, the stories, which can take another while. Then you have to stitch it together in such a fashion that the theme actually stands up and walks like some Frankenstein monster. That's where so much of the work of filmmaking, in the writing and editing, takes place. And you keep comparing what you've done to what you intuitively know it could be and should be.

When and how does the storytelling take shape?

You create your first description of what the film is. Sometimes it's in the form of a letter to a colleague, sometimes it's in the form of a two-page proposal to get seed money. But every iteration in some sense is a version of the film, and you try to give that iteration as powerful and intense an articulation as you can. And then, when you move to the next articulation—longer, more detailed, more structured, more intense, hopefully more involving—you don't abandon the previous iteration. You use it as the point of departure. And as you do that, it begins to vary. Not four episodes but five; not one hour each but two. In my case, it's never shifted in a way that has retroactively obliterated the original intuition; it elaborates it. It's very much like rolling a snowball down a variegated hill. The snow is sort of wet here and dry there and dirty here and pristine there, and as you move, the snowball acquires its own eccentric shape and velocity. But it's always growing organically in relationship to the material and the hillside that it's moving down.

When there's a potential to research indefinitely, how do you know when to stop?

I think any successful creative project exists within an oscillation between obsessiveness and decisiveness, and you can't abandon either. The obsessiveness that makes you keep on looking for more material, another photograph, shoot another interview, delve deeper, is in a sense always there. A metaphor might be Odysseus strapped to the mast, listening to the sirens singing, and what they're singing is, "There's more stuff here. There could be more material. There must be more." But you create a structure in which you're not only Odysseus strapped to the mast with his ears unwaxed, you're also a disciplined crew moving forward, making decisions. "We're going to use this and go with it." Anytime anything works, you never let go of it. And that's the decisiveness. You say, "Right. It really works." Always rare. That's not to say that at some point you don't discover in the process that the things you like best are no longer going to fit. But you hold onto them, and by holding onto them, they take up space and begin to delimit what you can do.

Do you write a draft of the script before you shoot?

It's really happening in tandem. For example, right now we're working on a biography of the World Trade Center, an eighth episode to NEW YORK. We have a very clear outline of what the film is, and a kind of a treatment that's about fifty pages long, a corralling of the material likely to be in the story. But it's not a script. It's a chronologically-arranged treatment of what feels like the principal historical materials, an iteration that has enough structure in it to tell you where the themes of the film are going to emerge, where they develop to their highest point, and where they transform.

Armed with that, you can do interviews; you know how to craft questions. And you can always go out and shoot live cinematography, whether it's cinéma vérité shooting or live shooting of landscapes. The ideal thing is to do at least some of the production, in addition to interviews, while you're doing the script, because you're going to find that there's material you didn't expect.

For example, everyone knows of Philippe Petit, the man who walked on the tightrope between the Twin Towers. What I didn't know until doing an interview with him was that he's going to be a huge part of the film, not just a little five-minute moment halfway through. Here was a man who in 1968 conceived, sitting in a dentist's office in Paris when he was 18, the fantastic ambition that he wanted to be a high-wire artist and walk between the two towers of the World Trade Center, which had not even been started. When he did it, in August of 1974, the buildings were reviled for their brutality and their kind of inhuman scale in lower Manhattan. And suddenly here was this slender, unlikely Frenchman, dancing on the edge of nothing, as crowds of New Yorkers looked up in astonishment. That juxtaposition of fragility and power—and sort of vertiginous aerial theatricality—is the essence of a crucial aspect of the World Trade Center. So you discover that this person you thought was a little footnote expands to become part of the psychological center of the film.

Six months ago, if someone had said, "Will you interview Philippe Petit?" I would have said, "Probably." But luck is a residue of design. The design comes from that intuitive conviction that the story is powerful, and from the themes that you articulate on the basis of that conviction. That design then allows you to go out in the world and chance, so to speak, upon all sorts of elements: interviewees, places that you might shoot, quotes from a book, episodes of the history that you knew nothing about. And that's why that interplay between obsessiveness and decisiveness is so crucial.

Tell me about your process of editing.

The analogy, I think, is writing, by which I don't mean to say that it's verbal. You're trying to create a sequence that is as powerful and intense and engaging a sequence as you can. And in a way, that's what writing is. You start out with a sentence, and then you elaborate it into a paragraph, a few pages, a treatment, a script. And all the while you're collecting material for the film. When you sit down to edit, in a sense, you're writing—not with words and ideas alone, but with words and ideas, images, interview moments, spoken material, archival newsreel footage, sound, music. You're still trying to sequence them, still trying to elaborate that sequence which, like a five-word summary of your film on paper, sings a little bit and has some shape to it and engages somehow.

Do you use a dramatic act structure?

I think that that's a very sophisticated way of thinking about it, which probably one does whether one knows one is doing it or not. If you get to the point where you're actually driving forward the process of creating a story—and it's getting better—that's what you do. We have a very simple, very homely formula, which came up in the editing room of THE CIVIL WAR fifteen years ago, which is, just give and take away. It moves by the old structure of contrast. Now, if those contrasts were simply alternating back and forth, the film would be completely repetitive, like a red light going on and off and on and off. So that dynamic of giving and taking away has to itself have an arc of change in it. A value is posited, you care about something, some problem is put in its path, and it develops and transforms over time.

And your protagonists aren't necessarily human. In the series NEW YORK, the city itself is the protagonist.

Right. You have to be true to your subject. A mistake that's often made is to confuse the component parts of a subject for the subject itself. Say for instance you were doing a film about the West, the conquering of the American West in the second half of the 19th century. Immediately, the building of the transcontinental railway, the Battle of Little Bighorn, George Armstrong Custer, Sitting Bull, or the events leading up to Wounded Knee—all those stories, events, people, moments, clearly compete to be part of your story. But what can happen is you can be seduced into thinking that your film is really about that person or that moment or that thing. It may very well be fine to spend all your time talking about George Armstrong Custer. But if you've determined that you're doing a film about The Way West between 1845 and 1893, you can't take the cheap and easy solution of just being beguiled and distracted by the most dynamic, dramatic, component part. And I think that what happens in historical documentary films very frequently, to their detriment, is that the people who make them get diverted and don't stick to their guns, which is, "I started with this subject. There's only one hero to this story." That's the most challenging thing, I find, in doing these films the part is always seductive and the whole is very elusive. Yet it's the whole which is your subject. It's the thing that creates coherence and narrative trajectory, relates incidental components to deeper themes. It's the whole that gives you dramatic movement. Not a kind of dramatic movement that keeps you penned within the circumstances of a local story, but dramatic movement that sends you arcing out across a vast amount of space and time. And if you discover that there's even as many as two heroes, you've got two stories. You've got two films.

How do you ensure that a film is balanced in its storytelling?

One big difference between a certain kind of written history and historical documentary films is that the former can afford to be discursive and self-qualifying and nuanced, without jeopardizing, necessarily, their power. The latter, films, cannot afford to do that. In my view, the way complexity gets into film is not by trying, at the same time, to say something is five different things, but by over time showing the many different facets of something.

I gnash my teeth at academic historians who seem to have dipped into ten minutes of a film and say, "You claim that New York is all about commerce and greed. Doesn't that seem a powerfully capitalistic position to be taking?" Well, right, there are those moments where that was the facet of New York that we were holding up. Because film is, in certain ways, a reductively simple medium. It wants you to be transfixed at every moment by one simple thing. So how do you get complexity? Not simultaneously, but consecutively. You get the banker now, and then later you get the labor leader. You get the poet here, and later you get the master builder. When you're with the poet, don't say, "And at the same time, there was a master builder and there was a politician." To try to do more than one thing at once compromises the intensity, which is the promise of film's engagement with the audience.

I think viewers, filmgoers, TV watchers, understand that film works best by engaging you very powerfully in a sequence of "nows." Now we're here, and now we're here, and now we're here. New York turns out to have the logic of capitalism, but also the logic of alternatives to capitalism. It's a place about building fantastic public works, but it's also a place about stopping the building of fantastic public works. It's about powerful men who rule for 50 years, and about 144 disenfranchised women who in their fiery deaths catalyzed tremendous social change. It's all those things. And I think that what filmmakers are always vulnerable to is that any moment extracted from the flow of a film seems to be reductive. If it weren't reductive, it wouldn't work as film.

Do you think about what you want the audience to take away from a film?

The illusion that film performs, when it's powerful, is it gets people to confuse the experience of the film with the experience of the past. To get audiences to almost unconsciously confuse the aesthetic experience they're having as the film unfolds with their imagination of what it must have been like to be there in the past. In a way, I think that for historical documentary filmmakers, that's the way you animate the past. By creating, paradoxically, a present, which is the film that you're watching now, which is so aesthetically and psychologically and emotionally and intellectually engaging, ideally, that people say, "Right, that's the past. How amazing Coney Island was at the turn of the 20th century." But of course it's not the past. And that's the great poignancy of historical films. You're using the elements which history has handed down to us, or which we have created in the present, to stand in for those things.

The thing I've always found most difficult to describe about filmmaking, which I think is the most important thing, is that you must get people to believe in the existence of something other than what they're seeing on the screen. They have to believe that beyond that frame they're looking at—up above it, off to the left where they can't see, before the moment they're looking at, after the moment they're experiencing—there's something more. If you do that, which is, I find, very difficult to do, then what you see is that people are transfixed. They're not just looking at a shining screen. They believe that these are real people, real events, real moments, caught in a whole dynamic which is infinitely mysterious and dense and they're not sure where it's going but they sure as hell care about the outcome.

Which means you've engaged the viewers; they're active, not passive

Right. It's easy to tell people what a story *is*; it's very difficult to tell a story. When films simply tell you what the story is, they're basically two-dimensional maps rather than four-dimensional universes. Storytelling is "once upon a time." It's a ship that comes around a corner, and you can see it and you're somehow thrilled by it, caught in the "now" and a whole bunch of potential futures which haven't yet occurred. You're saying, "What's going to happen here?" When films tell stories, when they engage you in the process of a story, then they work.

In terms of the ethics of using archival material, are there guidelines as to what you will or won't do in your work?

I think there's kind of a contract which any film or filmmaker establishes with the viewer. And that is you, the viewer, trust me. I will always use the thing that's closest to the truth that I possibly can. Now, that may turn out to be not very close at all sometimes. The purity of the intention of the filmmaker is crucial. And the intention is double—the truth, but the intensity of its presentation as well. If you're on the Donner Party trail, which took place 150, 160 years ago, there were no cameras there. Therefore, if a shot of a wagon train—which is, in fact, a still shot from a film made by the Church of the Latter Day Saints in the 1940s— works and is not a lie, it's because a moment's reflection will tell people there were no shots of the Donner Party. So why do we believe it? Because we're being taken there by an assembly of story elements: verbal elements, facts, artifacts, quotes, interviews, shots that are plausibly, clearly, demonstrably, from the route.

I think that there's a way in which you can be absolutely faithful to the archival elements and ruin a story. There are historical documentary filmmakers who apparently believe that having the original photograph is all you need to bring somebody into the truth and to make the film powerful. That's nonsense. It may well be that the shadow of a hand of a live actor, at a certain moment, will bring you closer to the truth of Abraham Lincoln than all the Brady photographs in the world. Conversely, maybe it won't.

Maybe the reenactment will be terribly done. So it really has to do with the ingenuity of the filmmaker. Sometimes, you might actually choose to use an element that's less historically authentic, because it works better and is therefore a better thing to do. The essential purity of the intention of the filmmaker—to tell you the truth but to bring you intensely into the dynamic of the story—is being honored.

What about the underlying research?

Not only do you do book and archival research, but you always work closely with academic advisors. Tampering with the facts is absolutely inconceivable. It doesn't mean that you don't make a million mistakes, but you fact check and you change it. When filmmakers begin to play fast and loose with a fact, they begin to rupture the essential contract that they make with the audience. Even though the audience can't quite tell where or how or why, they may not have that knowledge, they swiftly and intuitively understand that somebody's bullshitting them. You need to feel the integrity of a film. It's solid. It's well-wrought. It's made of materials that seem apt. It's well balanced. We bring an enormous amount of expertise, we viewers of films, when we sit down and let the lights go low. And in that sense, viewers are the best critics of films.

How do you begin to think about visualizing a subject for which there is no photographic record?

[Photographer] Alfred Stieglitz formulated the idea that a photograph was not an objective representation of an outer external reality but was an equivalent of an inner state, an emotional state. And I think that film, being a sequence of images, is in a sense simply a more elaborate version of that. Sometimes a plethora of available archival visual imagery can make you think that that's what the movie is, and not pay as much attention to the fact that it's always about finding an equivalent. When you're obliged to invent the imagery, it in a sense focuses you on what your job should be anyway.

The great example of this is Custer and Crazy Horse. The most photographed American of the 19th century, except for Abraham

Lincoln, is George Armstrong Custer. And there's no photograph of Crazy Horse. I'm not convinced that it was easier to bring the emotional reality of George Armstrong Custer to life just because there were all those photographs. With Crazy Horse, you were obliged to go to landscape shots and modest recreations to find the psychological resonance. There was no easy way out.

Will you talk about the rhythms of editing, how you know when to fade to black for a moment, or when to let a sequence play?

The units of construction of films are scenes that have beginnings and middles and ends and their own rhythms and climaxes. In a story like *The Donner Party*, when you've had one climax, you need to fade out and have that moment of emotional pause and closure. Film is essentially musical, like any temporal art form. It's all about incremental progressive effect of all the events that make up the flow. Do you need a beat, will the flow become too relentless if there's not that pause? Do I need to receive the information I was receiving in that last scene at a slightly statelier pace, or do I need to speed it up? What you're trying to enhance, it seems to me, is the axis of clarity and the axis of emotion. Because the two are totally related. The clearer the event, the more powerful the emotional impact of it.

What I love about the final phases of making a film is when you can just feel everything is exactly right. Not that there couldn't have been something else which was also right, but that given what you've chosen to do, it's right. The language, for example—that there's no gap between articulation and understanding. That's what makes these scripts so mindbogglingly difficult. It's not the concepts or research that are the challenge, it's finding the articulation within the flow of this particular film. What are the words that are clear, in the simplest, best way for this moment in this film? I think of that line of Geoff's [writer Geoffrey C. Ward] from THE CIVIL WAR: "The spring rains had washed open the fresh graves from the year before." You're done. You could come across the same historical fact or moment and articulate it differently, and maybe that different way would be just as good in its own context. But you're done.

16

Jon Else

In addition to numerous filmmaking awards, including four Emmys and several Academy Award nominations, filmmaker Jon Else was honored with a five-year MacArthur Fellowship in 1988. Jon's films include *The Day after Trinity: J. Robert Oppenheimer and the Atomic Bomb, Yosemite: The Fate of Heaven,* CADILLAC DESERT, and *Sing Faster: The Stagehands' Ring Cycle*, winner of the 1999 Sundance Filmmakers Trophy. He was series producer for the first season of EYES ON THE PRIZE and a consulting series producer for the second season, and has served as cinematographer on hundreds of films.

Jon is head of the Center for New Documentary at the University of California, Berkeley's Graduate School of Journalism, a program created to explore "affordable and innovative" models of documentary film.

Is the common thread in documentary a need for story?

The common thread that we've overwhelmingly embraced for the last fifty years is story. We haven't figured out a way to do documentaries very successfully without stories. The adoption of the devices of *dramatic* film—that's a relatively new thing. If you go back and look at *Nanook of the North*, the story in *Nanook* would never fly at HBO today, or on public television. It clearly fulfills the need to have a central character, to have some forward motion. But it doesn't really come to any sort of resolution. And documentary, particularly television documentary as we know it, abhors ambiguity. Documentaries now, if executive producers are going to sign off on them, have to be resolved at the end, and they generally have to be redemptive, even though real life is often unresolved and unredemptive. That's something new.

Story, in the sense that I think we all bring to it from Western literature, from the theater, from a good novel and narrative films that in fact has served us extremely well. It's kept a lot of viewers from changing channels to watch a soap opera or *E.R.* But in a way, that's our deal with the devil, our Faustian bargain. I've spent a lot of my career trying to make real people in the real world behave like Lady Macbeth or Hamlet or Odysseus or King Lear. Trying to sort of force them to not be quite so messy and non-chronological in how they go about their struggles with life, and to try to make it fit a Shakespearean mold.

When I did the film *The Day after Trinity*, about J. Robert Oppenheimer and the building of the first atomic bomb, we had people on the production staff read *Hamlet*, and there was a lot of discussion around the big table as we were shooting and editing about the similarities between Oppenheimer and Hamlet. What we ended up doing, I think, was kind of bend whatever Oppenheimer's real-life character was so that it more closely approximated a tortured young Danish prince trying to figure out what to do. The same was true with Henry Ford [*A Job at Ford's*], in THE GREAT DEPRESSION series. There was a great, I think, unconscious effort on my part to make Henry Ford's reversal of fortune at the hands of his workers reflect King Lear's reversal of fortune at the hands of his daughters.

But isn't that a valid biographic device, as long as your work is also accurate? Print biographers do it.

Both films are structurally very successful, I think. But whether they're successful history or not—time will tell. Robert Oppenheimer and Henry Ford are an awful lot more complex and their lives are messier, in terms of their forward motion, than either *Hamlet* or *King Lear*. And the real problem in both of those films is that I attempted to make myself invisible, jumped through a lot of hoops to make the filmmaker invisible.

Even then, shouldn't viewers should realize that someone is telling the story?

But I believe very firmly that audiences take documentaries to be somehow truer than nearly everything else they see on television.

And that at the end of a film, when the lights come on or the commercial comes on, there are certain events that the audience believes happened in a certain order. The audience doesn't say, "Well, that's Jon Else's version of how the events in Henry Ford's life unfolded." People are going to take it to be the actual God-given way in which actual events happened. I try to get it right; there's nothing in either of these films that hasn't been fact checked to within an inch of its life. And that's why I feel comfortable putting out my version. There are other versions that also can be fact checked.

What I don't have patience with are stories that get put out there in which the filmmaker is too lazy to fact check it or the story is too good to be fact checked. To kind of let it go and then say, "I'm not a journalist, so it doesn't matter." I don't buy that.

As a director and director of photography, how much do you plan your storytelling in advance?

In approaching a film, I always try to find at least two stories that unfold simultaneously. One of them almost always is a very simple, straight-ahead, forward motion through time. For instance, in *Sing Faster*, the forward motion is just the simple story that is told in Wagner's *Ring Cycle* in the operas. It's this crazy soap opera about the gods fighting, a giant Aristotelian drama with characters and rising conflict and resolution and all that. And then parallel to that is the much less linear story of the stagehands preparing this production for opening night.

In CADILLAC DESERT, the same was true. In setting out to tell what, on the surface, were not enormously riveting tales of how canals and irrigation were developed in the West and how dams were built, I first looked for a narrative. Just a simple, forward-moving narrative that went through time and involved people in conflict. And it turns out that there was a lot of that, in Congress, that had an enormous affect on how we live in America today.

The second thing was to find some sort of a visual chronology, something visual on a grand scale. And it turned out that was fairly straightforward. The American West was at one time very, very dry. What we did was that we slowly, in the course of each hour, showed the water being re-engineered. Helicopter photography was extremely important in CADILLAC DESERT, in getting up above these landscapes to see how much they had been changed.

You really can't tell how much the plumbing system in the West has been turned on its head until you get up above and look down and see that the rivers and canals are running in the wrong direction. It's dry where it should be wet, and it's wet where it should be dry.

Do you ever storyboard your work? For example, the scene of the workers at Yosemite National Park, in Yosemite.

Never. What I do is I plan very carefully and work extremely hard to figure out, what is the concept behind this particular sequence that we're shooting? Why are we watching these people blowing up a boulder on a particular trail in Yosemite? What is this shot or sequence telling us within the developing narrative of this film, and what is this shot or sequence telling us about the world? Are we there with the trail crew and the dynamite because it's dangerous, and that's the drama? Are we there because all the dynamite in the world is not going to make a bit of difference in this giant range of mountains, that people are really insignificant here? Are we there because these people are underpaid and they're trying to unionize? You've really got to figure out what the concept of the sequence is, otherwise you just fire hose everything.

How would answering those questions change how you shoot the scene?

If the sequence is about man against nature and the futility of trying to tinker with these billions of tons of granite, it may be important to show that the boulder is either very large or very small. And you can choose to do that by how you place human beings in relation to the boulder, and in fact we did that with that particular boulder. The thing I remember about that particular scene is that it was to some extent about danger, that people were using dynamite to clear a trail so that hikers could enjoy their Sunday afternoon going up to the lake to catch some trout. I remember having a lot of communication with John Haptas, the sound guy, to make sure he was getting this grating and—to me—very scary sound of a pocketknife cutting through a stick of dynamite, because of the danger involved.

If that scene was also to some extent about the camaraderie between the members of the trail crew, all of whom had lived in these mountains together, in camp, for many months by that time, you try to do a lot of shots in which the physical relationship between people shows. You show people touching each other, looking at each other. They weren't trying to unionize, but if in fact we had been doing a sequence about the labor conditions for trail workers in Yosemite, we probably would have made it a point to shoot over the course of a long day, to show how long the day was, show them eating three meals on the trail, walking home really bone-tired exhausted.

There's a factory scene in the Henry Ford film about how rough it is to work in an automobile factory. And one of the devices is to have all of the talk between the workers made inaudible because the sound of the machinery is so loud. The same is true in the opening of Barbara Kopple's *Harlan County*, down in the mine. If the opening is about the danger of working down in the mines, the fact that the roar of these coal-boring machines drowns out all human speech is important. And you may not sit there in the theater and say, "Oh, I can't hear what the guy is saying," but I think it really sinks into your bones that this is an atmosphere in which you would not want to work and for which you would want to be paid adequately if you did work.

Basically, the more you're aware of what you want these images to convey, the richer the images are going to be. The danger is that we always have to be ready that the scene may be conveying something different from what we expected it to convey. Something may come flying out of left field and then you begin shooting differently. If a child had come wandering up that trail where the trail crew was, and we suddenly saw that it would be interesting to see this trail crew entirely from a child's perspective, I probably would have shot the whole thing on my knees from there, looking up at these people from the child's perspective.

So the shooting has a point of view.

Yes. In CADILLAC DESERT, we went on a tourist tour with a helicopter pilot who talks about celebrities' houses and about the casinos in the Las Vegas strip, and I made it a point to shoot all the aerials with a piece of the helicopter in the frame. I would shoot down through the bottom of the helicopter so that you could see the edge of the door; you knew you were actually inside a tourist vehicle, which is very different from other aerial shooting we did that was sort of a detached documentary gaze from the nose mount on a helicopter.

Now, it may be that you shoot a sequence and somewhere along the line you unearth some material in front of your camera or some research or a new angle that means that this stuff suddenly has a new meaning. That can be good or bad. It can be bad when the producers insist on bending it into the old meaning. I do a lot of camera work for other people, and I see an awful lot of sequences that I've shot end up on screen being pumped up to mean something which is really nothing to do with what they were at the time.

Why do you think this happens?

There's a lot of misunderstanding that tape is cheap and that it's a good idea with mini DV to shoot everything in sight and figure out later what it's about. That's one problem. The other problem is going out with a preconception, shooting a scene which doesn't match the preconception, and coming back into the editing room and trying to force it with narration, tricky cutting, or shooting bogus footage to add to it. We've gotten to the point where people's need to have things be dramatic and unambiguous often gets the better of them. I take a very firm view about documentary ethics in general, and I think that there's an alarming erosion. The great thing about low-cost video production is that it democratizes documentary. One of the downsides is that there's no oversight. And there's a danger that people's enthusiasm or rage or advocacy is going to get the better of them.

Do you write outlines and treatments before you shoot?

I do. Well—I do two kinds of films. I do films about things that have already happened, which are historical films. And films about things that are actually happening as we film. And you have to treat them differently.

The reason historical films are so popular with funders is that they know what they're going to get; they know what happened. And the same is true for planning the film. It's your job as a maker of historical films to spend whatever it takes, six months or a year, to figure out a way to write an engaging treatment that draws on every bit of research, to turn over every stone, find out who are the interesting characters, alive and dead, find out who are the good witnesses. I write very, very detailed treatments for historical films. All my historical films take place in the present, by the way, there's a huge present component to them.

On films about events which unfold as you film, it's nearly impossible to write a treatment; that's one of the reasons they're so hard to fund. What you can and must do is to write a document, a quasi-treatment that clearly lays out who the film is about and what the conceptual underpinning of the film is. If it's a film about a baseball team, are you there because you care about the mathematics of baseball, or do you care about the profit the owner makes? Do you care about the relationship between the players and fans? Are you there because there's a Japanese player on the team? Are you there because these players relate to the legacy of the Negro Leagues? Why are you there?

Then, whatever you write needs to lay out what might likely or possibly unfold as an order of events. It has to lay out pretty clearly who the characters are, what their relationship is to one another, and what's likely to change over the course of the time that you're going to be filming.

No matter how you do it there's a little bit of folly in doing it. Who could possibly have written a treatment for *Titicut Follies* or *High School* [Frederick Wiseman] or *Salesman* or *Gimme Shelter* [Albert Maysles, David Maysles, Charlotte Zwerin]? And the problem is simply the money, who's going to give you the money to go out and find out what's happening in the world? And what happens when you call your funder and say, "The film that you funded, which is about the Miners for Democracy movement, is now turning into a film about a group of miners in Harlan county?" I think the fact of the matter is that the vérité films that get made get funded almost solely on the reputation of the filmmaker or on the basis of a good sample tape.

So you expect students to write something up before they go out to shoot, even if there's a good chance the story will go off in an unexpected direction.

You bet. They'd have to write up what I just described, and I want them to go a little further and actually go out with some bomb-proof fallback plan, some plan where if everything goes wrong, there's some film they can come back with.

Do you shoot to the treatment?

I treat it sort of like the airplane evacuation instructions. When all hell's breaking loose and you're out on location and you're sick with malaria and half your crew has mutinied, you can glance at this treatment and figure out this fail-safe way of making the film. You hope that you'll find something vastly better, but the original treatment is a way of ensuring that you can get the film started on the screen, and most important, that you can figure out some sort of ending.

Do you work with an act structure?

I do, I try to always make it a point to have the rearrangement of time, the flashbacks and flash forwards, carefully worked out within that ever-advancing present tense in the film. That almost always gets changed in the editing, but at least going into it I have something that I know, if all else fails, I can use this model and it'll be at least a passable film that won't embarrass us all.

At what point do you know what you want your audience to get out of the film?

It's probably a mistake to begin a film without some notion of what the audience should feel and believe and understand at the end. Those are three different things. If you've chosen a complex and deep and robust subject, there are going to be things that emerge in the process of making the film that are going to change your notion, your idea of where you want the audience to be. You know, you spend 80% of your time on the first 10% and the last 10% of the film. The middle part's easy.

What about casting?

For better or for worse, casting is everything. We look for people who are—it's the "t-word"—telegenic. I used to describe it in much more charitable terms—we used to say, "Look for the good storyteller." In practical terms, most documentaries now require having two or three lead characters, and then sort of a second tier of the supporting players. You can look at dozens of documentaries, good ones, and that's the model that they use. It gets bent a little too often, particularly in historical films, in the direction of powerful leaders. The thing that's tough is to find the little people, but they're always there if you look hard enough. In CADILLAC DESERT, we tried to find people who worked on the dams, people who remembered the West as it was before the rivers were redirected.

In finding people to help tell a story, I'm always very direct about calling people who may have a different point of view on the story than me and encouraging them to be part of the film. Respecting what they have to say, putting it in the film. On the afternoon that we sealed up the deal on CADILLAC DESERT [based on the book by Marc Reisner], the first phone call I made was to Floyd Domeni, who is the dam builder from hell in Marc's book. He turned out to be a wonderful man who was more than happy to talk very forthrightly about what he did and why he did it. I make an attempt, in all my films, to either have the film be fair to everyone on all sides of an issue—and being fair doesn't necessarily mean giving everyone the same number of seconds on the screen—or to make it very clear that I'm doing a rant, that this film has a position, and not try to trick the audience into thinking that I have no stake in this.

But fairness is in the eye of the beholder. On CADILLAC DESERT, I thought that our story unfolded with enormous fairness, and it got a lot of people angry on both sides. Some environmentalists felt that we were too easy on the forces of development. There were a lot of big agricultural groups who thought we were way too tough on big agriculture. There were people in Los Angeles who thought we had disgraced the memory of William Mulholland. I disagree with them all. [But] it's okay if people don't like our films; it's not okay if we get it wrong, and it's factually inaccurate.

In your program at U.C. Berkeley, you try to identify the types of stories that lend themselves to lower-budget filmmaking (for more information, see http://journalism.berkeley.edu/program/courses/dv/cookbook.html).

In the system we're trying to develop at U.C., it's a mistake to first find a story and then figure out how to make it inexpensively. You have to figure out how much money you have to spend, and then figure out what story fits with that. It's the opposite of what we've been doing all our lives.

There are some straight-ahead litmus tests that you can apply. It's almost impossible to do inexpensive films which include archive material. You have to find stories that'll withstand moments of inelegant storytelling, that will not be destroyed by the loss of a particular character or location or action. You want to look for stories that can be done without travel. You want to look for stories that have a built-in narrative timeline, narrative arc.

Films don't go over budget because you paid a sound guy too much and put the crew in a hotel for an extra day. They go over budget because people waste two months of editorial time figuring out what the story is. If you're talking about doing inexpensive work, that's the single most important thing, finding a story that's not going to require that.

And it's probably cheaper to figure out the story before you shoot, not after.

It's much more cost-efficient to figure out the story beforehand. The downside of that is that you're never going to be able to make *Salesman* or *Soldier Girls* [Nick Broomfield, Joan Churchill] if you do that. And the fact is that it's very, very tough to do any kind of even vaguely cinéma vérité film—which really involves discovering the story—inexpensively.

A few other things. You want to do stories where you don't have to burn up a month getting any administrative access. You know, if you want to do a story about the history of Disneyland, that's a textbook example of something that's not going to be inexpensive no matter how you do it. If you want to do a story on the inside of a political campaign for a month with a PD150 [Sony miniDV camcorder], you probably can do that inexpensively. It's got a built-in story arc, two leading characters, somebody's going to win, somebody's going to lose. You've got rising action, rising tension.

You know, EYES ON THE PRIZE and THE CIVIL WAR and AFRICANS IN AMERICA and *The Farmer's Wife* and *Long Night's Journey into Day* and *Crumb*, those films are always going to cost at least a half million bucks [per hour], the going rate now for prime-time PBS or HBO.

What are some of the other challenges of making a quality film for less money?

I suspect then that the most important element and in some ways the most difficult element after that is how you break up time. How do you take the order in which real people have done real things in the real world, and how do you stretch and shrink different events to last more or less screen time? And how do you re-order them in a way that gives the greatest drama, without leading the audience to believe falsehoods, that certain things happened when they didn't?

The editorial process, which can stretch to months or in some cases years on documentary projects, that reordering of time, that's what burns up money. It's all about, first of all, finding the point at which you enter the story. I always try to begin documentaries in the present, with something going on now. And the mysterious art is then figuring out at what points do you flash back to reveal portions of the backstory, and at what point do flashbacks within flashbacks?

In real history, Harvey Milk and the man who eventually killed him, Dan White, were both elected in the same election at the same time. But Deborah Hoffman and Rob Epstein, in structuring *The Times of Harvey Milk*, carried the audience through the first third of the film, getting Harvey Milk elected to his seat on the San Francisco board of supervisors, with hardly a mention of Dan White. It's only after Harvey Milk has been elected that we then flash back to the same election and meet Dan White, and go through Dan White's ascent to power. And those two men will eventually meet and White assassinates Milk.

Yosemite: The Fate of Heaven tells two stories as well; the story of the park today and the pressure it's under from tourism, and the park as it was encountered by Lafayette Bunnell, on an Indian raid in 1854. *Yosemite*'s an interesting case because all of the footage on screen is in the present; it's a historical film which takes place entirely in the present. All of the narration is from an 1854 diary that I discovered about halfway through the pre-production period.

Did you excerpt and use passages in the order in which they were written?

The unfolding of events in the diary, the story of what Lafayette Bunnell and the Mariposa Battalion actually did—arriving at the valley, chasing Chief Tanaya and his tribe, and finally burning Chief Tanaya's village—those in fact are in the correct order. On the other hand, Lafayette Bunnell's ruminations about Yosemite and his transformation, his transcendental experience—those paragraphs are shuffled around pretty substantially. And I don't know; I teach in a school of journalism now and I take a much tougher view of all this than I did five years ago. I sometimes lie awake at night wondering if that was the right thing to do.

Isn't there a logic that these are his thoughts, which were likely ongoing?

Yes, I think that's true. But when the lights go on, we are responsible for what the audience believes to be true. And that includes not only what happened and what things looked like, but the order in which they happened, which is crucial to cause and effect.

Do you think that the standards for what is journalistically sound are changing?

Don't get me started. In public television, the voracious need for ratings that has developed over the last ten years, when Congress decided to abandon any substantial support for public television and public television ended up being dependent on ratings just like *Cheers*—what happened then was that an awful lot of public television executives embraced the idea that they had to make things as dramatic, as overly dramatic, as possible. It's an insult to the intelligence of Americans to think that you have to turn history and science into soap opera in order to get people to watch the show. But it's a direct result of politics; it's a direct result of the defunding of public television and the galloping dependence on corporate underwriting. That's advertising, and they want eyeballs for that.

Are there common structural problems that you encounter in your work with students?

The most common one is difficulty in finding where to enter the story. We find that almost all first-time filmmakers start their film at what later turns out not to have been the best place in the chronology. If they have five or six characters in their film, they'll start with a roll call of all the characters, sort of the film equivalent of having everybody stand up and introduce themselves. So you're five minutes into the film and the story hasn't begun because you're still meeting the people and seeing little vignettes about them, and it's often not very satisfying. If you're following some-one on a journey, it often makes sense to begin the story with the journey underway and *then* do the introduction of the characters and the backstory.

The second most common difficulty is a reluctance to give the audience enough basic information because students are very re-luctant to use narration of any sort. They've grown up exposed to nothing but bad narration and often have trouble imagining narration that's brilliant and artful. But words in a film can be wonderful or horrible, just like camerawork or sound or music or editing. Very often the films are pretty good, but you want to know a little more.

The third most common problem is the ending, getting a film to end. And that's the one we have the least success in solving.

Last question. You've talked about the role of documentaries in advancing public awareness of issues and events. Can you explain?

I'll limit myself to discussion of documentary as something that's important in civic dialogue, in the national conversation. The role of documentary is to provide the American public with a basis for conversation, a basic and accurate understanding of what the issues are and what the basic facts are. Documentary in fact does have a secret life among policy makers. President Clinton was famous for always watching lots of documentaries in the course of briefing himself for a particular issue. When he went to China, he watched several public television documentaries including *Gate of*

Heavenly Peace [Richard Gordon, Carma Hinton]. When there were debates about tobacco subsidies, he watched *Tobacco Blues* [Christine Fugate, Eren McGinnis]. When there were debates about farm subsidies, he watched *The Farmer's Wife* [David Sutherland]. I found out years later that there was a screening of the Yosemite film in a Senate caucus room for seven senators, even before it was released on PBS. CADILLAC DESERT had a screening on Capitol Hill in a Senate caucus room with about 100 people in attendance from the White House, OMB, the Congress, the Senate, the Department of the Interior.

If you go to the sixth grade in California, you have to watch CADILLAC DESERT. Now, there's no question that public television is also hugely important, simply because of its large but diminishing reach. CADILLAC DESERT was seen by about nine million people on the night it was broadcast. The book only sold 50,000 copies. By the time the sun sets on my life, the series will probably have been seen by 50-70 million people around the world. Fine with me.

17

Susan Froemke

Susan Froemke, chief administrator and principal filmmaker at Maysles Films in New York, has been with the company since she joined Albert Maysles and his late brother, David, on the production of *Grey Gardens* (1976). In the years since, she has made more than 20 nonfiction films, including the Academy Award-nominated *Lalee's Kin: The Legacy of Cotton*, a look at poverty and education in the Mississippi Delta, and the Grammy Award-winning *Recording* The Producers: *A Musical Romp with Mel Brooks*, a PBS film about the making of the Broadway hit's cast album.

I've heard direct cinema described as "the drama of life—without scripts, sets, interviews, or narration." Many people think this means you just go outside and start filming.

Right. But that's not at all what happens. It's one thing if we're recording an event, and the client wants us to be somewhere at a certain time and we show up with our cameras. And as you start recording that event, you see, "Wow, this could be a really interesting film; there's more than just this Rolling Stones concert that I'm filming [*Gimme Shelter*], or there's more than just these meetings with the Gettys [*Concert of Wills: Making the Getty Center*]." Pretty soon, you have to start thinking as a filmmaker and ask yourself, What story are you telling? What direction is your subject taking you in, and is that something that's going to make a good film?

What about films that begin as a general topic or idea, such as Lalee's Kin?

The genesis of *Lalee's Kin* was HBO calling me up saying, "We'd like you to take a look at poverty at the end of the millennium." So how do you start to find a story? We researched and researched. We had to become educated about the current issues of poverty. We wanted an answer to the question, "Why is there so much poverty in this rich country?" This was 1997; the welfare reform bill had just been passed. Initially, it seemed that the obvious story line was to follow three welfare mothers and see how the changes in the welfare laws were affecting their lives. But as I researched the topic more—and it wasn't just me, I had two smart assistants on staff here—I realized that I wanted to look more at the systemic causes of poverty.

Through talking to a lot of academics and policy makers, including Senator Paul Wellstone, we identified the systemic causes of poverty as illiteracy, illegitimacy, and racism. Larry Brown, who had written the book, *Hungry in America*, told us, "If you're doing a film about poverty, you've got to be in the Mississippi Delta." He said, "There's this one school superintendent that you've got to meet, Reggie Barnes." And when I called Reggie Barnes, I got that intuitive feeling over the phone that this is my subject. Reggie said, "If you can educate the child of illiterate parents, you can stop the cycle of poverty." And that struck home. It's a simple statement but it's a powerful statement; let's investigate this. I went down to the Delta and met Reggie, who had a Herculean task ahead of him, getting an impoverished school system off academic probation. This was a real narrative, the first I'd found after searching in four different states for almost six months.

So you have the genesis of a story, what then?

At Maysles, we say that casting is everything. We choose to call it "researching," because people think that casting means actors, like a Hollywood film. But we do have to find our subjects, they don't just fall in your lap. Once we found Reggie, we needed to find a family whose lives were going to intersect with the school superintendent's story, so you could see how difficult it is to try to stop this cycle of poverty that's been passed down for generations. Since this is the Mississippi Delta, we couldn't find any production personnel who could help us cast, so I asked Jim O'Neill, who was affiliated with the Delta Blues Museum in Clarksdale, to drive me around the cotton fields.

When we drove through Lalee's neighborhood, I saw her family pulling down a house, an old wooden structure next to an old trailer she was living in. We stopped and watched, and Lalee soon invited me inside. We sat down at the kitchen table, and she just talked. And I thought, "This is the dream subject." Because I could say one or two words, and she would start to pontificate. Also the fact that she was giving me access to her house, the first time I met her, is exactly what you need when you're doing vérité. It's all about access and getting the trust of your subject. I think Lalee started trusting us very early on in the shoot. And she'd never seen a documentary in her life, so it's not like I could say to her, "Just let us film your life, and if you don't like something that we're filming, you can always tell me."

We also loved Lalee's children; they just charmed us. That was another reason why Lalee was cast. Main and Redman were the first two kids that we met. Redman was so curious and adorable, and Main, although somewhat withdrawn, really opened up around us. And it was after the second time we filmed that we met Granny [another child]. Right away I thought that Granny was a fascinating character and had a lot of potential as a main or secondary story line.

You filmed Lalee's Kin *over a period of time, traveling from New York City to Mississippi periodically to shoot. What would motivate a trip?*

We went down to film Lalee soon after I met her because she was getting a new trailer [from the government]. And it's really a metaphor for poverty. Lalee's so excited that this new house is going to arrive, she's full of hope and expectations, and when she finally gets it she realizes it's this rat-infested dump. It was a year before she could get a stove, a refrigerator that worked, and electricity. I mean these are gargantuan efforts for a family to overcome. And you see her crushed, which is what we experienced filming this very poor population. They couldn't have hope for long. But they had this resilient spirit; they would say at the end, "Well, I thank the Lord for whatever I've gotten."

The story kept changing every time we went down there. It was really hard to track. We would go down for events, like the arrival of the new trailer or the beginning of a school year. We went down on Granny's birthday, which also happened to coincide with the school announcing that it was going off probation. We would always check in with Lalee and Reggie, especially with Lalee, and get a lot of textural things. And oddly enough, a lot of things would happen on birthdays or Mother's Day, I guess because a lot of people would come into the household. On Mother's Day, she found out that Eddie Reed, her son, was in jail.

We would often go down thinking we were going to film one thing and something totally different would happen; a whole new chapter would unfold. And I just would not worry about it. Your subjects, in many ways, are directing the film. You follow the directions their lives take; it's always much more interesting. Even the minutia of daily life fascinates me, like when Lalee is teaching Granny how to cook. It tells so much, that there's no meat in the house, and what Lalee ends up cooking with is bologna.

As a direct cinema filmmaker, a style that's observational or "fly on the wall," how do you approach issues of storytelling?

We're trying to make scenes, because we're trying to make nonfiction films. I never think that we're making a documentary. I think that we're making a film, just like a feature film director makes a film. I've got to get cutaways, I've got to get an end point of the scene, and I've got to get into the scene some way. Usually you're going to miss the beginning of the scene, unless it's total serendipity and something unfolded while you were filming. Often you're sitting waiting and something happens and you just miss that first line. You've got to get it some way.

For instance, the scene at the end of the film where Lalee breaks down. We went into the trailer and Lalee was incredibly upset. She's talking to her daughter. And so Al [Maysles] and I just started filming because we could see that something had happened, something very emotional was going on. As I started to understand—a neighbor had come to tell her that Eddie Reed had been taken back to jail—I knew that I didn't have a beginning to the scene. I had to get a beginning, but I didn't want to just ask Lalee, "What's going on?" I don't like to do that, to cut to an interview to explain what's going on in this beautiful emotional scene, and we're not going to be using narration, so I have to figure out how to nudge Lalee to give me an opening line.

That's, to me, a real skill that you develop after you've shot a lot of vérité and you know what you need to bring back to the editing room for the editor to be able to craft a scene together to tell a story. Lalee didn't know what Eddie Reed had been taken to jail for. So what I did is, I asked Jeanette, Lalee's daughter, "Why don't you call the police, to find out?" As soon as I said that, Lalee said to Jeannette, "Why don't you call the police?" That allowed Jeanette to talk with them and then tell Lalee [as we were filming] what had happened. So that we did have a beginning to the story.

So you're working on several levels—as the technician recording sound, the producer worrying about Lalee, and the storyteller watching for a scene's beginning, middle, and end.

Completely. I feel like that's something I learned very much from being able to watch David Maysles work. When David and Al were shooting *Grey Gardens*, there was no one in the house but the two of them. But I worked on the editing, and so I saw how David talked to the subjects, and I'd seen it on other projects, too, where David would get certain information out of a subject. And so I know you have to do that. You're like a psychiatrist, you say things like, "How did that make you feel?" When Lalee was telling about the death of her son George, that was a situation where she was so emotional, it was very hard not to intervene and comfort her. But being sympathetic and hardly saying anything keeps the scene going to where you feel like you have an ending. And to me the ending was where she said, "You want to love your children but don't love them too hard," which is a really amazing line.

What other storytelling issues do you face?

I'm always trying to figure out how to tell the backstory. Often over the course of shooting I'll just throw out a question: "What about your mother?" Or, "What about Redman?" Especially if there's someone else around and some comment about the past goes into a discussion about the present. You throw out a thought and let the subjects bounce that around and see where it goes. That's how the "school or jail" scene started, with me just chitchatting. Lalee talks about how she started caring for Redman, and then she says, to Redman, "You know, you're gonna have to go to school or you've got to go to jail." And Redman says, "I want to go jail." And so the scene offers a way to explore one of the film's themes; that these little boys are being programmed to jail.

I don't think it pays off to try to manipulate in vérité; it doesn't ring true. We would never ask anyone to do anything other than, for instance, I noticed that Lalee didn't have any water. She was always pouring water out of a Clorox bottle to wash her dishes and things like that. She'd go to the jail and get it out of a hose that was attached to the building. And so one trip when we were down there, not much was going on, I said, "Well, are you going to go get water today?" Because I knew I wanted to get that scene of them hauling water. But that's something Lalee's family does all the time anyway.

How much footage did you end up shooting?

I think the ratio was 70:1 [70 hours for each hour of the final edited film]. But that's 16mm. I think *Grey Gardens* was about the same. *Grey Gardens* was shot over six intensive weeks and I think it was about 36 to 40 shoot days. *Lalee's Kin* was about 42 shoot days.

It's funny, because when we were at Sundance with *Lalee's Kin* [Al Maysles won the 2001 Excellence in Cinematography Award for the film], there were other filmmakers who would tell me they had 400 hours or 300 hours or something. You should be making choices. That's what filmmaking is all about, making choices in the field. What a handicap going into the editing room with that much material. Because to me you really have to explore your footage.

Tell me about editing Lalee's Kin.

We started editing about a year and a half into the shooting. Our approach to editing is that you screen everything and then you make selects. These films are not easy to structure. We screen all the footage, and then we talk about what we think is strong. The content dictates the form, the way we approach it. What you originally think might be the story, you realize you might have a much stronger story but it's going to be harder to craft. And so there's a lot of experimentation and restructuring and recutting.

Do you use an act structure?

We often call it Act One, Act Two, Act Three. We'll say, when we're screening, "This is Act One information"—it's setting up the situation. We don't yet know where it's going to appear in Act One, but we put it in that section. And then Act Two and Act Three.

Act Two is always the hardest in vérité, it's the hardest part of the film not to sag. You've got to get a few of your feisty scenes into Act Two. Reggie with the pep rally, where you see Reggie's passion, really held up the middle of the film and kept the story going, which is so important. In vérité you don't often have a lot of scenes that tell the story, you have to be very careful how you place them.

Were you still shooting when you started editing?

Ideally, it's better to start editing once you have shot. We usually try to cut the end of the film, the climax, so we know what we're building to. We want to have some kind of a dramatic arc, whether it's a story line arc or an emotional arc of some sort. Some realization that the character has, or some understanding about life, something like that. But with *Lalee's Kin* we hadn't finished shooting, so we just started cutting scenes. Let's say that there are 10 moments, or maybe 20, that we think really could make great scenes, so we cut those together. And then we do a very rough assembly, like four hours long. And you see how the scenes play against each other.

At this point, a scene could go in many different directions. Sometimes you have two or three points in a scene; often you try to assign a value to the scene. For example, "This scene is going to tell Lalee's backstory, her family upbringing." Or, "This scene is going to explain what Reggie's dilemma is." Or, "This scene, you're going to understand Granny's despair." One scene may stand for something for a two-month period, and then you completely re-edit it to stand for something else.

That's why we give our editors director's credit because they work very closely with us in structuring the film and giving the film a beginning, middle, and end. We do the selects and then the scenes, and once we cut the scenes, we start to put them in an assembly. Right away you start to see which story lines are working and which ones are weak. And you keep editing down, you keep sculpting, down and down. The hardest part for us has always been the opening. Trying to set the scene and introduce a lot of characters.

In general, direct cinema expects viewers to work a bit to follow a story, to figure out the players and themes.

Charlotte Zwerin—a phenomenal filmmaker to have learned from—said to me early on, "I don't see what's wrong with making people work a few minutes in the beginning of a film." And I think we all feel that way. I think it's different when you're cutting just for television. In a theater no one's going to get up and leave; they've committed 2 hours or 90 minutes, part of their day, to going through this experience and they're ready to sink into a story. Television's a lot different; you'd better grab them right away. It's a different way that you start to edit.

How do you keep track of the material as you're editing?

I think most filmmakers use 3x5 cards. You write the topic of the scene and one or two points of what the scene's going to accomplish, and you have a bulletin board and keep rearranging these cards About 10 years ago, [editor] Deborah Dickson and I started taking notes and putting them into the computer. It's much easier to look at your structure on paper and quickly see, for example, I've got a lot of Lalee, good Reggie, now I've got to weave in the kids. You can see what you're missing.

What kind of editing schedule do you follow?

We *Lalee's Kin* edited in a little less than two years. *Grey Gardens* [a portrait of Edie Beale and her mother, Edith Bouvier Beale, reclusive relatives of Jacqueline Kennedy Onassis] took two and a half years; it took a whole year just to figure out what you had in the footage and what story line you were going to go for. Nothing happens in that house in *Grey Gardens*. So how do you structure a film about it? It took a long time to figure out that there was a balance of power between Little and Big Edie.

Vérité is a time-consuming process.

I think you get a much richer, more layered, more complex film in the end. You have to see where your subject is taking you. You've got a kernel of an idea and an intuitive feeling that this is going to lead you somewhere really interesting, but you have to have nerves of steel while you're making it. A lot of stuff doesn't happen the way you thought it was going to happen or in a timely manner. This is where the faith and the experience of making these films comes in, where you just know that life is going to reward you in some way. Sometimes you can get really lucky with a subject, like *Gimme Shelter*. The Maysles got an assignment to film a Rolling Stones concert at Madison Square Garden, one concert. And then they asked the Stones if they could, on their—the Maysles'—own money, follow them on tour, and then the Altamont concert happened.

In *Lalee's Kin*, when the school district got off probation, Reggie's story, you could have stopped the film there. But Lalee's story . . . We thought one of the most revealing moments was when Lalee said, "I don't know much about love." It's really an amazing thing to hear a woman say; she's never really experienced romantic love. But you realize that she does love her children very much. She doesn't show it so much, but deep down she loves these children, and she especially loves her son. You see her devastation when her son is going to go to the penitentiary, probably for life. And that's when Lalee breaks down. But then she raises up again and it's her "keep on keeping on." When Al and I walked out of the trailer after we'd filmed that, we looked at each other and said, "We have an ending." And Deborah Dickson felt the same way.

Let's move on to Recording The Producers, *which you filmed as Broadway stars Nathan Lane, Matthew Broderick, and of course Mel Brooks made the cast album for* The Producers. *How was that film to make?*

That was all about gaining the trust of these celebrities. They have to do this very difficult recording of a cast album in one day, because of the union rules, and here's this film crew that I think everybody thought, "This is going to really prevent us from getting it done." Mel Brooks was very skeptical at first. He even said to me, "I hate cinéma vérité."

But Nathan Lane was a big fan of D.A. Pennebaker's film, *The Company*, and so Nathan right away was very willing to wear a mike, and then Matthew Broderick came right on board. And what surprised us—and that's what's great about doing this because you never know what you're going to get, it's always a sense of discovery that's so exciting—is that they were very close, and big fans of each other, and they were very funny together. Nathan kind of interviewed Matthew, and Matthew played the role of Marlon Brando, and it's just this wonderful kind of vérité moment that you would never have anticipated. Talk about holding up the middle! It gives you a whole new insight into who these men are and how clever and bright and fast on their feet they are, in terms of humor.

Mel didn't want to be miked, but he was sitting next to [director/choreographer] Susan Stroman and she was miked, and so I could hear him. And as he could see that we weren't interfering, he said, "Look at this film crew, they have so much patience." We started at 7 in the morning. I would say by 2 in the afternoon, he started to relax with us being there. There was a lot of chitchat going on, it was an off moment, they weren't recording, so I just threw out, "Mel, I'm curious, was there really a Max Bialystock?" And Mel just lit up and told us this great story. I mean he's a showman, obviously, and it was a wonderful story, and we all laughed, and then he came up to me afterwards and said, "You know, I think this is going to be okay." And I said, "But you know Mel, we *are* going to need an interview." And he said, "Oh, I don't know."

It wasn't until 7 at night that he agreed to be interviewed, and then he basically did a stand-up monologue. As soon as I got that I said, "I've got a film, and I've got a great film." And afterwards, he was willing to sit and talk to us, and it was very heartfelt, and we got another layer that way. And then it was just a joy in the editing room; we edited that film quickly. It was wonderful material.

What kind of gear and crew did you need?

When you only have one day to shoot, there's a lot of pressure on you as the director to make sure you're getting everything. We could have used four cameras, but we only had the budget for three—two in the recording studio and one in the control room. I used the most experienced vérité cameramen, I think, in existence: Bob Richman, who grew out of Maysles; Don Lenzer, who's done years of work with us; and Tom Hurwitz. You had to go in with people who are also filmmakers in their own right because you couldn't be everywhere at once and there was almost no way to have a communication system because it would interfere with the recording process.

Last question. How has your work been affected by the emergence of digital video?

It's been hard for me to get used to the rhythm of shooting in video. I grew up in 16mm. I like the fact that you have to change film [magazines] every 10.5 minutes because it makes you really think about what you're shooting and what you're getting and what you need to get. A half an hour [a video cassette length] goes fast—when you're shooting it's all very intense—and then I think, why did I keep shooting?

In terms of editing, it has made a tremendous difference. With *Lalee's Kin* [which was shot on film and edited on video], we did selects and digitized selects. I don't really understand how we ever edited without the Avid, to some degree, even though I miss being able just to get on a Steenbeck and look at footage—not selects, dailies. But all the different versions you do in the [nonlinear] editing room, I mean, you can work it out so much quicker.

Still, you've got to have time to think about what's really the best story to tell with your footage. Any team in the editing room is going to tell a different story. You could have cut *Lalee* in a variety of ways. You could have cut *Grey Gardens* differently as well. You've got to think about what you're doing, and you need time to process the material. To me, that's never going to change. Telling a story is telling a story, and it's not always easy—especially in vérité—to see what structure is going to be best; there's a lot of working with material that's required. I've been in editing rooms where the editor gets a call from a cable station, "We're hoping you're available, we've got one month to make this hour-long film." And we're always just stunned. The truth is that *Lalee's Kin*, whether you're shooting in video or film, was going to be big budget. You needed the time in the editing room. You needed to pay a good editor. You needed to be going on many trips into the Delta to shoot. Those are expensive. And you can't run a film company on these tiny video budgets, either.

18

Jeanne Jordan and Steven Ascher

Jeannie Jordan co-produced and directed *Running With Jesse* for the PBS series FRONTLINE, and her documentary editing credits include two films for the acclaimed PBS series EYES ON THE PRIZE. Jordan has also edited several dramatic films, including *Blue Diner*, *Lemon Sky*, and *Concealed Enemies*. Steve Ascher recently updated *The Filmmaker's Handbook*, a best-selling text that he co-authored with Ed Pincus. His work has appeared on NBC, HBO, PBS, and the BBC; his films include *Del and Alex* and *Life and Other Anxieties*.

Together, this husband-and-wife team produced, directed, and wrote *Troublesome Creek: A Midwestern*, the story of the Jordan family's struggle to save their Iowa farm. Steve was also the principal cinematographer; Jeannie edited. *Troublesome Creek* won the Grand Jury Prize and Audience Award at the 1996 Sundance Film Festival and was nominated for an Academy Award.

The filmmakers are now working on a film about the Heywood brothers, Stephen and Jamie. After Stephen Heywood, a builder, was diagnosed with Lou Gehrig's disease (ALS) (which claimed the life of Jeannie's mother shortly before *Troublesome Creek* was completed), his brother Jamie created the ALS Therapy Foundation in order to expedite the search for treatment or a cure.

I spoke with the filmmakers separately for this interview.

You began Troublesome Creek *in the spring of 1990, after a receiving a phone call from Jeannie's father Russ. Can you tell me about that?*

STEVE: Russ called and said he thought this would be his last year of farming. If we were going to call ourselves filmmakers and not make a film about this, there was something wrong. To be able to do a story like this, to have that kind of access—I thought of it as both an opportunity to tell this story and also for Jeannie to be able to tell some of the wonderful stories she'd been just telling around the dinner table for years about growing up in Iowa.

He felt that he'd have one more year of planting and harvest followed by an auction. [The Jordans' plan was to auction off their livestock, equipment, and personal belongings in order to pay off their debts and keep the land itself, 450 acres.] That gave us the possibility of a narrative spine. It would have been much harder if not impossible to just make a film about day-to-day life on the farm, and be able to get into the kinds of issues that we did. We filmed four times over the course of about a year and a half.

How did you plan for the visual storytelling? Did you write up outlines, a treatment?

STEVE: We had to write up various things in order to raise money, but they were never really part of our thinking. With stories like this, in part you're following events and the events dictate what you're filming. But you have in your mind certain themes that you're interested in. In this case, the year on the farm, which included all the tasks that had to be accomplished—planting, harvesting, preparing for the auction, the auction. Then there are themes about Russ and Mary Jane, their marriage and their raising of children; there were themes about Jeannie's childhood; and themes about the changing landscape all over the Midwest, all over rural America. You're kind of advancing all of these fronts together, and you shoot things that can work toward them.

At the start of the film, there's a sequence in which a cat jumps from the roof of a barn into the arms of Jeannie's brother, Jon. It serves as a metaphor; as Jeannie says in voice-over, "my family in a nutshell— incredible luck, incredible timing, and teetering on the brink of disaster." It's certainly not a metaphor you could have planned.

STEVE: That's a real tribute to editing. We had been filming for over a week, on the first shoot, and nothing had happened. We filmed mostly just goings-on at the farm. A cow had died, and we were doing a stakeout, waiting for the rendering truck to pick it up. Just waiting, for hours. And then we heard people shouting, and there was this cat on the roof. At the time we were just incredibly depressed. If the big event is a cat on the roof, we're really in trouble.

JEANNIE: Plus, when the cat jumped, we were moving the camera. I saw the cat jump, and Steve got the end of the cat jumping. But we didn't get the cat jumping. So it was a disaster. We filmed the wrong thing and we didn't get the climax of it. But in *Troublesome Creek*, I cut every inch that we shot. So I just went at that. I thought, I'm going to see if I can find a way to make "missing the cat" work. I know we have "after missing the cat," and I know we have "before jumping," so let me just cut it and look at it. And I realized that missing it was part of the story and the metaphor, and that the metaphor was unbelievable. The fact that Jon would even walk up there and say, "Come jump into my arms, little kitty," was absolutely a thing about my family that's always driven me nuts. Totally unrealistic, and it worked.

Once I got it cut and realized it was a metaphor, I also realized that if this were the first thing you really saw in the body of the film, it would set you up to be ready for anything. I knew—because we'd been trying to raise money for the film for years at that point—that people had the most prosaic, small-minded reaction to what farming is or what people who farm are and that I had to fight that.

STEVE: The problem with doing a film like this is as soon as people hear the words *farm* or *farm documentary*, their eyes glaze over. They assume it's going to be a sentimental film or something very earnest and probably depressing. A distributor told us that we were dealing with a "double D" here, documentary and depressing, which equals death at the box office. So we were really anxious to make it clear that this was going to be a different kind of film. Our hope was that the film would resonate with universal themes in a way that it would rise out of its literal self as a "farm documentary" and become something that's about the passing of time, and about a marriage, and about the history of America. At times we referred to *Troublesome Creek* as a nonfiction drama, in the sense that it has a dramatic arc and feels very much like a movie.

You shot only 27 hours of film footage, in 16mm, for a program that runs about 88 minutes. That's very conservative.

STEVE: That was mostly imposed by budgetary problems. Every time we'd get out there, we'd budget a certain amount to shoot, and invariably we would have shot that amount halfway through the time. And then we'd have these agonizing meetings up in the bedroom trying to decide how much more stock we could order, which we knew we couldn't afford to process. Most of the footage of the film we never saw for about a year. [It was stored in the freezer at their home in Massachusetts until they could process it.] The joke was that instead of having dailies, we had yearlies.

Would you shoot it in video today?

STEVE: Probably we would, but at the time we felt strongly that the landscape of Iowa and the texture of the farm would only come across in film. The beauty of the landscape, the feel of the animals, and the smells and the corn in the summer—all of those things are an important part of why farmers do what they do, because it's such a tough life. That had to come across, mixing the financial tension and strain with the rewards of being a farmer; it played into the structure of the story. So we made sure that the seasons were very much a part of the film. Ultimately, we blew the film up to 35 mm. There's no comparison between the beauty of the 35 mm image even to 16 mm projection.

But by the same token, there were a number of scenes that we missed or gave short shrift to because we were so limited in the amount of film we could shoot. In a typical evening, we might shoot a roll or a roll and a half of film. That's 10 minutes or 15 minutes of material, which is hundreds of dollars. If you were to do it in video, you would feel remiss if you hadn't shot at least two or three tapes at an hour apiece, just because it's so much easier. In video, you have to have a reason to turn off, as opposed to with film, where you really have to think before you pull the trigger.

You filmed the Jordan family during an extraordinarily difficult time. Were you ever concerned that the filmmaking would add to their burden?

JEANNIE: I have a very political family. The farm situation, the farm question was something I was raised dealing with, a really viable big political issue in this country. So trying to capture what it was that we felt was so tragic and shortsighted about it, through what was happening to us, I knew they'd all be behind that. I also knew I wasn't going to betray them in any way. I wasn't going to show anything that they didn't want me to show or say anything that was a breach of their privacy.

The only time that I felt bad was when we asked my parents to go to Rolfe, where I grew up. [The filmmakers bring the Jordans to a farm they'd rented for several years before taking over the family property.] I knew that the house had fallen apart, and they didn't. It was very painful for them. They were blue, as my mother would call it, for a couple of days afterwards. And my father was angry at the guy who owned the land. So when we edited it in, I asked them if they didn't want that there. My mother wasn't talking by that time [because of her illness], but she agreed with what my dad said, which was, "If you don't see what eventually will happen, you don't understand what you're talking about. You can say farmers go out of business and farms go away. How do they go away? They fall apart. They tear them down." And he said, "You have to show something like that; this is as good as anything else."

STEVE: They never asked us to stop filming. We're very careful even with subjects that we've been filming for years, we still feel very hesitant about what we film and when we're being intrusive. In Jeannie's family the most you would get might be a look of, "Why are you filming this?" or as we approached the time of the auction, one of the reasons that Jeannie becomes more of a character on screen is that her sisters were saying, "You don't think you're going to be able to just film this without helping, do you? You're not going to get off that easy." So Jeannie had to participate more in preparing for the auction, and during those times I filmed single-handedly.

Some of the best scenes [just happened], such as the scene prior to the auction in which Russ and Mary Jane are talking about whether this woman from the bank is going to come to the auction. And she's defending her friend and Russ is saying, "Well, she's perfectly nice, but she is from the bank and she will be looking at this thing from the bank's perspective." That was breakfast; that wasn't a film scene. I just kept the camera on the floor and kept a mic clipped on a coffee cup; it started to get interesting and so I started shooting. You don't feel like it's a scene about being filmed, you feel like you're sitting at the breakfast table with us.

The idea that you can respect the privacy of your subjects and still present an honest story might surprise some filmmakers. Do your students ever ask about that?

JEANNIE: It's not so much that they ask about it as that I tell them. A lot of students do personal films; that's kind of what all of our first instincts are. Lots of times they'll have crossed the line. A young filmmaker I know did a film about her mother dying of cancer, and it was very raw. Her mother was a very beautiful woman who, when she knew she was being filmed, would get really done up, as much as she could. But sometimes her daughter would walk in the room filming, and her mother wouldn't be prepared for it, and she'd complain a bit. One of the things I said to the filmmaker after I looked at one cut is, "I want you to look at this through your mom's eyes. And I want you to look for moments where she looks good. As much as you can tell the story with those, I think that it will still work and you don't have to embarrass her. You don't have to make her feel like, "Oh, I look so horrible." Her mother probably wasn't going to see this film, but still, it's trying to instill that kind of respect. We all have a natural instinct to protect, but I think that a lot of students, when they're young, think that means you're not being honest; that you have to show something bad or raw to tell a good story.

The stories in Troublesome Creek—*both the overall story of the Jordan farm and the individual stories that Jeannie tells, such as "Daddy Date Night," in which she recounts nervously preparing for one-on-one time with her father, even writing out talking points on her hand— manage to be both very personal and universal.*

STEVE: When I think of the universals that mean the most to me in the film, they're about time and family connections and the passing of history, a history that means so much now but will be completely gone in a certain number of years. You're looking for true moments. Part of it involves giving the audience room to think and images that are suggestive of those themes. The drive from the house to town, the shot is out the back, facing backward, and you're seeing this beautiful plume of dust that was kicked up, backlit by the sun. And I remember shooting it, hanging out the car door, and thinking it was beautiful, but it's also clearly a visual metaphor for leaving the past behind. And it's while Jeannie's narrating this wonderful Daddy Date Night story.

As their daughter, are you revealing information to your parents, through this film, for the first time?

JEANNIE: Yes, absolutely. Mother knew that I was scornful of her Pollyannaish view of the world, as in the scene of me giving her shit because she thought that Charlotte at the bank was her best friend. But Daddy, we were all scared of him when we were little. We aren't anymore; he's mellowed incredibly. But he was moody, he was worried, and he was just a formidable guy. He was also 6-foot 4 and has those eyebrows. So in doing the film, the one thing I could not do is depict our childhood without some hint of that.

So there were two places in the film: Daddy Date Night, and the Bergman reference. ["Russ came to the idea of optimism late in life," Jeannie says in narration. "The Russ I knew growing up could give a Bergman film a run for its money in the Moody Darkness Department."] But if you say something good right afterwards, which is, "He's completely turned around and is the optimist of the family," he comes away from it thinking, "I'm the optimist." But he noticed the other. He didn't say anything to me about it until about two years ago. We were visiting Steve's mom and stepfather. We were sitting on the porch on Martha's Vineyard, and my dad said, "Bergman." I said, "He's this Swedish filmmaker, makes really, really, depressing films, but really good films." And he said, "When you were little, did you think I was like that?" And I said, "You *were* like that Daddy, I didn't *think* you were like that." And he said, "Did you really write things on your hand?" And I said, "Of course I did, I didn't make that up"—how could you make that up? Then we had a really interesting talk. One of the things I asked him was, "Did that hurt your feelings?" And he said, "No, because everybody seems to like me anyway, who saw the film."

Tell me about the westerns that we see the Jordans watching throughout Troublesome Creek.

JEANNIE: The first time we were there to shoot, it was like, they're going to watch TV every night. They're not going to talk about anything. This is a disaster. And then part of us started realizing, wait a minute, what they're watching, by and large, are westerns. We decided we could use that as a metaphor.

STEVE: Russ loved westerns and watched them whenever possible, and the whole issue of his struggle with the bank is informed by cliché storytelling notions of good guys and bad guys, cowboys and farmers, and making a stand against your enemy. We were trying to show that the reality is more complex than that, but that in certain ways those stories really did inform Russ's approach to the bank and the battle that he was engaged in with them. For example, *Lonesome Dove* was on the night before the cattle auction. And it felt like some incredible piece of serendipity or fate that this story about the end of the West would be on the night that Russ was about to shed the cowboy part of himself. When you're a farmer with animals, you're partly a plant-grower and you're partly an animal-wrangler. And this was going to be the end of his wrangling days.

The film's first-person narration, in Jeannie's voice, carries viewers through farm policy and family history with a light and often humorous touch. Did you always know the film would be narrated?

STEVE: Jeannie thought that hopefully the film could stand on its own without narration. I think I always had it in the back of my mind that it would need a narration. In the end, the narration is a very important part of moving the story along and giving you access to layers of knowledge and storytelling that go into the past, that you just can't film. Jeannie would sit down and write stories about, for example, Daddy Date Night. She'd write a few pages and then she'd give it to me and I'd pull things out of it and then she'd rephrase them and place them; it's a kind of an organic back and forth. Collaboration can be hard, but there's so much about how you interpret the material and what's really going on in a scene, and what does the audience need to know and when, that it's very hard to make these films alone.

I think of the film as both biographical and autobiographical. And it's always walking the line between "as seen through" Jeannie's eyes, she's narrating; my eyes, because I'm shooting; but also seeking to make that presence disappear at moments when we want the audience to just be immersed in Russ and Mary Jane's story without thinking about the perspective from which you're viewing them.

The film also conveys a strong point of view without becoming a rant.

STEVE: One of the strategies that informed the storytelling also was that as partners, Jeannie and I had very different perspectives on what was going on. Jeannie had lived it and knew it intimately, and I was from New York and didn't know anything about farms; I knew what I'd read. So we combined an insider's and an outsider's perspective. The film by turns takes you deeply inside the family and then steps outside it and looks at them in a more distanced way and looks at the story in a more distanced way. I think that's another way that you can take a personal narrative and help the audience to see it in larger terms.

JEANNIE: To be a political film, *Troublesome Creek* had to be charming. You had to like these people, to identify with them. If I had ranted, which was in me to do, I would have lost a part of the audience because the bias would have been too obvious. The bias is obvious, but it's tempered. I'm not positive I'm right. I had to show that I was angry that there are only three million farmers left, but I'm not saying I know how to fix it or whose fault it is. It's history; it's just happening.

STEVE: We felt that the film's biggest influence could be if it were a compelling story that people would want to watch. A lot of the early funding for the film came from humanities councils, especially in the Midwest, and one early rejection we got was from somebody who saw an excerpt of the film and said, "This film doesn't raise any questions, it's not about anything, and it's not a humanities film." But when the film was done, because it's a compelling narrative that people want to watch and are moved by, all of the other issues that would make it either a political film or in that case, a humanities film, emerge from the story and *are* there to be talked about. We took it around the Midwest, and the fervor of the discussions that would come after the film—it raises the questions to a level that people feel passionate about. We saw that as its biggest kind of political contribution.

Is that why you avoided some "traditional" documentary elements, such as interviews?

STEVE: We didn't want to do interviews. We absolutely did not want any expert testimony about anything having to do with farming or economics that would make it seem like that this was a subject being studied as opposed to a subject that was being lived. At one point, [though] we felt we had to sit Russ Jordan down to try to get him to tell us his side of the story—

JEANNIE: —Steve and I had this whole list of questions to ask him—

STEVE: —And the result of that is the banker joke that he tells. And that's it. That was his response to, "How are you doing? What do you think is going on with the bank?"

JEANNIE: That's denial, but it's a good way to do it. At least it's funny.

You went to see one of the bankers yourselves, and it's noticeable that when he starts talking, the narration interrupts and talks over him.

JEANNIE: I hate when people are identified with their lips flapping, in talking-head movies. It's like, "Oh, pay no attention to what this person is saying." I've always been a real stickler about that. So the fact that I did it here, I was saying something. I was saying, "Pay no attention to what this man says because he's not saying anything." But the only way that I could cover him over and talk over him was to acknowledge that he had a right to feel this, and that this was just business, this was not personal.

To what extent, if any, does the film play with chronology?

JEANNIE: There is only a certain amount of that you can do in documentary. The example that I would use is the westerns. Is that the western they're watching at that exact moment every time you see them? No, it's not. I would say that my attitude about it is, it didn't change the basic truth, which was my parents escaped into westerns. But the fact that they weren't always doing it exactly when, or watching exactly what it looked like they were watching, I don't think matters.

The only one that I was absolutely dead set on was *Lonesome Dove*, because it happened the night before the auction, and I didn't want to mess with any chronology about the auction. Someone once asked us if it really snowed the morning of the auction. I was so offended by that, to think that someone would think we would, what, stage that?

You've just begun editing The Heywood Boys, *a feature-length documentary. How did that project get started?*

STEVE: When we heard about the Heywoods, we saw the possibility of making a dual portrait of someone living and coping with ALS, and his brother, who's trying to find a drug that will slow or stop the disease. There's hope and energy on the science side as well as access to the scientific process, alongside with Stephen's experience living with the disease. It's very painful to see Stephen's condition declining, but there's also an enormous amount of vitality in his family and his personality. Because it's a dual portrait, we knew that it would open up a lot of narrative possibilities that wouldn't have existed otherwise.

JEANNIE: We know that it's about these two brothers and one of them has ALS and one of them has started a foundation to cure it. That's the bottom-line description. Other than that, we don't really know what it is. But in the same way that with *Troublesome Creek* there was kind of a plot—we had a year that my parents were going to make or break—we have a disease that they're going to beat or not. And everything that's going to make the film is going to come out of them, out of what we shoot of them and their personalities and the sort of twists and turns of the family story.

As you approach material in the editing room, do you think about act structure?

JEANNIE: Act structure? No. I tend to be a natural storyteller; it's something I kind of grew up with. I start from the beginning of the footage, and I'm cutting whenever I see any kind of a story. The story might be Wendy, Stephen's wife, gets tired of watching [their son] Alex try to open his sippy cup and goes over and opens it for him, but there's a whole back and forth between them. I'm probably not a good person to talk to on some level just because I really don't want to think about the big picture until I have all the little pictures together.

Isn't that the same as editing sequences?

JEANNIE: It is, it's making sequences. And I'm stringing them together and then I'll get Steve to come in and we'll watch them together. So that whatever reactions I have already in my mind, he'll have his own. Because he had his own to begin with because he shot them. So we just kind of leapfrog over each other and try to sneak up on whatever is in the material that the other one doesn't see.

Any last words of advice on storytelling?

STEVE: Think before you shoot, know what it is you're looking at, and have a sense of what you want a shot to convey. Shots don't just happen; they're an expression that is concocted between the camera person, the subject, and serendipity. And you should always be thinking, "What is it that I want to take out of this scene, what do I want audiences to see?" You're always putting yourself in a seat in the theater when you're shooting, or you should be, and thinking, "What am I revealing? When do I want you to know that this character is sitting over here or that this person is frowning?" And that's a calculation that you're doing both when you're shooting and you're editing. How to structure a scene to reveal things.

JEANNIE: Be respectful of the privacy of who you're covering, especially if you're making personal films. Even if you're doing a very intimate film you can do that. Unless there's some real evil that you're dealing with, I think that people need to be careful and respectful of who they're shooting in personal films or in cinéma vérité films.

19

Sam Pollard

Sam Pollard has won three Emmys and numerous other awards for his work as an editor, producer, and executive producer on both dramatic and documentary films. A frequent collaborator of filmmaker Spike Lee, Sam co-produced and edited Lee's Academy Award-nominated *4 Little Girls* (HBO), about the 1963 church bombing in Birmingham, Alabama that claimed the lives of 11-year-old Denise McNair and 14-year-olds Addie Mae Collins, Carole Robertson, and Cynthia Wesley. His other documentary credits include *Goin' Back to T-Town*, THE RISE AND FALL OF JIM CROW, AMERICAN ROOTS MUSIC, and *Brother Outsider: The Life of Bayard Rustin*.

Sam and I worked together on two PBS series, I'LL MAKE ME A WORLD and EYES ON THE PRIZE.

As an editor, what's your role in structuring the film's narrative?

You get three types of documentary producers. The first type will say, "I went out, and I'm doing a film about these four girls who were killed in Birmingham, Alabama. Here's my script, here's my structure, we'll screen the dailies together, and I want you to follow that template."

Second type of producer says, "I went out, I shot this footage about four little girls who were killed in Birmingham in 1963. I filmed their parents, their nieces, their cousins, I talked to ministers in the community of Birmingham, I also talked to Andrew Young and other people involved in the civil rights movement, because Dr. King went there in 1963. I think the story is going to be not only about the girls, it's also going to be about the historical event of Dr. King trying to break down the walls of segregation in

Birmingham. That's my story. I haven't written anything down, but that's the idea." That's the second approach.

Third approach, the producer comes in, says, "I shot all this footage about the four girls killed in Birmingham, I'll be back in eight weeks, you let me see what there is—create something." I've done all types of documentaries, all three types.

In the case of *4 Little Girls*, Spike was like the third producer. He basically said, "I've got to do this story about these four girls; it's been in me about fifteen years, I need to do this story." And he went down and he shot. He never really figured out what the arc of the story was, but he'd been carrying this story around with him so long—and his aesthetic is so artistic. He just knew he didn't want to make an ordinary-type documentary. Just not his style.

He came up with a list of people he wanted to interview, and after he shot for a month, the family members and people involved in the movement, we went into the editing room. For about three weeks, from 7 to 11 in the morning, we would screen dailies and talk. I came up with the idea of trying to do the parallel story. On one track we have the girls' lives unfolding; on the other we see the movement as it moves into Birmingham, and then they collide with the bombing of the church. And that's how we basically approached it.

One of the strengths of the film is the stories and storytellers, particularly Denise McNair's father, Chris.

They were good stories. But you know, it was interesting. I was on that shoot when he did Chris. This was like a feature shoot. Spike had a truck, he had tracks, he had dollies, he had all these lights. I said, "Jeez, what's all this equipment?" And Spike had done a lot of research, but when we got to the interview that day, he didn't have any questions on paper. I was sitting behind him, and I had my own sheet of questions. And I swear, I thought he was so haphazard in how he was asking questions, his style is, to me, so indirect, I thought, "He's not going to get anything good out of this guy." But Chris really connected with Spike; he was able to convey emotion and was such a good storyteller. Mrs. Robertson [Alpha Robertson, mother of Carole] was also a good storyteller. They'd been living with their children's deaths for so many years, and they had stored so much, probably, things they wanted to say. And they all trusted Spike.

From your own experience, how do you think filmmakers establish that kind of trust? I'm thinking, for example, of Big Black (Frank Smith), a former Attica inmate you interviewed for EYES ON THE PRIZE, and renowned poet Gwendolyn Brooks, interviewed for I'LL MAKE ME A WORLD.

You know, it's a funny thing. Sometimes when I interview people, there's a kind of connection where I feel like I'm with family. I feel just very open myself. I don't feel couched; I don't have anything to hide. And I think people feel that and connect. Sometimes, I don't feel that comfortable with the person I'm interviewing, and it comes through. I interviewed Nell Painter for this JIM CROW show. I didn't feel I had done my homework in terms of what questions to ask, and I never connected with her. Everything was very stiff.

What if you're interviewing someone whose views you strongly oppose?

You still try to be as human as possible. For THE RISE AND FALL OF JIM CROW, I interviewed this white gentleman in Florida who, when he was 16 years old in Georgia, saw four black people killed. At first I said [to the other series producers, Richard Wormser and Bill Jersey, both of whom are white], "You want *me* to do the interview?" Because this guy was 70 years old, he's still a redneck; you can see it, he still carries that baggage. But somehow, when I sat down and interviewed him and really touched on some areas that were so painful for him to remember, and really understanding his ambiguous relationships with black people—this guy opened up to me. Because there was some kind of unspoken kinship that we had. At first you could feel that he was a little hesitant. He's going to tell a black man about how, when he was young, his father, his uncle, told him, "You can't hang out with niggers because they're going to think they're uppity"? Did he really want to say those words to me? But then he did because I said, "Just be yourself."

The only person that we knew I wasn't going to interview was in northern Georgia, this gentleman named Gordon Parks [no relation to the filmmaker]. He tells a story in Bill Jersey's show, in show three, about how when he was 15, his grandfather took him to a lynching of a black man. And even now he's unrepentant. I mean, he's surrounded by young white guys who are Klansmen, he's still a Klansman, so they knew that one I wouldn't do.

How do you feel about projects where the footage is handed off to an editing team and the initial connection is lost? Someone like the old man in Florida could be treated very badly

Mutilated. I've been fortunate enough to not yet have someone else take the footage that I've shot. I feel it's my responsibility to be the one to help shape their story, and tell that story in the editing room. If somebody in JIM CROW says, "Well, I never said it like that," then I'm the one they're going to have to deal with. It's a delicate thing. You have to make editorial adjustments, sometimes, to try to get the story across clearly, concisely—because it's always about trying to be concise.

The problem is that most times when people do their interviews, they don't quite understand that they're going to be edited. I've had it happen so many times. Someone will look at the interview and say, "What happened to what I said? I talked to you for two hours and you used two minutes?" I had one guy stop talking to me, on *T'Town*. We screened that film at WGBH [in Boston], and he came up from New York to see the film. We had interviewed him for an hour and a half, in his house. I used all of one minute. And this man, he did not talk to me on the flight back. Because what happened to his interview?

How much of the story do you work out before you film?

With *T'Town*, I did a treatment, and then when I got back, before I gave the footage to Betty [Ciccarelli, the editor], I worked out a complete structure. So I gave her a 20-page template as a guide. With JIM CROW, Richard Wormser had done scripts, so we had scripts.

You shot to scripts? How was that?

It was like what we did at Blackside [filming to written treatments]—we completely changed it. Basically, I had a 40-page script from Richard. When we went into the editing room, I followed the script, and when we looked at it, it was terrible. Slow. Meandered. And then we went back and restructured, and then we looked at it again; it looked a little better. It's a process. He went and reshot; we put a whole new element in that was never in the script.

But the thing is, it's always better to have a foundation, a template. So you know you have something there in front of you.

Most documentary filmmakers, even the students, go out and shoot and they don't have a clue what the story is. I mean, I'll do it. I've been trying to shoot something about my father, and even though I know I'm not doing it the right way, I'm still just going out and shooting. But I don't have any money, no deadlines, I don't feel constricted. When someone's paying me, before I start editing I will always write down the structure.

I did AMERICAN ROOTS MUSIC with Jim Brown. Jim's one of these documentary filmmakers who shoots and shoots and shoots. He had shot with Arlo Guthrie, Pete Seeger, a bunch of people, and he had all this archival footage and stills. One of the segments he gave me was about Woody Guthrie. He didn't tell me how to put it together structurally, he just said, "I want to convey that Woody was a great man, a great musician, a real humanitarian." Oh, okay.

So then I sat and I watched all the interviews with the transcripts, made my selects, looked at all the archival footage, looked at the stills, and before I started to cut, every sequence I did, I would take out my tablet and write out a structure. Maybe I'll start with Woody singing, "This land is your land," and then I'll transition to Arlo saying, "The first time my father sang this song . . . " I always use a three-act structure motif; you've got to make sure that within each sequence you build to something in terms of a beginning, middle, and end.

In this particular case, with AMERICAN ROOTS MUSIC, we were doing this sequence by sequence, and then I tried to figure out an order of the sequences for each show. This wasn't too difficult, in that it was almost chronological. I knew that in the beginning show I had to start with musicians in the early 1900s. And then I transitioned to Ralph Peer finding the Carter Family, and then from the Carter Family, I went to how country music evolved, and then from country music in the 1930s, there was gospel music, Thomas Dorsey. You try to transition—and with this film it was narration that was going to do it—you try to make a narrative transition that doesn't say, "and this happened." You say, "The music that was happening in Memphis in 1927 was profound, it moved people to . . . " You write into it.

Do you look for a story arc?

I usually do. A transformation of a state of being. Sometimes I don't have to have a character take me through. And sometimes I can feel there's a sense of artifice. Part of me with Ali [a story about fighter Muhammad Ali, in EYES ON THE PRIZE] always felt that—even though Ali's a great character, even though it's his real story—it feels a little jerry-rigged. It doesn't feel like it quite unfolds, it feels like you see the hands of the filmmakers moving the pieces. And that always throws me.

4 Little Girls *begins in a cemetery, with Joan Baez's "Ballad of Birmingham" on the soundtrack, relating the tragedy that's about to unfold. How do you feel about the need for a "hook" at the start of a film?*

I have two feelings about it. Sometimes you've got to give them a hook right up front, like the bombing. Years ago, I did a film about Langston Hughes. We basically kill Langston off at the beginning. "He's a wonderful poet, but then he died." Then we backtrack and tell you the story. I always kind of liked that, that old movie thing. But I thought it was a mistake in retrospect; it underwhelmed the whole film, dramatically. Sometimes if you give them the hook up front, then when you build up to it again you say, "Oh, I already know that." Sometimes the hook can be detrimental. In *4 Little Girls*, it wasn't. The reason we started with Joan Baez was because the song was so great. And Spike had had [director of photography] Ellen Kuras shoot the cemetery footage in that very weird style. He didn't know it was going to be at the beginning, but he shot it.

How do you approach issues of balance in your work?

Even when we were doing EYES, I always questioned that, having to get the opposing point of view to give you the balanced perspective. I think the word shouldn't be "balance." I think that if you interview people that have contradiction, that to me gives it a more textured perspective. In *4 Little Girls*, people said we took a cheap shot at [former Alabama governor] George Wallace. Well, I don't think so. He was not in the greatest health, as we know. But it wasn't like he had just been thrown the questions and didn't know what to say. He knew. Before he even consented to do the interview, Spike had to send him all the questions. And when I look at the outtakes—I put the whole outtake of the interview on the DVD—I really didn't cut that much out. So I didn't think we did him a disservice. It's a funny thing about people. Part of the reason George Wallace did the interview, I think, is because Spike Lee wanted to interview him.

You've edited in both film and video; have changes in technology changed how you approach storytelling?

I was talking about this with an editor friend of mine the other day. On a Steenbeck, when you approached the editing of a sequence, any time you had to restructure scenes you would pull your film down and unsplice it. The physical process of doing that would force you to contemplate what you had done editorially, or what you were about to do. You had a moment to think. Then, when you finished your splice and looked at your sequence, you might have come up with another approach because you'd had a little respite to think about it. That's number one. Secondly, because you're editing on film, there was a pacing that was given to your material because of the equipment you worked on, that in today's age is probably a little archaic.

What has happened with the nonlinear technology—which I don't know anything about except how to cut—what's happened is that as schedules have been tightened, the idea of thinking has suffered. You don't have 24 weeks now; you'll be lucky if you get 12 weeks, from start to finish, editing the film. You don't have time to sit back and think about your cut. "What am I trying to do, what's the arc of the story, where's it going?" Now, you get a cut really fast, and most times now, what I'll do on the Avid is, I'll do another version. Because you can do it. You hit duplicate, you just do another version. Someone will say, "Well, that doesn't work, Sam." "Oh, I know how I can do it."—and you do another version, and another one.

Everybody needs a chance to process the material. And now the way we make films, because of this technology and the cuts, film storytelling is becoming more and more a mosaic: talking heads, quick bites, archival footage, blah blah blah. If you don't have good storytelling skills and you don't have a good story, it all becomes bells and whistles.

What are the biggest storytelling issues your students face?

The biggest pitfall is understanding what their film's about right from the beginning. Before they set down to write a page of the narration or script, what's the theme? And then on the theme, what's the story that they're going to convey to get across the theme?

For me, the theme of JIM CROW is how a people of color who were given their freedom in 1863, with the Emancipation Proclamation, had to struggle mightily against tremendous odds to be able to find that window of opportunity, and the things they had to do on all levels to move themselves forward. Richard and Bill may have a different approach, but that to me was what it was always about. So the next step was to find the stories that were going to help convey that. What I liked about JIM CROW is that there's an ambiguity in these real-life characters. Look at Booker T. Washington. On the one hand, he's this great man who starts this wonderful school [in 1881] to help black people. On the other hand, he basically says to black people, "Don't try to go but so far; take it to a certain level but don't rock the boat." None of this is simple. I always believe that nothing is black and white, that it's textured, shades of gray. To me, if that comes through, we did our job.

How do you evaluate story ideas?

What makes an idea great for a documentary is if you're introducing me to a world I've never heard about, and there's some story within that world that's going to be new and attention-grabbing. A student of mine who's Muslim came to me two weeks ago; she was down in Trinidad last summer and shot all this footage, so she wanted me to take a look at it. When you say Trinidad, my assumption, the first thing I think of is, Carnival. People in costumes dancing, having a good time; everybody's trying to do a film about Trinidad and Carnival. So I figure this is what she's going to show me.

She puts the footage up on the TV, and, it's about a Muslim sect in Trinidad that's been in conflict with the government about being able to have freedom of choice in their own mosque, their own communities. Their government feels that they're like a terrorist group and they've been clamping down on them. There's been violent struggle, shootouts. So all of a sudden I'm saying, "Wow, this is interesting. I never knew there was a Muslim sect in Trinidad. I didn't know there was all this tension that's been going on for about 12 years." It's very interesting material for a documentary. Her problem is, she just went out and shot. Her father's Muslim, he knew about this group, introduced her to some people. Now she has no clue how to put the film together. What I said to her is, it's like doing the homework in a backwards way. You have to sit down and write down on paper, "What am I trying to say? What's the arc of this film?"

As a filmmaker, do you work to ensure that your storytelling is inclusive, that it covers voices and experiences that might not be readily available in archival material or secondary research?

I met filmmaker St. Clair Bourne in 1980, when I did his film about the blues in Chicago, *Big City Blues*. He basically became my mentor, in making me understand, as an African American, that the voice of "the other" is an important voice that has to be conveyed because you rarely hear or see it. Since that time, I've always believed strongly that, be it films about African Americans or Native Americans or Asians, women, it's important to be involved in those films. And if you're involved in a film that doesn't have that, you try to find that in the material.

Bennett Singer came to me a few years ago, wanted to do a documentary that I'm now executive producer of, *Brother Outsider: The Life of Bayard Rustin*. That to me was important. Not only because Rustin was so active in civil rights, but because he was a gay man who wasn't afraid to say that, no matter what the consequences. That probably drew me more to it than the fact that he was the main cog for the March on Washington.

With any documentary, music is an important part of the storytelling. At what point do you start to think about it?

All the time. I love music. I did a travel show for WNET a few years ago, GOING PLACES. Al Roker was the host. And one of the first segments I produced was about going to London. First thing I did, there's a music store on 12th Street off Third Avenue in New York, I bought about $100 worth of music. To find the moods, try to convey the different moods I wanted to have in the piece. I ended up having to take it all out because they wouldn't pay for the rights. But music is always important to me. You have to be a little careful because sometimes music can overwhelm the storytelling and undercut the drama of just letting the images play.

Years ago, when we were doing the EYES show, you were opposed to a piece of music, "Keep On Pushing," that we put in at the end of the Ali story. You thought it was going to detract from just listening to Ali and the narration. And Betty and I argued with you, "No, no, Sheila, you're wrong." But in retrospect, you were right. I watched that show recently—the music was too specific, too on the nose. You've always got to be careful about how you use music. I like it to be a little more indirect now, as I get older.

20

Kenn Rabin

An archivist, filmmaker, and writer, Kenn Rabin is one of the nation's leading authorities on audio-visual research and the use of archival materials. His credits include the series VIETNAM: A TELEVISION HISTORY, which involved over 90 archives from a dozen countries; EYES ON THE PRIZE, for which he received an Emmy nomination; 500 NATIONS, Kevin Costner's saga of Native American tribes; and Barry Levinson's *Yesterday's Tomorrows*, on which he served as writer and associate producer.

As someone who's a storyteller and an archival film expert, what do you see as the strengths of using archival material to tell documentary stories?

I think that we've become more and more a visual society, and our storytelling relies so much on wanting to see what people are talking about. If we see it, we believe it's true, which is a tricky trap to get into, especially in this digital world. But we're raised on visual images, so we tend to think that that's the only way that stories can be told, and it's funny how you start crying out for those moving images if you don't have them.

What people don't realize is that moving images contain embedded in them certain types of information that is different than information in printed material. It's not a strength or a weakness, it's just different. To give you an example, I know of an archivist who's got a local news collection, and she's adamant about not throwing away stories on local fires, that kind of thing, because it shows what a fire truck looked like in 1950, how the firemen dressed. And she's got a point, that there's all this social information that's encoded in those visual images.

If you're telling a story with archival material, at what point should you start finding that material?

There's an interesting chicken or egg thing that the producer faces when dealing with the kind of cross talk that you get between archival footage and the interview process. Very often the interview subjects will suggest where to look for archival material or what to look for. Examples: "I was there with my friend and he had a movie camera," or "I remember NBC News was there." And what you find in the archival footage will sometimes suggest, "Oh, here's a lot of coverage of a particular event, let's expand on that." Or you'll see someone in archival footage and say, "I wonder if we can find that guy, is he still around, can we interview him?" That's the kind of cross talk you get when you really do your homework. You've got some of your team going after the archival and part of your team doing preinterviews and shooting interviews. That kind of ideal way of doing it often implies the need for a higher budget and particularly more lead time in pre-production and more time in the edit room. There's no time to do that when you're doing one of these short-form, assembly line things that has to be done in six or eight weeks for a miniscule budget.

With schedules and budgets that tight nowadays, are producers taking shortcuts with archival research?

Generally speaking, most filmmakers I am contacted by don't understand that the way you make a stock-footage documentary is that you go to the original creators of the archival footage (the networks, newsreel houses, collectors, filmmakers) and hunt around for it, see what they shot, look through cards, look through computer printouts, screen material, order it up, and bring it all into the edit room. Their understanding of the process of making a compilation documentary is that your research consists of finding all the other documentaries that have been made on the subject, getting copies of them on tape, screening them, identifying the shots that you want, and then lifting them, or at best trying to get the producers of those films to tell you where they got the shots. Or contacting someone like me to try to find those shots, somehow, by just looking at them and intuiting where they originally came from—usually about a week before the show has to be delivered.

As wonderful as it is that the technology has become less expensive, in a way it helps to feed this idea [that] the whole process is cheap, including the research. The ideal thing is of course, "We don't have to spend on answer prints and syncing [since we're working in video], so let's put the money into really good research." But it doesn't work that way.

There also seems to be a change in how archival material is used, especially in lower-budget films.

Because of the quickness and cheapness with which documentaries are now being produced, people use what's called "wallpaper," which is generic images that stand in for narrative points that are being made. So when you say, "the city of Saigon," you can show an image that may be the city of Saigon, but it may not be the time period you're talking about, or it may be a city that looks like Saigon that you kind of get away with. It's really just an image that you're putting up on the screen to occupy the viewer's eyes for the three or four or five seconds during which the narrator is finishing their sentence. Sometimes people wallpaper with the correct image and sometimes they wallpaper with the wrong image. It's not very good storytelling however you do it, because it's not organic. It's "pegs and holes" filmmaking; in other words, it's trying to fit a peg into a hole, rather than letting the process unfold organically in the editing room.

What about either slowing down or speeding up archival material?

This is something that's routinely done today. Changing the speed of archival footage, particularly slowing it down, will subtly or not so subtly change the emotional flavor of a piece of archival footage. It will make something seem more heroic, more sorrowful, more gruesome, depending obviously on what the content is. And that's something that people don't think much about when they think about whether they're using archival footage honestly. They don't think it's a cheat.

Is your bottom line that you just don't manipulate archival material, period?

Well, that used to be my bottom line. I would say something a little different now, a little more complicated than that. My bottom line now is, there are a lot of different kinds of nonfiction projects you can do. If you are doing the standard historical documentary and you are setting up that type of storytelling vocabulary, and that's the expectation you want your audience to have of you, then yes, you follow these journalistic rules and you use your footage with complete integrity. If you're doing another type of documentary, then you create it in a way where you are setting *those* rules up for your audience, and your audience understands that you're going to be playing a little different game. Slow down the footage if you want, just make it clear that's what you're doing—that's not what the event looked like, you're editorializing. I've worked on a lot of very good documentaries that slowed down footage, including a film on Cesar Chavez, *Fight in the Fields*. But it's really obvious that they slowed down footage, and they weren't doing it to make it into something it wasn't. We didn't do it in VIETNAM: A TELEVISION HISTORY because the subject was so emotionally loaded, especially at the time we did the documentary, which was a lot closer to the end of the war. We were very careful not to editorialize.

I'm excited by the idea that filmmakers are finding new and different ways of using archival that set new rules that break the old rules. I like the fact that some people are using archival to make very personal documentaries; other people are using it to make what once upon a time was called video art. The only rule is that you've got to tell your audience what your rules are. I really like Jay Rosenblatt's work; you watch one of his films and you know he's trying to do something that's emotional and visceral and is not some representation of historical accuracy. It's something else; it's an art piece.

We often see early film footage—Charlie Chaplin, the Keystone Cops—played very quickly. Why is that?

Turn-of-the-century footage was, at the dawn of the technology, mostly shot at about 14 frames per second, approximately. If you screen *The Birth of a Nation* [D.W. Griffith, 1915] correctly, you're screening it at about 14 or 15 frames per second. And then as you go through about 1916 to 1918, it starts to standardize on 18 frames per second, which really is what the standard was for silent film through the 1920s, and then you get to sound film, which is 24 frames per second. Of course things varied; before there were electric motors, the cameramen were hand cranking the cameras. Even as they filmed one shot, their hand motions might change slightly.

So it's an inexact science, but if you present early motion picture that was filmed 1917–18 through 1928–29 at 18 frames per second, then the motion will look normal to you, and it will look like what it looked like to the people who watched it at that time. I worked with the original copyright frames of Griffith's film *Intolerance*, when I did some work for the American Film Institute. These were the frames of the film that were submitted for copyrighting in 1916. One frame of each shot of the film was stapled to a card and submitted to the Library of Congress, and we could see how the shots were tinted and toned. [The filmmakers] had people hand painting each frame of the film; for the Babylon sequence they would have someone paint the king's throne with gilt. These things were stunningly beautiful. They're not the scratchy, dark, black and white, running-too-fast things we usually see; they're tremendous works of art.

Have the visual archives for the 20th century been kind of picked over, or are there still surprises to be found?

The archives have been picked over fairly well for the subjects that everyone has done, that's true. But having said that, there's still the rest of each shot, and there's still, how do you use the shots and how do you put them together and how do you put together all the different elements that you have, and why do you pick the subject that you pick? I mean you have to go back a step and say, "Why do you want to make another documentary about the Kennedys? Do you have something new to say? Does the world need another documentary about that?" People should ask themselves, "Why am I picking the subject I'm picking?"

But the other thing is, they've not only been picked over, they've been conglomerated and overly computer-catalogued, because they've been retrieved so often. The same keywords pull up the same footage again and again. Creativity is being taken out of the search process.

An example of that: when we were doing Vietnam: A Television History, we got down to the last episode, about the fall of Saigon. I was at Sherman Grinberg, which held the ABC News footage at the time, and I was looking for all the footage I could find on the evacuation of the American embassy. I pulled everything I could find in the computer, and then I started putting in some other words like *Saigon, embassy*. And then I started putting in phrases like *embassy roof*, that would not necessarily have been put in if, like today, you're no longer at the archive but telling some sales rep at the archive what you're looking for.

You can't go to the archive?

It depends on the archive, but less and less can you go to the archives. As collections get bought up by these conglomerates, they have their people who are paid little and who turn over every six months, who sit at computer terminals and do these searches for you. So you tell them what you want, and they punch in the most obvious keywords. And then they pull that stuff, they put it on a VHS cassette, and they send it to you. And that's your film research.

Are you allowed to suggest unusual keywords?

You can if you can think of them, although you don't know how their computer systems work. One of the things about film research was that you pull some reels, you look at some stuff, and then you think of other things you want to pull. You also put in date ranges and personalities and things like that.

And so I was looking for everything on the fall of Saigon and closing down the American embassy, and because I put in some unusual keywords, I came up with this one fairly large reel of film. I put up the picture on the flatbed and started watching it, and it looked like chaos at the embassy. People trying to climb over the fence to get into the embassy, people trying to grab onto the bottom of the helicopter as it's trying to take off from the roof, and all this. And I'm watching it and all of a sudden from chaos everything stops, and everybody becomes calm and walks away and sits down at tables, and then there are random shots. And I'm thinking, what's going on here? To make a long story short, I discover that what I'm looking at is footage not of the embassy in Saigon but of Thailand, where Michael Cimino is shooting *The Deerhunter* and recreating the fall of Saigon. And he had yelled, "Cut," so all these actors had stopped recreating the fall of Saigon and had gone back to a cup of coffee from the craft services table. It was the eeriest thing.

The previous episode of the series was ending with the fall of Saigon, and we were going to pick up there at the beginning of the last episode and go on to talk about the legacies of the war. And we thought, this is amazing, we'll start the last episode with this thing, which is a recreation of this event that we'd seen the real footage of at the end of the previous episode. And I never would have found it if I'd had to phone in, you know, "Give me what you've got on the fall of Saigon."

Is it possible to make an archival film on a low budget?

It's possible, but it has to be something for which the archival materials are relatively inexpensive and accessible, and are not owned by heavily commercial third-party sources or bound by increasingly strange legal encumbrances. There are now all kinds of rules and laws regarding likenesses of famous people, which get you into all kinds of financial trouble. I worked on a film recently that wanted to use a clip from something that normally would be in the public domain by many years. But because an actor appearing in it had their likeness trademarked, the use of that clip was going to be prohibitively expensive or not even available.

So these kinds of middle-of-the-road projects financially are possible, but the producer has to be very savvy and talk to the right people to know whether the subject is feasible, particularly if it's going to rely on very specific pieces of third-party material that they can't do without. I would like to see the government step in and be heroic—issue exemptions to the copyright laws that allow nonfiction filmmakers working on primarily educational projects to be less encumbered by various restrictions—but I don't see it happening. Congress is moving in the opposite direction, favoring corporations maintaining control over their copyrights for longer and longer periods, which is not the original intention of the law.

What should storytellers know, and how should they compensate for, the various biases that are inevitable in archival or third-party material?

Producers should know about the material they're using—where it comes from, what the history of that company is—at least enough to know what the bias might have been. The more you know your subject, the more you're going to know how things might have been manipulated.

As an obvious example, if your subject is the Stalinist era in the Soviet Union, you're going to know that the materials produced out of that environment were manipulated in certain ways and showed certain sides of issues and not other sides. As a producer, you can include that as an actual subject. You can do a section on the use of propaganda in the Stalinist era; you can show photographs that have been doctored, before and after. You can show film footage that was released in the Soviet Union and then show footage of the same event as it was released in another part of the world.

It's really your responsibility to educate yourself about these kinds of things—knowing, for example, the history of the newsreels. A lot of documentary filmmakers rely on newsreel footage if they're dealing with the early or mid part of the 20th century. Newsreels ran from about 1910 through the late 1960s in various countries. They were manipulated in lots of different ways, and of course narrations of the newsreels were heavily propagandized and newsreels were often restaged.

One of the great newsreel moments in my research was when I was at the National Archives looking at some *March of Time* newsreels, produced by Time/Life. I found outtakes from the story on Kristallnacht, the night when the Nazis raided all the Jewish shops. Actors dressed as SS storm troopers were sitting around a studio smoking cigarettes while prop people brought in glass plate windows with Hebrew writing on them, that were obviously meant to be windows of Jewish shops. And they were setting up to shoot a scene that was supposed to be Kristallnacht.

Above and beyond that, anyone using audiovisual materials should understand in general that these materials have a point of view. Things are edited. What is in the frame and what isn't in the frame, what shots are and aren't being used. Whenever you inherit audiovisual materials, you are inheriting something that's been edited in a variety of ways. That's a basic fact that anyone working in media needs to understand.

Another issue we noticed during the making of EYES ON THE PRIZE was that the quality of archival news coverage changed fairly dramatically between the 1960s and 1980s, and beyond.

This is a problem more and more, since network news has become a part of the entertainment division and budgets have gotten cut back. I saw Paddy Chayevsky's *Network* the other day, which was made in the mid-70s. It's amazing how prescient it was. I remember thinking how outrageous it was at the time, and now half of it's actually happened and the other half is just around the corner.

You look at stories, particularly from the 1960s and particularly from NBC and CBS, and you have these incredibly in-depth stories where reporters followed people around for long periods of time. And in the 1980s and 90s, you have basically leading up to a sound bite. It's almost like the newsreels, which are often frustrating to use because you've got these short shots that you can barely edit into a sequence—one minute on each story.

There are two different types of changes here: the changes in nightly news, and the changes in network news documentaries. The 1960s were also the glory days of such long-form documentary series as CBS REPORTS and NBC WHITE PAPERS. These were researched and shot over months and then presented as periodic specials. They're a great source of archival footage, and that kind of source doesn't exist anymore. I'll look and say, "Well, there isn't footage of this race riot on campus but there's the aftermath of it." Or, "There isn't footage of economic strife but there's the aftermath of it." Apart from war, what other long-form issues are being covered by American news in the kind of detail that say, the civil rights movement was?

So I think that one of the things that begins to happen as you get good committed documentarians in the 1990s and beyond is that they start covering their own stories. If you're interested in more contemporary history, you're probably not making archival films. I'm generalizing, but I think there are a lot of people out there interested in what's been going on for the last 20 years, and they're not making archival films.

And this work, in turn, becomes an alternative to archival news material for the next generation of filmmakers

Yes, and that footage will be wonderful, intimate footage that is not like anything the networks would have shot. People have been making their own films all along, but I think that now, more people are making their own films about contemporary subjects.

$$\text{21}$$

Susanne Simpson

Susanne Simpson has been executive producer for Nova Giant
Screen Films since 1990, and was nominated for an Academy
Award for her work as producer/writer on *Special Effects*. Other
giant-screen credits include *Island of the Sharks, To The Limit, Storm-
chasers,* and *Shackleton's Antarctic Adventure,* winner of the Best Film
and Best Cinematography Awards of the Giant Screen Theater
Association.

Previously, Susanne produced several documentaries for the
Nova science series, winning an Emmy for *Can the Vatican Save the
Sistine Chapel?* As an independent, she was the associate producer
and editor of *Eight Minutes to Midnight: A Portrait of Dr. Helen
Caldicott,* which was also nominated for an Academy Award.

What makes something a good idea for a giant-screen film?

Even though IMAX® films have been around now for about 25
years, it's been an industry for which the art of storytelling has
been a slowly evolving thing. When people first started making
IMAX films, they were enamored with having their images 90 feet
high, and storytelling wasn't really a part of it. The ones that did
very well in the beginning were films that were about places that
people could go to and experience in a way that they might not
otherwise experience. It was in some ways like a slide show, where
you would see images and the narrator would talk about what you
were seeing. Some of that remains true in the industry, which
makes it a different kind of filmmaking than you might make for
television. The image is all-powerful, and the words have to
support the imagery. In television, sometimes the images and
words don't have to match. I'm not saying that's the best type of

storytelling, but people listen to the narration on television. In the giant-screen industry, you have to use many fewer words.

One of the changes that started to occur is that many of these giant-screen theatres became part of science museums, and the science museums were interested in science content films. So there were early films, one called *Genesis* [1979, 32 mins], where there was information being talked about in this short format. In more recent years, people have been challenged by the medium to create a story instead of an information-based film. There have been several approaches to doing that. One has been to go to dramatic recreations, sometimes with dialogue. But even the dramatic recreations tend to use a narrator, because of the short format. To move the story points along, you oftentimes need a narrator to make those points for you.

Tell me about Shackleton's Antarctic Adventure, *the giant-screen film you produced about the ill-fated expedition of Sir Ernest Shackleton.*

It was clear to me that the way to tell the story was with dramatic recreations. We wanted to use real documentary elements and weave it together in a dramatic story. There were archival images, there was 35mm film footage from the original 1914–1916 expedition, and there were many diaries that the men had written, including Shackleton. The story at that point was well known; there'd been a lot written about it. The important thing for us was to figure out what were the dramatic turning points and how could we visualize them on screen.

Having been in the IMAX industry for a long time and seen many different versions of people using dramatic recreations, what became clear to me was the most successful ones were the ones without dialogue, where the characters were representational, [rather] than speaking on film. It became important to use the diary material, the personal storytelling of the men, and to put that in the voice of actors. And so then we had to make a decision about, what is the narrator doing in this film, and what are the voices trying to accomplish? I set out to use the narrator to help move along the story points and the men to explain emotionally what was happening to them at that moment in time, feeling that if we used those voices well, we could get more of the emotional quality out of the story. Because it's an incredible story, and we knew we could tell it.

One of the things that's very difficult in an IMAX film is that because images are overpowering, you have to be very careful about what you show on screen, like the men suffering, starving, being cold, having a difficult time. So we had to walk a careful line—use the men to tell emotionally how difficult things were, but be careful with our imagery not to make something too graphic. There was one point at which we had to decide whether or not we should graphically illustrate on screen the shooting of the dogs, which are put to death before the men get into lifeboats. That can be overwhelming to an audience, that kind of violence. And so with IMAX you're always making sure that you're providing imagery that is descriptive of the story but doesn't go too far in terms of some of the graphic details.

Is that also because there are likely to be children in the museum audience?

It's because of the audience demographics—40% of the audience are kids, schoolchildren—and it's also historically what people have experienced. Many people [who] have made wildlife films have had to pull back on scenes of the hunt and things like that, because it turns out it's just much too much on a 90-foot screen to show things that are graphic and difficult to see.

The WGBH website (http://www.pbs.org/wgbh/nova/about/gsfi. html) makes clear how massive an undertaking the Shackleton shoot was. How did you plan for the storytelling?

We started out with a film treatment. And the idea was to look at, again, the key points in the story and how we might dramatize that. IMAX films are much closer to, say, making a feature film. It's very important that you take your film treatments and actually storyboard them. We went through the process of storyboarding the film and looking especially for transitions where we could use the documentary archival footage and then use a match dissolve to bring us into the dramatic recreations, as a way of easing people into the different storytelling techniques.

How extensive are the storyboards?

Very extensive, hundreds of pictures. Every shot needs to be storyboarded. In the case of IMAX, it takes so long to set up every single shot, and especially with a film like this that had a lot of weather conditions that could change in a minute. We had to know exactly what shots we absolutely needed for the film, and what shots we could do without. And so we had to go from the beginning of the film to the very end, storyboard all that out, and know what our options were if we weren't able to accomplish certain shots.

What went into determining those "must have" shots?

The Shackleton story is one of the most remarkable stories I've ever come across. And because it's so well told and well known, there are some obvious turning points. The ship gets stuck. The ship sinks. The men leave the ice floes to get into their boats. They arrive at Elephant Island, to discover that in fact, they'll never be rescued. So Shackleton has to set out with five men to South Georgia. They run into a hurricane along the way, and when they arrive they're still not done, and therefore have to cross South Georgia, finally to arrive at the manager's villa. Those were the essential story points that had to be told. We needed to decide whether we had the archival footage to tell it, or whether we needed dramatic recreations to tell it. [The expedition] was very well documented in the beginning, before the ship went down. And then it became less and less well documented. So that we knew that the latter half of the film, from the time the men got into the boats, was going to have to be a dramatic recreation because there was no archival footage to tell the story.

   The other thing that I knew from the beginning is that I wanted the story to end at the rescue. There are many other elements of the story, in terms of how Shackleton was received [afterward] in Argentina, Chile, and England. But a 40-minute film in a museum, it's meant to be an inspiration to the audience, so we knew from the beginning that we would leave it on the rescue.

You start the film with some very dramatic black and white stills of the Endurance *at night, caked in ice, and then quickly move to spectacular aerial shots of Antarctica. How did you decide on a point of attack?*

We did a kind of prologue, where we use some of the most dramatic archival footage shot by Shackleton's photographer, Frank Hurley, [using] strobe lights, and we set up the fact that there was a ship stuck in the ice, 28 men were in danger, and the audience is about to see a film about that. And then we needed to set the stage in Antarctica. IMAX is incredibly dependent on images, and Antarctica is such an exotic place for most people. And then we get back to how Shackleton began his *Endurance* expedition.

In IMAX, you're always having to juggle the fact that people are there for the dramatic imagery, they're there for a real experience, meaning they have to feel shaken around a little bit, a little bit seasick, have the sensation of flying. We felt that helicopter images were extremely important in establishing not only the scale of Antarctica, which is so important, but also for the audience, because there's this expectation that they will have an experience. I think the surprise for people when they came to see the Shackleton film was that it's one of the very few films in the medium that does tell a story from beginning to end and has some emotional content. People are afraid for the men and what's going to happen to them, they're sad when Shackleton has to leave some men behind, and they're of course euphoric when he's able to rescue them.

So you're telling the story while also building on the unique strengths of large-screen presentation?

Absolutely. There was a way to tell this story and yet have it be experiential. We had to build a special kind of camera mount on pontoons, because we wanted the camera to be at sea level. When a small boat, 22 feet, is at sea level, you can actually experience what the waves and the currents and all of that are about, and that way then you can understand what these men are up against. So, the camera techniques were also a way to get the audience to experience the story and what these men were really up against. Both have to work hand in hand all the time.

So the entire crew is thinking about the story, even early in the planning?

At absolutely every single stage, the story is important. Filmmaking in general is about choice making, and when you start to develop something, you have a million and one choices to make. And whether you're developing a script, shooting the film, or editing, you're remaking those decisions all the time. Because you start out with an ideal of what you want to accomplish, and by the time you've shot the footage you've only been able to get what you could financially, or what you could accomplish from a logistical sense. At every point in time you're asking yourself, what are the most essential elements I must have on film to tell this story? Because you're going to have to reallocate your resources—your people resources, logistical resources, money resources—to accomplishing those shots that you must have.

From the very beginning, you want everyone on your team to be invested in that. Your camera team, art department, editor—everyone has to understand what those essential elements are, because you're going to need everybody to help you accomplish that. "Here's where a crane shot would really be the best; here's where a dolly shot would help move you into the elements of the story." Your job is to hold the entire vision in your head, to be able to visualize this entire film and know what's the most important thing to be accomplished. The producer's the one who's made the commitments to the science museums about what this film is going to be; the producer's working with the writer and director to make sure that that vision is going to meet the needs of the ultimate audience because as creative people there are a lot of ideas that are being thrown around, and at some point somebody's going to have to make a decision about whether those ideas actually achieve the ultimate goal or not. And you need to be able to communicate that to your team at every stage, because so much of what you want to get you can't. You have to work with people and be able to explain to them why this is more important than that.

It all seems rather daunting, especially considering that the production was shot on location in Antarctica

It was entirely daunting. We were told that even though we had allocated something like 30 filming days, with the changing weather we might end up with half of those. So before the crew went on the first filming trip, we created a list of 15 shots, thinking, if we could only get 15 shots for this entire film, what are the 15 shots we must get? And then we had satellite communication, so the line producer who was in Antarctica could call me if those shots could not be accomplished. There was one shot that we wanted to get—Shackleton and his men, when they were crossing South Georgia, had to get down the mountain very quickly, and so they actually coiled up a rope and slid down. What a fabulous IMAX shot, a point-of-view shot of them going down the mountain. We had decided that we would leave that as our last shot in the first filming trip. But when the team got there, they realized that the ice conditions had changed dramatically. Everything was heavily crevassed; there weren't these nice sweeping snow slopes. The line producer and the director of photography felt that it was much too hazardous, and so did our group that were basically our safety and expedition leaders. And so that shot was dropped. Would it have been a great shot to have? Absolutely. Could we risk anyone from the team to do it? No. And you have to make those decisions all the time.

How much planning was needed before you could go to film?

The project idea was brought to us a year in advance of the first filming trip. So we had approximately a year to raise the financing and probably six months of that was devoted to developing the storyboards and treatment. We made two filming trips to the Antarctic, and we always planned for that because we didn't think we'd have as many filming days available to us as we eventually did. And then about 20 to 25 weeks to do the edit of the film.

Is the editing process similar to that on a regular documentary?

A lot of it is, in that you take IMAX film, which is 15/70mm; you print down to 35mm and you transfer that to Beta and input it into the Avid editing system. And then at the end of the process, you take your edit on Avid and output it to Beta, have your film expediter cut the 35mm negative, make a 35mm print, and screen it on a large screen, sitting very close. Because the one thing that you can't tell on an Avid system is the pacing of the shots. Even though the pacing is right when you're sitting in your Avid room, on the big screen you need much more time to absorb it, so you often end up lengthening shots. One of the other differences is that it's very hard to tell if there are any technical problems with your original IMAX film. So that's why we print down to 35mm, because you have a film expediter who looks to see if there were any camera problems with what you did, and if there are, you can swap out shots. Sometimes you don't see things until you've actually printed it up in IMAX and you have to go in and swap shots at that point. It's a long post process because you're having to check at many different points in time whether your images are really of the highest quality.

What were the biggest structural changes during the editing?

One was, when Shackleton left Elephant Island, he left 22 men behind. We needed to tell the story about the boat journey that Shackleton was taking to reach rescue on South Georgia Island, but we also needed to tell the story of the men who were left behind. The question was, how many times and when to go back to that story? We tried every configuration you could possibly do.

The other big decision was that in our second filming trip to Antarctica, we had filmed three world-class climbers recreating [in modern-day gear] the trip that Shackleton made across South Georgia. Originally, we had thought that we were going to introduce those climbers in the beginning of our film and then come to their trip at the very end to explain what South Georgia's like today. When we looked at that—and again, we tried many different ways—our decision was to leave it until the end of the film. In the beginning, you so wanted to get into knowing the Shackleton story and what happened in Antarctica that it was too much of a detour to spend time in the present day. So that was a very hard decision. Those were probably, structurally, the two hardest.

But films speak to you; it's very clear whether something is working or not. And sometimes, because you're so stuck with the way something should be, you try a lot of different ways to kind of jam it in, to see if you can make it work. That's one of the most challenging parts of putting a film together in the edit room. You have this basic plan that works on paper; whether that plan works on film is a whole new experience.

It's very interesting to watch the material and try to identify what does work and what doesn't work, and then to make adjustments based on how you analyze that. And again, this is where a lot of choices come into play because now you're juggling again. Is that such a great shot you must use it, even though it has no place in the story? We had a 3-minute shot in the beginning of the film, a helicopter shot going close to the pack ice and then rising over icebergs. I would never think of using a 3-minute shot in anything, but the shot is so fabulous, we had to find a way to tell the story around that 3-minute shot.

How do you balance storytelling with scientific content?

Many of the giant-screen films being made are really not stories, they're subjects—volcanoes, rainforests, sharks—because of the mandate to include the scientific information. Usually a story falls secondary, or what you're doing is you're creating three or four stories in a 40-minute film to carry across the information that you need to carry across. To have a story with a beginning, a middle, and end, like Shackleton, is unusual, and we made a decision from the beginning that the story was so compelling, and there was so much the science museums could do to support the story in educational programs that we were going to leave the science to the support materials. That was a difficult and unusual choice for us to make, but we felt that there were so many elements—whether it be Antarctica, survival, geography, or any of those other things—that could easily be dealt with by teachers or through other programs, and that our goal was to achieve a good story.

Does your experience on Shackleton's Antarctic Adventure *change your storytelling approach to your next giant-screen project,* Pompeii?

It sets a pretty high standard; [Shackleton's] one of the best stories I've ever heard. But certainly when we started to put together our next film, we've looked very hard at creating characters who existed in Roman times. We now have evidence of those characters through the work the archeologists have done. We're going to use dramatic recreations and show how these people lived, and use the documentary evidence of Pompeii as it is today to show that we know everything we do about these individuals through the artifacts they left behind.

How do you find a story when what you're really dealing with is a subject, like Pompeii?

It's always the hardest part. And yet if you find a good story, it's also the most satisfying part. Traditionally, how people have solved the problem is to take a 40-minute film on a subject, whether it be special effects or coral reef or anything like that, and put maybe four or five different stories together. So in the case of *Special Effects*, it was going behind the scenes on four different films and [doing] a story about the making of those films and the special effects. Each of those stories was meant to demonstrate something about how effects are done and how the brain perceives those effects. The overall story is about how the eyes can deceive the brain, in terms of the effects.

To come up with that, to say what the message of the film is, is a very difficult process. [But] you have to start by knowing what the message of your film is, what you want your audience to know. And if the reason for doing *Special Effects* for science museums is because you need to teach people something about perception, then the important thing is to find stories that demonstrate how the eyes can deceive the brain, how illusions are created. If you can teach people that your eyes and brain can be deceived, then you're teaching them something that's a very good analytical tool for the rest of their lives. Not just with respect to special effects but to any of the digital manipulation that goes on in our world today.

When we were putting together *Island of the Sharks*, we had to look at the question of, why are we going to make a film about sharks? And it came down to a story of one particular island in the Pacific [Costa Rica's Cocos Island, which is home to more sharks than perhaps anywhere else on earth]. We wanted to do a film that showed how sharks have existed and evolved for billions of years, and tell the story of Cocos Island, and convey to people that we're losing these kinds of sanctuaries and we may lose some of the creatures on earth that we value. Whether or not you actually say that message that way in your script, you have to know going into it what it is that, by the end of the film, you want people to know, or to feel.

From there, what's your process for developing a story?

In my treatments, scripts, or films, I try to recreate the exact same feeling that I had when I first heard the story or the information. So if some information really piques my curiosity, I try to remember that that's what the audience is also going to respond to. When pulling together the Shackleton film, I tried to remember exactly the points of the story, when I would tell people the short version of the story, [that] really drew an audience in, and not to lose sight of that. That for me has always been the single guiding principle in making choices for the parts of the story that I want to tell. Because how you tell your story to other people is really a way of knowing what elements are important, what elements really interest you, and you can see in the reaction in others what elements in the story really attract them, too.

So it's many months later, everybody's exhausted, you've shot and now you're editing. How do you hold onto or remember that initial enthusiasm?

I have to say, I'm a sucker, emotionally, for films. It doesn't take much for me to be very responsive to films and emotions that come through. So that's a pretty easy thing for me personally; I fall for it every time. In making the Shackleton film, there are three places that we were very keen on making heart-wrenching moments. And they still get me.

One is when Shackleton's leaving Elephant Island and he leaves a letter with Frank Wild that says, basically, you're to take care of the party and if I don't come back, tell them, tell my people I tried my best. [The second is] when they finally arrive at the manager's office, and they've actually succeeded in making it. And third, when Shackleton arrives to rescue the men on the island. And those were designed into the film but they were also moments where, when you're making the film, you know you've got it. And I certainly knew we had it when I heard the actors' reading of those moments.

Part V

ADDITIONAL MATERIAL

Books and Films

BOOKS

Ascher, S., & Pincus, E. (1999). *The filmmaker's handbook: A comprehensive guide for the digital age.* New York: Plume.

Barnouw, E. (1993). *Documentary: A history of the non-fiction film.* London: Oxford University Press.

Bruzzi, S. (2000). *New documentary: A critical introduction.* London: Routledge.

Dolan, S. B. (Ed.). (1994). *Telling the story: The media, the public and American history.* Boston: New England Foundation for the Humanities.

Howard, D., & Mabley, E. (1993). *The tools of screenwriting.* New York: St. Martin's.

Jacob, L. (Ed.). (1979). *The documentary tradition* (2nd ed.). New York: Norton.

Rabiger, M. (1998). *Directing the documentary* (3rd ed.). Boston: Focal.

Rosenthal, A. (1996). *Writing, directing, and producing documentary films and videos* (revised ed.). Carbondale: Southern Illinois University Press, 1996.

Stubbs, L. (2002). *Documentary filmmakers speak.* New York: Allworth.

SELECTED FILMS

Betty Tells Her Story: Produced, directed, and edited by Liane Brandon.

Blue Vinyl: Produced by Daniel B. Gold, Judith Helfand, and Julia D. Parker; directed by Judith Helfand and Daniel B. Gold; edited by Sari Gilman.

Bowling for Columbine: Produced, directed, and written by Michael Moore; additional producers Kathleen Glynn, Jim Czarnecki, Charles Bishop and Michael Donovan; edited by Kurt Engfehr.

Brother Outsider: The Life of Bayard Rustin: Produced and directed by Bennett Singer and Nancy Kates; edited by Veronica Selver and Rhonda Collins.

Cadillac Desert (hours 1–3): Producer, directed, and written by Jon Else; based on Marc Reisner's book, *Cadillac Desert*; (hour 4) produced and directed by Linda Harrar; based on Sandra Postel's book, *Last Oasis*.

The Civil War: Produced by Ken Burns and Ric Burns; directed by Ken Burns; written by Geoffrey C. Ward and Ric Burns with Ken Burns; edited by Paul Barnes, Bruce Shaw, and Tricia Reidy.

Daughter From Danang: Produced by Gail Dolgin; directed by Gail Dolgin and Vicente Franco; edited by Kim Roberts.

The Day After Trinity: J. Robert Oppenheimer & The Atomic Bomb: Produced and directed by Jon Else; written by David Peoples, Janet Peoples, and Jon Else; edited by David Peoples and Ralph Wikk.

The Donner Party: Produced by Lisa Ades and Ric Burns; directed and written by Ric Burns; edited by Bruce Shaw.

Eyes on the Prize: (hours 1–6) Produced by Orlando Bagwell, Callie Crossley, James A. DeVinney, Judith Vecchione; edited by Daniel Eisenberg, Jeanne Jordan, Charles Scott; (hours 7–14) Produced by Sheila Bernard, Carroll Blue, James A. DeVinney, Madison Davis Lacy, Jr., Louis J. Massiah, Thomas Ott, Samuel Pollard, Terry Kay Rockefeller, Jacqueline Shearer, Paul Stekler; edited by Lillian Benson, Betty Ciccarelli, Thomas Ott, Charles Scott; both seasons, series writer, Steve Fayer; executive producer, Henry Hampton.

4 Little Girls: Produced by Spike Lee and Sam Pollard; directed by Spike Lee; edited by Sam Pollard.

Gimme Shelter: Directed by Albert Maysles, David Maysles, and Charlotte Zwerin; edited by Ellen Giffard, Robert Farren, Joanne Burke, Kent McKinney.

Grey Gardens: Produced by Albert Maysles and David Maysles; directed by David Maysles, Albert Maysles, Ellen Hovde, and Muffie Meyer; edited by Ellen Hovde, Muffie Meyer, and Susan Froemke.

Harlan County, U.S.A.: Produced and directed by Barbara Kopple; edited by Nancy Baker, Mirra Bank, Lora Hays, and Mary Lampson.

A History of Britain by Simon Schama ("Dynasty"): Produced and directed by Clare Beavan; written by Simon Schama; edited by Michael Duly.

Hoop Dreams: Produced by Frederick Marx, Steve James, and Peter Gilbert; directed by Steve James; edited by Frederick Marx, Steve James, and Bill Haugse.

Journeys With George: Produced, directed, and written by Alexandra Pelosi; co-directed and edited by Aaron Lubarsky.

Lalee's Kin: The Legacy of Cotton: Produced by Susan Froemke; directed by Susan Froemke and Deborah Dickson with Albert Maysles; edited by Deborah Dickson.

The Multiple Personality Puzzle: Produced by Holly Barden Stadtler and Eleanor Grant; directed by Holly Barden Stadtler; written by Eleanor Grant; edited by Barr Weissman.

Murder at Harvard: Produced by Eric Stange and Melissa Banta; directed by Eric Stange; written by Eric Stange, Melissa Banta, and Simon Schama; edited by Peter Rhodes.

New York: A Documentary Film: Produced by Lisa Ades and Ric Burns; directed by Ric Burns; co-directed by Lisa Ades; written by Ric Burns and James Sanders; edited by Li-Shin Yu, Edward Barteski, David Hanswer, and Nina Schulman.

Recording The Producers: A Musical Romp with Mel Brooks: Produced by Susan Froemke and Peter Gelb; directed by Susan Froemke; co-directed and edited by Kathy Dougherty.

Roger & Me: Produced, directed, and written by Michael Moore; edited by Wendy Stanzler and Jennifer Beman.

Shackleton's Antarctic Adventure: Produced by Susanne Simpson, Scott Swofford, and George Butler; directed by George Butler; written by Mose Richards, Chrystal V. Spijer; edited by Stephen L. Johnson; executive-in-charge, Paula Apsell; executive producer, Susanne Simpson.

Sherman's March: A Meditation on the Possibility of Romantic Love in the South During an Era of Nuclear Weapons Proliferation: Produced, directed, and edited by Ross McElwee.

Sing Faster: The Stagehands' Ring Cycle: Produced, directed, and written by Jon Else; edited by Deborah Hoffman and Jay Boekelheide.

Sound and Fury: Produced by Roger Weisberg; directed by Josh Aronson; edited by Ann Collins.

Southern Comfort: Produced, directed, written, and edited by Kate Davis.

The Sweetest Sound: Produced, directed, and edited by Alan Berliner.

The Thin Blue Line: Produced by Mark Lipson; directed and written by Errol Morris; edited by Paul Barnes.

Troublesome Creek: A Midwestern: Produced, written, and directed by Jeanne Jordan and Steven Ascher; edited by Jeanne Jordan.

Vietnam: A Television History: Produced by Judith Vecchione, Elizabeth Deane, Andrew Pearson, Austin Hoyt, Martin Smith, Bruce Palling; edited by Eric W. Handley, Carol Hayward, Ruth Schell, Eric Neudel, Glen Cardno, Paul Cleary, Mavis Lyons Smull, and Daniel Eisenberg; chief correspondent, Stanley Karnow; executive producer, Richard Ellison.

Yosemite: The Fate of Heaven: Produced and directed by Jon Else; written by Michael Chandler and Jon Else; edited by Michael Chandler; executive produced and narrated by Robert Redford.

About the Author

Sheila Curran Bernard is an award-winning filmmaker, writer, and consultant with credits on more than forty hours of documentary programming for public television, commercial and cable broadcast, and theatrical release. In addition to an Emmy Award, her work has been honored with the prestigious George Foster Peabody Award for Excellence in Broadcast Journalism and the Eric Barnouw Award from the Organization of American Historians. She has been a fellow at the MacDowell Colony and the Virginia Center for the Creative Arts.

Index

- indirectly intimidate other civilisations
- other races stole from Iranian civilisation
- indirectly (showing no clips of present empire) make
   comparisons against Iran